I0560233

ATTITUDE AT
ALTITUDE

ATTITUDE AT
ALTITUDE

The
People's Guide to
Park City and Summit County

BY MICHAEL O'MALLEY

Lady Morgan Press

Copyright © 2025–2026 Michael O'Malley
All rights reserved.

First edition October 2025
Second edition May 2026

The people and places described in this publication are real.
No artificial intelligence was deployed in the creation of its text or
illustrations. All photos and images, unless otherwise noted, are by
the author. Any errors are the author's, and any statements that put
somebody's knickers in a twist are probably intentional and, as satire
and parody, are likely to be protected free speech.

Published in the United States by
Lady Morgan Press, LLC
Olympia, Washington
ladymorganpress@xmission.com

ISBN: 979-8-9994164-0-7
Library of Congress Control Number: 2025943040

Book cover design by: Michelle Rayner, Cosmic Design
Interior design by: Katie Mullaly, Surrogate Press®
Proofreading: Callie Miller, Peak & Pine Press LLC
Story editing: Stacy Dymalski, Memoir Midwife

DEDICATION

In thanks to Keith Droste, Hal Compton,
and the other history hikers.

They all have taught me so much.

TABLE OF CONTENTS

Transportation

Civics and Politics

Wealth and Real Estate in Park City

Water and Weather

Recreation, Health, and Wellbeing at High Altitude

Liquro and Churches

Critters

Art, Music, Film, Museums, and Things You Have to See to Believe

The Future is Here

End Bits

INTRODUCTION

Read this work front to back, or feel free to bounce around to what interests you the most. Lord knows it wasn't written systematically. Why should you have to read it that way?

Who Is This Publication For?

Attitude at Altitude: The People's Guide to Park City and Summit County is your down-to-earth companion to this vibrant mountain town and its stunning surroundings. Whether you're visiting for the first time, returning for an annual getaway, ensconced as a full-time resident, or splitting time between here and elsewhere, this guide has something for you.

Packed with historical, cultural, economic, and natural insights, as well as practical tips, it will enrich your experience—no matter how long your stay.

Michael O'Malley has lived through all four stages of life in Park City—first-timer, repeat visitor, part-timer, and full-timer. His perspective will help you navigate the area's charm and challenges. By understanding its past and present, you'll gain a deeper appreciation for this special place.

Please note that there's a modest amount of content spillover into the neighboring areas of Salt Lake City and Wasatch County. This should be forgiven since both have a big influence on quality of life in Summit County, and both are home to many of the workers who make Park City what it is.

Unlike the glossy brochures, this guide offers an honest, spicy take on Park City. Dive in and discover the real scoop!

GUIDING PRINCIPLES

"In general, set your life to a slower rhythm and renounce all 'me-first-gotta-get-mine' attitudes. There's plenty for everyone around here, so just relax and receive life as it comes to you." – Adam Strachan, Park City lawyer and civic leader

"In the United States, Main Street has always been two things—a place and an idea." – Miles Orvell, professor of English & American Studies at Temple University

"We have probably 1.5 million user days on those trails and a lot of types of users. A good thing to remember is ten seconds of kindness goes a long way. You can have your Strava on and smile at the same time." – Charlie Sturgis, former executive director of Mountain Trails Foundation

"Your Vacation Is My Life" – Red Rock Brewery T-shirt

"If this was reality it would be something." – Snorkel Bob, Hawaii-based author and businessperson

FOREWORD

I didn't dare ask one of my famous Olympic Medalist friends to write a foreword, knowing that nobody ever reads forewords. Nothing to see. Move along.

FUNDAMENTALS

Let's look at the big picture.
Here's the Who, What, When, Where, and Why
from the Paleozoic Era to the present.

SPACE

Summit County, Utah, comprises a 1,882-square-mile area (4,870 km²), and much of it is forest in the rugged Uinta Mountains. For perspective, this county's size is three times that of Summit County, Colorado, and 20 percent bigger than Rhode Island's 1,545 square miles (4,001 km²). And why do we always pick on Rhode Island for these kinds of geographic comparisons? Sure, it's on the petite side, but it's got great seafood.

Summit County, Utah, gets its name from the thirty-nine peaks within its boundaries topping 12,600 feet in elevation, more than any other Utah county. "Get high, stay high" should be our county motto. Our average elevation is 8,388 feet above sea level (2,557 m), or roughly the elevation of the Montage at Deer Valley.

The county's area is contained in a funny-looking, flintlock-pistol shape that came about in 1868, when the creation of the Wyoming Territory swiped some of our dirt. As a result, Utah forever pines for Colorado's square shape because, let's be serious, we're way squarer than them.

Paired with Summit County as part of the Wasatch Back, Wasatch County is 1,206 square miles (3,120 km²) and averages about 7,500 feet in elevation, so it's no slouch in the vertical department. Jordanelle Reservoir and Deer Creek Reservoir are major draws.

TIME AND GEOLOGY

The oldest rocks in Summit County are more than a billion years old. Back in the Paleozoic Era, about 300 million years ago, the Park City area was submerged by shallow tropical seas, but you had to wait millennia to get beach-side drink service.

With apologies to my geologist friends and at the risk of oversimplification, the game really got interesting a mere sixty-five million years ago, when the Farallon Plate crashed into the North American continent. According to state geologists, the collision created massive compressional forces that forced large slabs of rocks formed in basins to the west to be moved eastward. Thrust faults arose and can be seen in Summit County, and are related to the county's oil, gas, and metallic resources.

This is unrelated, but perhaps correlative, to the massive compressional traffic we're observing today, what with all the Californians moving eastward to Park City.

About thirty-five million years ago, there were enormous, active volcanoes to the east of U.S. Route 40. The Keetley Volcanics (a great band name) were a factor in creating conditions conducive to deposition of silver, lead, copper, zinc, and gold in our soils. This is a complex process.

Here's your geology class at 78 RPM: cracks in the strata, superheated water, dissolved minerals. We'd go into more detail but we'd like you to read further.

No description of Park City's geology is complete without quoting J.M. Boutwell, who wrote the seminal *Geology and Ore Deposits of the Park City District, Utah* in 1912: "The greatest geologic activity in the Wasatch Mountains took place in the middle portion at its junction with the great east-west Uinta Range. Within this area the most diverse formations are found on a prominent spur which extends eastward from the main divide. Extensive and irregular intrusion, widespread extrusion, thorough contact metamorphism, persistent and recurrent faulting, and glaciation have produced in a comparatively small area highly varied and complex results. At the heart of the area, in the focus of these contending factors, have been formed the most extensive and richest ore bodies in the range. This area is known as the Park City district."

In other words, there was a long-running, slow-motion car crash between the Wasatch and Uinta ranges—but "persistent and recurrent faulting" sounds like a description of a typical local *Nextdoor.com* thread.

Speaking of glaciers, Summit County has experienced waves of them. The Quaternary Ice Age peaked about 18,000 years ago around here, with a slight uptick in the 2022 to 2023 ski season when we topped 600 inches of snowfall. Glaciers carved much of our surrounding hillsides into their current shapes. When you fly east over the Uintas, you can observe the scooped-out basins and ridges to see the effects from on high. Better yet, hike to the Notch above Trial Lake and see the glacial striations on the ledges beneath your feet.

From the highest points of Summit County originate Utah's major rivers—the Bear, Provo, Weber, and Duchesne (which, for you newcomers, are pronounced "Wee-ber" and "Doo-Shane," not "Web-er" or "Doo-Chess-Knee"). The Provo and Weber flow right through our backyard and supply a lot of our drinking water and river tubing accidents.

Park City Proper

The municipality of Park City itself (and the coveted 84060 zip code) is only 19.99 square miles (51.77 km²). Things get confusing because a) the Park City school and fire districts extend into unincorporated county land; b) the U.S. Postal Service lets much of the Snyderville Basin, which is the area north of Park City proper, appropriate the "Park City" moniker; and c) in 2017, Park City Municipal bonded for and purchased the Bonanza Flat open space, which is—wait for it—in Wasatch County.

A good rule of thumb? When you pass the big white McPolin Farm barn on the right while going south on Route 224, you're in Park City proper. When you ride to the top of the funicular at the St. Regis, or ski down Deer Valley's Nabob run, you've crossed into Wasatch County.

Should we rename the unincorporated areas north of municipal Park City "Snyderville" in accordance with postal delivery? To make that happen, you'll have to fight a mass of unincorporated county residents led by a battalion of real estate agents. They love the Park City brand.

When my wife and I moved here in 1997, we didn't realize our Summit Park home was not actually in the city of Park City. We can understand the confusion and the adamancy to remain under that moniker.

Note: There is a smaller white barn on the east side of Route 224 closer to Kimball Junction. Unrelated to the McPolin barn, this structure was part of the Swaner family's ranching operations, and is part of the Swaner Preserve.

THE PEOPLE

From a standpoint of human history, people showed up in Utah about 11,000 to 12,000 years ago. Perhaps due to its harsher winter climate, there's no evidence of year-round habitation by Native Americans in Summit County. The Fremont people apparently spent some time in temporary hunting camps in Summit County as early as 5,000 years ago. Visit the Coalville Ledge to see some of the petroglyphic evidence, but please don't leave any artwork of your own at this sacred spot.

About 700 years ago, the Northern Shoshone and Ute tribes appeared on the scene, using Summit and Wasatch Counties for hunting and fishing in the milder times of the year. So it's possible that the pattern of part-time residents in our counties—so prevalent today—started centuries ago.

White men showed up in the 1820s, when fur trappers and explorers Jedediah Smith, Jim Bridger, Kit Carson, and others passed through, taking advantage of springs in Peoa for fresh water.

Members of The Church of Jesus Christ of Latter-day Saints (aka Saints, Mormons, LDS) showed up in Utah in 1847. A year later, Parley Pratt and Samuel Snyder explored Snyderville Basin and ran cattle on its verdant flats. In honor of "the LDS St. Paul," the area was called Parley's Park City, and was settled in 1850. The Pratt family tree still thrives in the county.

Other communities followed shortly: Oakley in 1853; Wanship in 1854; and Coalville, Hoytsville, and Henefer in 1859. Kamas and Peoa were settled in 1860, Francis in 1862, and Woodland in 1867. The Coalville settlement (officially founded in 1859) was a population center, and became and remains the county seat. Its founding was driven largely by the discovery of—no surprise—coal. Leader of the LDS Church

Brigham Young was more interested in having his adherents search for industry-supporting coal and iron versus precious metals.

The big bang occurred in the late 1860s, when Ephraim Hanks and a separate group of federal soldiers from Fort Douglas in Salt Lake City made discoveries of an ore called galena, a combination of silver, sulfur, and lead—mostly lead. Galena has a dark sheen, prompting prospectors at the time to say that "Lady Silver rides a dark horse."

Soon, out-of-state fortune hunters converged on our hills, scouring them for signs of ore. The completion of the transcontinental railroad in May 1869 opened the floodgates, and the newly arrived heathens dropped "Parley's" in favor of the linguistically economical "Park City."

Back in the 1870s, Park City was one of Utah's first non-Mormon towns. We still take pride today in not emulating Kaysville, Sandy, or Alpine, which are all prime possible locations should Hollywood ever remake "The Stepford Wives."

The discovery of precious metals in 1868 prompted the growth of Park City. It endured booms and busts for decades, and by 1900, the town's population grew to 7,500 souls versus today's count of 8,300. The transition from a mining economy to a recreation economy passed a major milestone when Treasure Mountains (yes, plural) launched in 1963. Treasure Mountains was renamed Park City Ski Area in 1966.

Recent census data put Summit County's population at around 43,000, much of which can be found in the check-out line at the Smith's grocery in Kimball Junction on Friday nights. Roughly two-thirds of that population is in the 84060 and 84098 zip codes. East of Coalville and Kamas, there's not much population density, but plenty of deer, elk, moose, badger, and the occasional lonely wolverine.

White (non-Hispanic) people make up about 85 percent of Summit County's population and 80 percent of Wasatch County's population. People of Hispanic descent make up about 11 percent of Summit County's population and 15 percent of Wasatch County's population.

Countywide in 2023, according to the Park City Chamber, there were enough hotel rooms to put 28,000-plus heads on pillows. Another 6,000 or more could find short-term rentals from private sources like Airbnb. In other words, on President's Day Weekend, the county can all but double our population. And that doesn't include the resort workers who are stuffed with eight or more workers into a two-bedroom condo during the winter.

PARK CITY PAST
-MINING-

Back in the day, Park City was a rough-and-ready mining town. Today it's a world class resort known worldwide. But as William Faulkner writes, "The past is never dead. It's not even past." You can't expect to keep hold of the things you love about a place and change the things you don't unless you appreciate that place's past.

Silver Camp Versus Lead Camp

I have a bone to "pickaxe" with the Chamber of Commerce. Mining started in the Park City area in 1868, and the last ore-producing mine, the Ontario, closed operations in 1982. According to the Park City Museum, over the course of a century of mining in Park City, the average ton of ore yielded about sixty-seven pounds of lead and one pound of silver. There's a lot of Park City lead spread around Europe and the South Pacific, thanks to the world wars. On a tonnage basis, we were a lead camp, but the Park City Chamber persists in promoting us as a silver camp.

On an economic basis, the Chamber can get away with this positioning . . . by a nose. According to research by the late mining engineer Keith Droste, the average dollar that Park City mines generated over about a century was split forty-one cents from silver, thirty-eight cents from lead, and the remaining twenty-one cents from copper, zinc, and gold, the other mineral byproducts in our region.

A little bit of sexy silver wins out over all that dull lead when it comes to tourism promotion.

Long before ski-town promotions by the Chamber scaled up, we acknowledged our lead camp past. My friend Lynn is a Park City native and a member of the Ivers clan, famous in mining circles. Her uncle Jim is honored by the miner's statue on Main Street.

When she was growing up, Lynn's parents told her stories about how the different mining towns in Utah would nominate representatives to compete in a mining town beauty pageant. Tintic (Juab County) would send Miss Gold, since that mineral was the mining district's *raison d'etre*. Bingham Canyon, where you can see the huge open-pit mine run by Rio Tinto, would send Miss Copper. When silver mining started, Alta got a jump on Park City by a couple of years, so they sent Miss Silver.

"That left Park City with Miss Lead," Lynn recounts.

This makes a lot of sense, because there are a lot of women who've been misled in this town.

Not So Much as a Hatful of Ore: A Lynching on Main Street

The term "lynching" arises from the American Revolution, when Charles Lynch, a Virginia planter, held irregular courts to punish loyalists with flogging. An extrajudicial killing, lynching is associated with hanging, but can encompass other forms of violence and death.

A factor driving "necktie socials" in the West was the lack of mature government structure, such as well-established courts and police resources. In that absence, "vigilante justice" ruled the day. As History Colorado notes: "Before Colorado's statehood in 1876, lynching was the main form of punishment for criminals in many mining towns across the Colorado Territory."

Utah has had at least a dozen known lynchings—most of which happened before statehood. At least five lynchings involved a Black or Asian victim. Other incidents illustrate the vigilante-justice theme, and an August 1883 Park City lynching falls in this category.

Overlapping mining claims near Iron Mountain were the cause of conflict between "Black Jack" Murphy and W.M. Brennan. Accounts vary as to whether Murphy got the drop on Brennan when the latter, armed with a shot gun, showed up at Murphy's cabin to contest ownership of the claim. Or, as several witnesses asserted and most researchers concur, Murphy took aim from hiding and ambushed Brennan as he rode nearby. In any case, Murphy turned himself in, and the sheriff transported him to Coalville for safekeeping.

Several nights later, a Park City mob took control of a Utah and Eastern train, rode it to Coalville, extracted Murphy from the sheriff's care, and rode the train back to Park City. The vigilantes then hanged Murphy from a telegraph pole near Main Street.

Ironically, one writer observed that the contested claims never produced so much as "a hatful of ore."

Were there any legal repercussions? As is typical in the national experience, post-lynching investigations (if any) were perfunctory, and no one was arrested or prosecuted. Such was the consent of the governed in the Wild West.

Dynamite at the Daly West Mine

In July 1902, an explosion rocked the 1,200-foot level of the Daly West Mine in Empire Canyon. Allegedly, mineworker John Burgy entered the forty-ton powder magazine with a candle that ignited the stored supply.

The force of the blast and resulting poisoned air killed twenty-five miners in the Daly West, and another nine in the Ontario Mine, which had a tunnel connection to the Daly West. This is acknowledged as the biggest tragedy in Park City history, at least until the advent of the Ikon and Epic passes.

This publication will not delve into the events of that day, as there are well-written descriptions to be found at *parkcityhistory.org* and elsewhere.

The explosion was impetus for the construction of the Park City Miners Hospital in 1904. Another outcome was the passage of a state law that directed mining operations to store no more than one day's worth of explosives below ground, with the rest stored aboveground. The long reach of that legislation was felt in 2008, when Layton Construction was building the Montage Deer Valley.

As company president Dave Layton relayed to me, a backhoe operator uncovered three cases of old dynamite. The foreman called the Park City Police. The Police said to call the Fire Department. The Fire Department said, "Here's the number for the Salt Lake City Bomb Squad." The Bomb

Squad said, "Hey, there's this company that works with mines, and they specialize in this sort of thing. They'll only charge you about $1,000 an hour."

The explosives-handling company spent a week or so on site, and allegedly unearthed and neutralized a total of seventeen cases of explosives. Whether Dave Layton's version of this incident is entirely accurate is not the point. Remember, never let the facts get in the way of a good story.

What's more important is how one good yarn leads to another, in this case about lawyers. A few years ago, I was leading a corporate hike out of the Montage. The company was a mergers and acquisitions law firm from New York. We hiked by the Daly West mine site, and after I told the explosives story, the head honcho pulled me aside and said, "Mike, that was a pretty good story, but I don't want you to think that $1,000 an hour is excessive."

THE LUCK OF THE IRISH IS NOT EVENLY DISPERSED

Park City in the heyday of mining was a diverse community with Germans, Swedes, Welsh, Chinese, Mexicans, Finns, and others contributing to our history. Your writer is of Irish descent, so please forgive me for focusing exclusively on the contributions of Hibernia.

Statewide in 1910, some 10,000 people out of a total population of 373,000 were born in Ireland or had one or two Irish-born parents (2.7 percent). The Park City area's percentage was probably higher, since mining attracted many immigrant Irish here. Park City continues to be shaped by this infusion.

The Irish are well known to have "saved Western Civilization" and this writer will not debate that point. According to historian Bishop Dwyer, the impact of the Irish in the Intermountain West has been above what a modest fraction of population would reasonably have produced. In that regard, their influence on Summit County and Utah is clear.

Consider the lives of prominent Irish-born or Irish-descended citizens, such as Colonel Patrick E. and Johanna Connor, Thomas Kearns,

John and Mary Judge, John Daly, Eliza Nelson, Dan and Isabelle McPolin, Rachel Urban and others. They were soldiers, mining magnates and millionaires, philanthropists, engineers, farmers, entrepreneurs, and more. From our own Miners Hospital, Big White Barn, and some still-producing drain tunnels, to Fort Douglas, the Governor's mansion, and Judge Memorial High School, their works affect us even today. (The Northern Shoshone would add "butcher" to Connor's resume; a sad tale for another day.)

Of equal importance but of far less prominence are the hundreds of hard-working Irish laborers who did the heavy tasks of drilling, mucking, and hauling in Park City's mines. Many are nameless, but their cumulative impact on our community was deep. Their labor made possible the wealth that coursed through and uplifted our town. Yet their stories often ended in tragedy.

A short walk through the Park City Cemetery off Kearns Boulevard will take you to a neat row of headstones facing west. They commemorate some of the Irishmen who died of asphyxiation in the Daly West explosion in 1902. They were John and Harry Devlin, James Murnin, John Carney, and Charles McAlindon (all of County Down), Richard Dillon of County Mayo, and Mike Conlon "Born in Ireland." The entire town turned out to honor their passing.

Or take the example of Michael McCarthy, who died horribly a few years earlier in the same mine. On November 15, 1899, at an early morning shift's end at the 900-foot level, McCarthy boarded a crowded hoist cage (nine men on each deck of the cage). "The cage came up smoothly and apparently the same as usual until about twenty or thirty feet from the top when a short 'Oh' was heard and someone remarked 'Mike is gone.' The men said they all felt the cage jar," noted the Park Record.

McCarthy had slipped off the deck, was crushed between the cage and the shaft, and his body fell 1,400 feet. When rescuers found the remains, a box was needed to convey all the mangled and fragmented parts to the surface.

The men standing near him had noticed nothing amiss when they all boarded the cage. Their testimony to the coroner speculated that McCarthy "had been working where the air was bad and when good air was reached, he was overcome, fainted, and fell off the cage."

Age twenty-nine and unmarried, McCarthy had spent time in the mining camp of Butte, Montana before moving to Park City. "He was a whole-souled, industrious, and well-respected young man and a splendid miner. Being of a mirthful disposition, his good natured natural Irish wit made him a favorite among men, and he will be sadly missed," said the Park Record.

The funeral took place at the Catholic church with Reverend Father Galligan officiating. The Park Record noted: "A large number of friends followed the remains to the city cemetery where they were consigned to rest." McCarthy's headstone is on the west side of the cemetery, on a slight uphill.

McCarthy had the character and background, but not the luck of a Kearns or Daly. On St. Patrick's Day, raise a toast to the famous and the not-so-famous Irish who built our community. All worked hard, and all made sacrifices, but Fortune smiled on some more than others.

Core Samples of Woe in Park City's Cemeteries

Park City has two historic graveyards: City Cemetery, located on the north side of Highway 248, just before you get to Highway 224, and Glenwood, at the very end of Silver King Drive behind Park City Mountain Resort.

In 2005, Park City historian Gary Kimball published an important work, *Death & Dying in Old Park City*. He spent eighteen months researching newspaper obituaries and mortuary records, producing a 126-page listing of a 1000 people who were buried in Park City from 1877 to 1954 and whose burials did not make it into cemetery records. There's no narrative thread, just core samples of woe paragraph by paragraph. "This is the story of the forgotten ones," he wrote.

A similar list is available for Glenwood, created by volunteers with the Glenwood Cemetery Association in the 1980s, using old handwritten records and other research.

What follows is a tabulation of those collective woes. This is not a statistically comprehensive expression of all death by all causes with all demographic data in place, as you would expect from a research study. In both data sets, there are many missing elements in terms of gender, age, cause of death, and even date of birth or death. The language used for cause of death can also introduce ambiguities. Like a core sample, the data indicate trending strata, not a delineation of the full body of ore.

With caveats in place, what were the leading causes of death in the cohorts described?

Far and away, the leading killer was not dramatic. It was pneumonia. Of the 773 deaths in Kimball's work that have sufficient data for our purposes, 20.4 percent represent deaths by "the old man's friend." But back then, pneumonia respected no age. Victims ranged from infants to those in their seventies. In Park City, pneumonia was a sweeping scythe that took many lives, decade after decade. Glenwood's records (748 mortalities with sufficient accuracy for our purposes) show a similar impact, with 17 percent attributed to pneumonia.

Numbers two and three among causes in the "Death & Dying" list reflect our mining heritage. Mining accidents represent nearly 10 percent of deaths. These include falls, cave ins, cage mishaps, runaway ore carts, explosions, and more. The horrible lung-damaging ailment silicosis, Miner's consumption, represents another 7 percent of deaths. The takeaway? Mining yields nearly a fifth of the deaths in Kimball's tally. Glenwood shows smaller but still significant numbers, miner's consumption at thirty-two and mining accidents at twenty-eight deaths.

In contrast, the number-two cause of death in the Glenwood cohort is heart disease (seventy-four deaths), while the number three spot is taken by stillborn births (sixty-four).

The number-four killer in the Kimball cohort was heart disease. Compare this to 2017, when heart disease was Utah's number one cause of death.

The other top causes of death in both data sets round out with ailments that today's medicine regards as addressable or controllable. These include non-mining accidents, tuberculosis, diphtheria, stomach ailments, and kidney failure. Of this list, only accidents are near the top of Utah's contemporary list (number three statewide in 2017).

Life in Old Park City had brutal edges. In the Kimball list, murder consumed eighteen lives, and suicide twenty-four lives. In possibly the most gruesome way to take one's life, Samuel A. Johanson shoved a stick of black powder in his mouth, lit it, and the resulting explosion splattered his head onto the walls of the Ontario Mine in March 1925.

Given that Park City was a silver-and-lead camp, it is an interesting side note that only two out of the 944 Glenwood deaths were due to lead poisoning. Apparently the galena ore mined here is not particularly bio-active, and posed a far lower danger than silicate dust kicked up by drilling.

The question of life expectancy in Old Park City is tricky. The most one can say here is Park City was a tough town, especially for women and infants. Approaching 30 percent in the Kimball cohort, the large number of deaths of those aged two or under from all causes drives the Park City life expectancy lower in both genders. Kimball describes the scale of infant mortality as "numbing." There are numerous family plots in Glenwood that tell the same tale.

The lesson for today? In 2020, the top causes nationally were heart disease, cancer, COVID-19, accidents of all kinds, and stroke, reflecting that people tend to live longer nowadays. So collectively, we share some but not all of the same dreads that our forebearers did, and here in Park City, we should all wear helmets when recreating!

We owe a debt of gratitude to the scientists, doctors, nurses, public health officials, and other healthcare professionals who have cornered and caged diseases that terrified our grandparents. While we face our own age's demons, life is less fraught today . . . give or take the odd leadership change at the federal Department of Health and Human Services. Thank your health care provider at the next opportunity.

The Deadly (and Miraculous) Quincy Avalanche

Avalanches took the lives of many Park City miners over the years. The slopes, barren of trees due to the mines' immense appetite for fuel and lumber, were frequent slide paths. If the miners weren't commuting to work via the drain tunnels, they were in dangerous territory.

"Terrible disaster has visited our camp leaving death and sorrow in its wake and casting a gloom . . . that is hard to dispel." These words in the Park Record spoke of a deadly avalanche that struck the Quincy Mine on January 28, 1903.

Deer Valley skiers pass the slide site when they carve their way down the Bandana run. The slide originated near what's now called the X-Files, a favorite glade area so named due to a planned but unbuilt tenth lift (Roman numeral X) at the far reach of the Daly Chutes.

The Quincy slide smashed into the hoist building just before noon, killing three workers and trapping six. "The heavy boards and timbers of the building were crushed in like an eggshell and the whole building filled with snow," the newspaper reported. "The roof was carried on the mass and the wonder is the whole hoisting plant was not carried down the gulch."

With the deaths of John Gafney, E.J. Cotter, and Charles Frink, the day was marked by tragedy. But it also had elements of the miraculous; for one, the Quincy boardinghouse, just a few feet away, escaped damage. The men inside sounded the alarm and workers at the Daly West joined the rescue effort. In minutes, "there were fully 300 men on the scene working frantically in the hope to taking out the entombed men alive." For another, had the slide hit a few minutes later, during the shift change, many more workers might have been in the hoist plant.

Of those six buried men who survived, Noble Bates, the top carman, was probably saved because he was eating lunch near a work bench that protected him from the crushing snow. Dave Coleman, timberman, was eating in front of the boilers, which apparently gave him enough breathing space to survive when the snow piled in.

In the meantime, shift boss Michael Wynn was sheltered by the structure of the building and, despite being buried waist-deep and in total darkness, he was able to find candles and dig himself out with a shovel. Upon making it to safety, he "aided materially in locating the other men in the hoist."

What of the men working below? Snow clogged the collar of the Quincy shaft, but the miners were well supplied with air. As soon as they determined that the cage conveyance would not move and the shaft bell-signals were not working, they exited into the workings of the Little Bell mine through a connection at the 200-foot level of the Quincy. They quickly joined the Daly West miners in digging out the Quincy hoist plant. The rescue effort took two and a half hours.

In summer, the Quincy hoisting works remains are still visible. About 100 yards uphill from where the Mid Mountain Trail cuts across the Bandana run, you can hike off Bandana to the skier's left. On top of the waste rock dump sits a rusting hulk of machinery, overgrown with brush. With the return of thick fir and aspen groves uphill, the machinery is at little risk of avalanche these days.

INVISIBLE DEATH IN THE DALY WEST

Many dangers within a mine are in plain sight: walls at the end of the drift poised to collapse, hoists with frayed cables, or the yawning abyss of a shaft. A tragic accident in the Daly West in April 1942 demonstrated a different kind of danger, an invisible one called "damp."

In hard rock mining, damp refers to the odorless and colorless gases, usually carbon dioxide and carbon monoxide, that build up underground. Some come from the rock itself and some from mechanical processes such as blasting or rotting mine timbers. These gases mix with or are heavier than air, and can build up in low-lying pockets of a mine where ventilation is not adequate. The word "damp" is from the German "dampf" for steam or vapor.

Carbon dioxide's danger comes from how, through mixing, it can displace the available oxygen in the air we breathe. In contrast, carbon monoxide is absorbed by the hemoglobin in the blood and reduces the amount of oxygen carried within the body's circulation system.

On April 23, 1942, miners were working on the 1,400-foot level of the Daly West section of the Judge unit of the Park Utah Consolidated Mines company.

Descending from the drift at the 1,400-foot level was a winze, or inclined shaft. The winze had a ladder and was about fifty feet in depth.

It was here, in a section of the mine that hadn't been worked for a week, that damp accumulated. A possible reason the winze hadn't been worked was the shortage of wartime miners; many had been drafted for military service.

In today's world, an advance in technology is not necessarily an advance in safety. By the 1940s, the use of candles by miners was greatly curtailed. Instead, carbide headlamps and newer, battery-powered head-lamps provided light to work by. Like candles, carbide gear only worked in the presence of oxygen, and could warn of atmospheric anomalies. Newfangled electric lamps, which came on the scene in the 1920s, were indifferent to the surrounding atmosphere.

A miner with five years of experience who lived in Oakley, Edmund Walker, thirty-two, had been using a blow pipe, a compressed air device to remove loose materials from blasting holes. His blow pipe ceased to function, so he entered the winze about 2:30 p.m., in search of a spare blow pipe that had been left there the week before. He was wearing an electric headlamp. There was a ventilation pipe into the winze to provide fresh air, but it had been disconnected and Walker apparently took no steps to reactivate the system.

Walker's work partner, Ted Johnson, twenty-five, of Park City was a mine teamster. He set out to the powder station to obtain additional blasting powder, then returned to the top of the winze where he was to rendezvous with Walker. When Walker failed to return, Johnson descend-ed the winze ladder. Johnson had two headlamps with him, one electric and one carbide. His carbide headlamp soon went out.

Johnson spotted Walker, who was unresponsive, and unsuccessful-ly tried to move him. Johnson began to feel himself lose consciousness. With great effort, he returned to the main level and staggered down the drift to where timberman Glen Dewey Lockhart, forty-four, and mucker Wallace Perry, forty, were stationed. Both Lockhart and Perry had fifteen years or more of experience.

Warning of the gas, Johnson explained the situation. Lockhart and Perry disregarded Johnson's caution, and immediately set out down the winze ladder. Like Walker, they did not or could not adjust the fresh air system.

Perry wore an electric headlamp, and descended first. Lockhart wore a carbide headlamp, which shortly went out. He returned to borrow Johnson's electric one, and resumed his descent. Recovering slightly, Johnson set off to alert a safety crew.

A safety crew of fifteen miners rushed to the scene. Given the labyrinth-like structure of the mine, it took them twenty to thirty minutes to reach the winze. There, a team of four equipped with breathing apparatus descended the ladder, retrieved the three unresponsive men to the 1,400-foot level, and attempted artificial respiration. That effort failed, and by 6:00 p.m. the bodies were removed from the mine.

State mine inspector C.W. Spence analyzed the accident and made some observations: "The two heroic would-be rescuers permitted their better judgment to be overcome by the sense of loyalty to a stricken fellow."

"All miners . . . should refrain from entering any temporarily abandoned or inoperative workings . . . without testing for air with an open light, candle, or safety flame lamp. Electric lamps are fine for illumination in places known to have good air, but there is a serious question about their advisability in uncertain places."

Describing the insidious damp, Spence stated: "When [the gases] reached a point lower than others they flowed as so much water would. The winze and adjacent workings were the low points and undoubtedly they were nearly filled to the brim of heavier-than-air, probably mostly non-poisonous, gases . . . ."

"The men were drowned in those gases," Spence concluded.

THE FATAL FLAGSTAFF FALL

Somewhere about the thirty-five-foot level of the Flagstaff Mine, and moments after he called his friends above for light, young Paul Parmalee's footing on the abandoned mine's old ladder gave way with a crash, and he plunged into darkness to his death.

It was the afternoon of Sunday, August 18, 1963, and the sixteen-year-old had traveled up from Salt Lake City to explore the area near Bonanza Flat with three other Salt Lake City youths. The mishap triggered a dramatic emergency operation that concluded that night with the retrieval of Parmalee's body from the 300-foot level of the abandoned mine.

One of the friends, Judy Brown, nineteen, drove her car to Park City and alerted marshal William Ryan. Soon, a team of law enforcement, mine company staff, and even "old-time miners who had worked at the mine" gathered at the site.

The first phase of the recovery operation involved one rescuer being lowered fifty feet, while attached to a heavy manila rope held by a team of men above. He cleared enough broken lumber to probe the bottom of the shaft with a light but saw no evidence of life.

Next, two other men were lowered to the bottom of the shaft. There they found Parmalee's body. Additional men were staged at intervals in the shaft to facilitate communication with the team above ground. The mine was "pitch black," the rescuers told reporters.

The body was raised, and delivered by ambulance to a mortuary in Heber.

Newspapers praised the operation as "one of the finest and most dangerous" ever performed in Park City's mines and complimented the "telephone operators for their splendid service" and the wives who provided hot coffee and sandwiches to the rescue team.

The Flagstaff Mine, located about a quarter mile to the south of Deer Valley's Cushing's Cabin, had not been operating for decades on that day in 1963, though there had been intermittent prospecting at the site over the years. The mine was the first producer in the district, with wagons of its ore delivered to the railroad facility in Echo in 1870.

The Utah Division of Oil, Gas, and Mining capped the shaft in 1991, as part of its Abandoned Mine Reclamation Program. Over thirty years, the program has closed about 7,000 of the estimated 17,000 abandoned mines in Utah. "Stay out and stay alive" is the agency's motto. We suggest viewing the Park City Museum's translucent, light-up display of local tunnels and shafts as a better method of exploration.

Deer Crest Views:
The East Ontario and Boiler Point

A Wasatch County aside: The next time you ride the Jordanelle Gondola at Deer Valley Resort, take a quick look to the north as your cabin starts to ascend. You'll see a large, rusted cylinder, the steam-power boiler of Boiler Point. Its story involves the Park City Consolidated Mine, East Ontario Mine, and the Deer Crest real estate development.

The workings of the Park City Consolidated underlie today's Snow Park, the St. Regis hotel, and Little Baldy Peak. According to museum researcher David Nicholas, the mine "commenced full production in August of 1929. Silver, gold, and lead reserves proved abundant, along with copious amounts of water. Unfortunately for the Park Con, it achieved the dubious honor as Utah's 'hard luck' mine. From 1929 to 1939 the mine was one of the most prolific producers in the state. However, the Great Depression ensured that historically low prices would be paid for its ores."

After a series of ups and downs, the Park City Consolidated purchased the St. Louis and East Ontario mines in May 1941, further expanding its reach to the south of the area. The acquisition did not particularly pan out, according to McKay Edwards, who was president of Park City

Consolidated from 1980 to 1990. Edwards executed the master plan and entitlements, which were the basis for the Deer Crest real estate project. In 1996 the land was sold to the developers of Deer Crest.

"The East Ontario shaft was about 700 feet deep. It was sunk in the days before drilling could either prove out an ore deposit or not, so it was an 'exploratory shaft,'" Edwards writes.

It was at this site that the boiler was originally located, presumably to run the hoist of the East Ontario shaft.

"At about 7,400 feet in elevation, the site was very scenic and a favorite of former Park City Consolidated Mines President Gordon Stott, who named it 'Boiler Point,'" Edwards continues. "On my real estate master plan I had designated the site as 'Boiler Point Historic Site' and hoped to leave the boiler in place, but the Deer Crest developers apparently had their own ideas."

While the boiler was relocated, one can be grateful that the developers and homeowners were far-sighted enough to preserve the historic artifact. According to Don Taylor, past general manager of the Deer Crest Management Association, the boiler "was moved between 1998 and 2000 by Heil Construction. At the time Deer Crest was being built there was a plethora of large equipment on site that could have been used to move it."

The boiler remnants have two main components. One is a large cylinder (about 150 inches long and fifty-six inches in diameter) that is held several feet off the ground by metal footings. An ancillary cylinder (about 120 inches long and twenty-four inches in diameter) lies nearby. A cursory examination unveiled no manufacturer's mark.

Maps from the United State Geological Survey (USGS) tell the story of the Boiler Point transition in a simple way. Between 1956 and 1987, the maps display the East Ontario alone on the hillside. The 2001 map shows the mine just west and uphill of Deer Crest Estates Drive, north of its intersection with Jordanelle View Drive. By 2014, the mine disappears from the topographic maps and the Deer Crest road system prevails. On the 1932 Colliers Claims map in the basement of the Park City Museum, the shaft is on the northwest corner of the Dewet #2 mining claim.

By today's landmarks, Boiler Point's location is between Tower 12 and Tower 13 of the gondola route, and roughly halfway between the gondola and the Jordanelle ski run. In other words, just a stone's throw from some hedge fund manager's living room window.

If you want to approximate the view from Boiler Point this summer, pick up the Deer Crest Trail near the St. Regis and follow it uphill to the Outlook Trail. At the end of Outlook, on the Jordanelle ski run, you get a fine view of Jordanelle Reservoir and the Uintas.

Geology and Labor in the Park City Consolidated

Launched in 1928, the Park City Consolidated Mine was a significant ore producer through the next decade. In 1936, the mine's general superintendent, Gloyd M. Wiles, wrote a detailed report for the U.S. Bureau of Mines on mining methods and costs in the mine. This technical document provides a look into the complexities of hard-rock mining hereabouts.

From its inception to November 1935, the mine produced 4,525 ounces of gold and 2.4 million ounces of silver from 155,135 tons of ore. This works out to about 12.5 ounces of silver to the ton.

The mine, located near today's St. Regis Deer Valley hotel, was served by the Denver & Rio Grande Western and Union Pacific railroads. The railroads shared trackage rights on the spur connecting the mine to Salt Lake City, and ultimately transported ore to a concentrating plant in Midvale, Utah.

Most of the ore mined at the Park City Consolidated was confined to lode deposits in three main fissures of Weber quartzite called the Silver, Roosevelt, and East Crescent. A vertical shaft was sunk to the 400-foot level, and then two winzes (inclined shafts) drove to the 1,000-foot levels of the Silver and East Crescent fissures. Drifts (side tunnels) were worked at multiple levels along the winzes. At the time of the report, a crosscut was being driven at the 900-foot level to improve ore transfer, water mitigation, and ventilation.

Exploration (aka "development") was carried on by what miners term as crosscutting, drifting, and raising. Diamond drilling for core samples into the shattered veins and native quartzite "country" rock wasn't worth the effort, Wiles noted.

One difficulty underground had to do with the swelling and sloughing faced when mining operations encountered porphyry and limestone adjacent to the fissures. "Swelling then takes place within a few hours after they are opened to the atmosphere," Wiles wrote. "Walls and ore matrices such as these demand individual attention in the various parts of the mine and present individual problems of wall support if safe, clean mining is to be accomplished."

In other words, the geology posed a danger of collapse. This called for cut-and-fill and open-stope mining with timber support. The report describes sophisticated eight-by-eight-inch Douglas Fir "post, bridge, and cap" timber structures and other carpentry necessary to shore up the workspaces. If this is hard to visualize, go see the fascinating scale model of a mine in the Park City Museum.

When it came to mining, pneumatic drilling and blasting were the order of the day. In the rock typically encountered, a miner and two muckers could advance a six-by-eight-foot heading as much as five to six feet in eight hours. "Usually twelve holes and sixty to eighty sticks of 30-percent-strength powder suffice to break the round," Wiles wrote.

Ventilation also proved a challenge. "The country rock contains an inert gas, probably nitrogen and carbon dioxide, which ebbs and flows from the workings in accordance with the barometric pressure. When the barometer is falling this gas enters the mine workings and so replaces the air to such an extent that even a carbide lamp will not burn. Conversely, when the barometer is rising, the air flows into the rock from the workings, and the most remote heading will contain pure fresh air."

Mines can breathe? Anybody who has stood in the cool breeze emanating from the Spiro Tunnel on a hot July day knows that is true!

The company had a thirty-horsepower centrifugal fan to draw air from the surface and deliver it to the working faces through galvanized iron tubes. "Four hours are allowed between shifts so that the mine air will be as pure as possible when workmen go on shift," Wiles noted.

The mine also had four pumps capable of lifting 1,100 gallons of water per minute, and an electrical system to power the various equipment needed.

Not surprisingly, the workforce reflected a range of talents. Beside a cadre of miners and muckers, job functions included an electrical/mechanical engineer, two electricians (and two helpers), three mechanics, three pumpmen, two timber framers, a blacksmith, and a steel sharpener. In administration, roles included geologist, assayer, cost-and-time clerk, and stenographer, among others.

Wages reflected the labor spectrum. For an eight-hour day, shift bosses earned $6.75. Master mechanics made $6.50, hoistmen $5.50, and electricians $5.25. The shaft timbermen and shaft miners made $5.75. Regular miners made $5.25 and muckers $4.75.

Rounding out the report is a dollars-and-cents analysis. It cost about $3.41 to produce and hoist a ton of ore. Development accounted for 29 percent of the cost, mining thirty-six, transportation twenty-two, general two, pumping six, and surface operations five. Across all those categories, labor accounted for 71 percent of the costs. Quite a way to make a buck! (To get 2025 purchasing power, multiply that buck by twenty-two.)

Bio breaks: People curious about mining in the old days sometimes ask, "How was human waste handled in the mines?"

Remember all that water Park City mines had to deal with? There was usually a flowing stream nearby where a miner could urinate. As for solid waste, the mines would designate an area for an underground outhouse, usually a section of the mine no longer being worked. In more urgent circumstances, a miner could use a pail or old dynamite crate. Someone with the job title of "honeydipper" would collect it and transport it out of the mine for disposal elsewhere.

THE METALLIC HISTORY SIGNS

As you hike, bike, or ski around Deer Valley or the Park City resorts, you may notice some metallic signs that share historical stories of our days past. These well-designed, attractive, and informative signs capture in brief the origins and outcomes of the Silver King mines and many more sites of interest.

That these signs exist in the first place is a *mea culpa* on the part of the United Park City Mines (UPCM) Company. In September 1998, UPCM dismantled the historic 1903 Keith-Kearns Mill near the base of the Pioneer chairlift. Apparently in doing so, they had failed to file any paperwork with Summit County. It was a "dark of night" destruction of a historic structure that was dilapidated, but still represented a significant part of our mining past. Rumor has it that the structure's timbers now grace Park City Mountain Resort's Legacy Lodge, which opened in 1999.

The Park City historical community had their hackles raised, and after a meeting with UPCM, County, City, Chamber of Commerce, and the museum, UPCM agreed to contribute $38,000 to mitigate the damage. The Restaurant Sales Tax fund matched that amount, and within a year, dozens of signs were in place.

We'll never retrieve the fascinating structure that was the Keith-Kearns Mill, but we can appreciate the incisive and interesting signage around our hills and town that resulted from UPCM's mistake.

Note that, in 2024, Friends of Ski Mountain Mining History installed five additional metal history signs at the relocated Daly West Headframe. These signs were not part of the original batch.

THE SILVER MINE ADVENTURE

Three common questions I hear about mining history in Summit County are: "Can you still go into any mines?"; "Do you remember when you could go into the Silver Mine Adventure mine?"; and "Do they still mine here?"

The answer to the first question is not really. Most of the mines or drain tunnels in the area have been completely closed up, either by gates or plowed earth. There are a very few open adits (mine openings, or a great New York Times crossword answer) scattered here and there. But the history crew doesn't talk about them, because the city or the state will then go close the adits up if they catch wind of their whereabouts. On the occasion when this correspondent takes friends to any of these clandestine sites, the friends are told, "We are entering an Instagram-free zone."

The answer to the second question is that the Silver Mine Adventure operated from about 1995 to 1998 in the Ontario Mine Number 3 Shaft off Marsac Avenue. It was the kind of carnival ride you'd do once. Guests would buy tickets to ride the creaky mine cage elevator to the 1,500-foot level of the mine, ride a small tram into the drain tunnel, and learn about operations underground. It was cold and claustrophobic, and guests were given flimsy plastic ponchos to ward off the water constantly dripping from the walls.

The entity that launched the Silver Mine Adventure was Leisure and Recreation Concepts (LARC) of Dallas, Texas, a consulting firm specializing in theme parks such as Utah's Lagoon. LARC spent $2.5 million in upfront capital, and claimed to the Deseret News that the Silver Mine Adventure hosted 60,000 people in its first five months of operation. LARC leased the mine from United Park City Mines Company (UPCM).

Groundwater impeding operations was a constant issue for Park City's mines. It was also an expensive constraint on the Silver Mine Adventure and impacted the bottom line—so were the costs of liability insurance and site and safety maintenance. And a "Tunnel of Terror" Halloween exhibit in 1997 stirred criticism from locals and unions, perhaps discouraging tourists from visiting. Whatever the causes, it seemed the underground "theme park" was, unlike the original Ontario Mine, bereft of profit.

Another possible factor: In the early 90s, UPCM was seeking development rights from Wasatch County for a hotel, golf course, and high-end residences in what would become the Bonanza Flat conservation easement. An attractive asset UPCM offered the county was the water flowing out of the Ontario #2 "Keetley" drain tunnel. When a deal was struck, having tourists traipsing about the culinary water supply infrastructure was no longer desirable, compelling the closure of the mine tour.

The Jordanelle Special Service District now maintains the Keetley drain tunnel. This allows the district to capture the steady flow of water exiting the tunnel, which is about three miles long, and terminates near the Mayflower Exit of Route 40. A yearly average of 6,500 acre feet of water is produced this way. The district treats the stream to capture the minerals that infuse the water. The district then sells the water to its customers.

So the answer to the third question is yes. We live in a drought-stricken state with high real estate prices, so "water is the new silver."

A closing pun: If you find ore, go adit.

PARK CITY PAST
-OTHER PURSUITS-

*Close calls and near misses, tragedy and healing,
and a cast of outlaws, bootleggers, real estate developers,
and other suspicious characters.*

THE PONY EXPRESS WAS HERE . . . FOR ABOUT SIX WEEKS

During the brief tenure of the Pony Express (April 1860 to October 1861), the main route took riders down Echo Canyon to Henefer, up over Big Mountain, down into Emigration Canyon, and then to Salt Lake City. A big winter closed the Big Mountain pass for a spell, and from April 3 to May 15, 1860 (the six weeks mentioned above), riders traversed from Echo to Rockport to Parleys Park and down Parleys Canyon to Salt Lake City. George Snyder (of Snyderville) and his wife, Rebecca, fed and provisioned the riders in that interlude.

You can find a memorial to Park City's role in the Pony Express at the Spring Creek trailhead in the Blackhawk Station neighborhood just northeast of the Kimball Junction exit on I-80. Just over a mile to the east is the Kimball Hotel Stage Stop, which was used by the Holladay Stage Line and the Wells Fargo Express Company. Built in 1862, the building may be the oldest structure in Summit County and is worth a look-see. Mark Twain describes the Kimballs in *Roughing It*.

You can also see a bigger-than-life bronze statue of a Pony Express horse and rider at the Redstone development, east of the Route 224 underpass. If you like the Frederick Remington school of sculpture, this is your jam.

The Pony Express was a victim of disruptive technology. In October 1861, transcontinental telegraph lines connected in Salt Lake City for the first time. Its nearly instantaneous delivery of information obviated the need for the Pony Express. You can find a plaque that commemorates the completion of the telegraph on Main Street in Salt Lake City, near the City Creek Mall. The Pony Express station for Salt Lake City was a block to the south.

BUTCH CASSIDY IN PARK CITY?

The coffee shop at the Park City Nursery on Route 224 is a delightful place to order up your favorite latte. The staff is attentive, the brew tasty, the pastries delicious, and you can take your haul into the big greenhouse and enjoy the greenery even in the depths of winter.

The only knock on the place is a small historical plaque explaining that the structure was the first general store in the Park City area. All well and good, and kudos to the Pace and Archibald families for running the operation back in the day (1880s to 1920s). Things get stretched a tad beyond credibility when the plaque states: "Local legend says that Butch Cassidy and the Hole in Wall Gang hid out in the floorboards while passing through."

First of all, can you imagine Butch and his roughnecks subjecting themselves to the indignity of hiding out in any crawl space anywhere in the western U.S.?

Second, there are essentially no archival references to Butch or his gang passing through town. There's not a word in any of the newspapers published in town from 1890 to 1920. It is known that Butch was arrested in Star Valley, Wyoming, in 1892 and spent a few months in jail in Evanston before facing trial in Lander. But Park City? Not a peep.

Third, there's the "George Washington" effect at work. Along the mid-Atlantic states, every historic country inn seems to have a sign that says, "George Washington slept here." Maybe so, maybe not. The "Butch Cassidy" effect is an analogous phenomenon in the western U.S.

There is a nicely wrought article in the newspaper and museum's "Way We Were" series that asks the question, "Did Butch Cassidy Rob the Oak Saloon?"

The article, written by Chris McLaws, postulates the following: "Legend has it that in 1910, Kid Parker – a common nickname for Robert Leroy Parker, aka 'Butch Cassidy' – entered the Oak Saloon at 12:30 a.m. and asked for a cup of coffee. He then pulled out a six shooter and told everyone to give him their gold. He got about $600 worth of goods and, as he was leaving, said he would be back for more. Or so it goes.

"In truth, this 'Kid Parker' was most likely a copycat of Butch Cassidy. Understandably, many young outlaws in the 'Wild West' took on the alias of their hero when committing their crimes."

Most sources place Butch's death in Bolivia in 1908. The Oak Saloon robbery took place two years later. So much for the floorboards.

Make sure to tip your baristas. It takes stamina to be that cheerful.

THE JORDANELLE JAPANESE INTERNMENT FARM

Shortly after Pearl Harbor, on February 19, 1942, President Franklin D. Roosevelt uprooted the lives of 110,000 Japanese Americans. His executive order authorized their relocation inland from the West Coast, despite a government report that concluded "there is no Japanese problem" and that they were loyal citizens. The order allowed for "voluntary" relocation for a short period before mandatory relocation by force.

Fred Isamu Wada, who ran a profitable produce business in Oakland, California, realized leaving as soon as possible would give his family more freedom in the long run. His wife was from Ogden, Utah, so he looked to Utah for a new home. His family joined fourteen others to form a farming cooperative, show support for the war effort, and avoid relocation to an internment camp.

Wada, thirty-five, scouted the Duchesne area but, despite a warm welcome, he settled on Keetley due to its proximity to rail lines. He negotiated with the local mayor and landowner, George Fisher, to sign a four-year lease at $7,500 a year for about 3,500 rocky acres and some buildings, including an apartment house. (That's about $145,000 in 2025 purchasing power.)

Locals did not take news of the Keetley Japanese Relocation Farm favorably. In a letter to Governor Maw, the Park City mayor, city council, and the Wasatch County sheriff, some locals requested the Japanese be kept away. Their request did not prevail, as Fisher had earlier checked with the U.S. Attorney to verify such a transaction was legal.

With government relocation and travel permits in hand, the group left Oakland around March 28, two days before the "volunteer" window closed and forced relocation became the policy. They traveled in twenty-nine vehicles, caravanning to Keetley in three days. Like many other Japanese Americans, they were never able to recover the homes and possessions they had to abandon.

Shortly after the group arrived in early April, someone in a passing car threw a stick of dynamite toward the farm buildings. Local miners were the suspects, and another blast followed, but things eventually settled down as the newcomers proved their worth in an area experiencing a labor shortage.

By moving quickly, Wada spared his followers a forced move to the harsher lands of Utah's West Desert, near Delta. The arrangement also benefited Fisher, whose land would improve. When the snow melted, Wada learned just how rocky the leased land was. "Hell," he said, "we had to move fifty tons of rocks to clear 150 acres to farm."

Throughout the war, the families in Keetley grew vegetables and raised chickens, pigs, goats, and beef and dairy cattle. They sold their goods to Safeway, ran a farm stand, and sent food to the Topaz internment camp. They cleared another 1,000 acres to bring in hay and built new structures. Some of the men hired out during the week to work on farms in Spanish Fork, Orem, and Heber.

At a macro level, about 5,000 of the 110,000 Japanese Americans affected by Roosevelt's order had the resources to move before forced relocations began. Accounts vary, but at the micro level, there were 124 to 140 people at the farm in Keetley. Of that group, more than fifty were under twenty years old, with at least twenty-five under the age of ten. When the harvest came in, everyone from ten-year-olds to elders joined the work in the fields.

A four-year-old at the time, Howard Yamamoto later recalled, "I don't remember that much, the hardship. But the parents, my God. Could I do it? No. I couldn't do it. I can't imagine myself doing it."

When the war ended, they brought in the last harvest and closed the farm. About one-third of the group remained in Utah, the rest returning to California. Jordanelle Reservoir, constructed by the Bureau of Reclamation, inundated the farm in 1995, but the rising waters did not wash the stain away from our nation's history.

Learn more at *historytogo.utah.gov/japanese-agricultural-colony/*

Copper Bottomed Conscience: The Michigan Bunch and Main Street

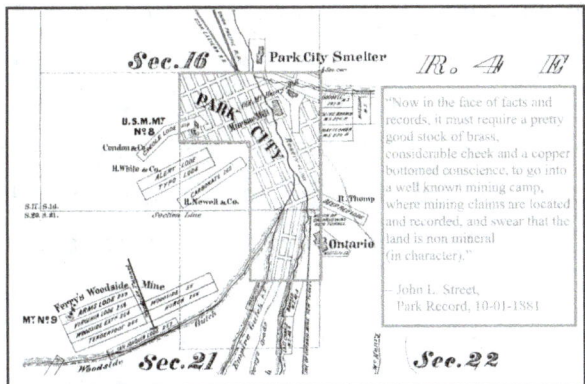

Image courtesy of the Park City Museum.

From the early days, the business of real estate has been a contact sport around these parts. In 1873, for example, little documentation of land ownership existed for Park City's Main Street area, creating a slippery business opportunity for a group of Midwest entrepreneurs including E.P. Ferry, D.C. McLaughlin and F.A. Nims. Known today as the Michigan Bunch, they were associated with the Marsac Silver Mining Company. The legal wrangling they engendered reached as far as the U.S. Supreme Court.

In May 1874 through an agent, Marsac co-owner Nims filed claim to four "quarters" of land, some 160 acres centered on the Main Street area. The application stated the land was unoccupied and not mining territory, though dozens of people who had built on it or prospected it would argue to the contrary.

Nims' purchase used certificates, called scrip, originally issued by the federal government to, in the words of the day, "*half-breeds or mixed-bloods*" of the Sioux Nation in Minnesota Territory. The certificates, known as "Sioux Half-Breed Scrip," could be exchanged by the original designee for other unencumbered U.S. territorial land. Nims ignored the stipulation that the scrip had limitations on transferability.

In October 1875, Nims, McLaughlin, et al. asked the federal Land Office to substitute more transferrable Valentine Scrip in place of the Sioux scrip. The Land Office overlooked the technicalities and allowed the switch, and in August 1876, Nims applied for a land patent. In November 1876, a group of Park City residents, led by lawyer and butcher John L. Street, appealed to the Interior Department, stating the land was occupied in 1874 and that some was used for mining and trade. (Parts of the Creole mine, Dugway claim, and Ontario Mill overlapped the 160 acres, and as for "lawyer and butcher," how can you tell the difference?)

At the national level, the fix appeared to be in. In February 1877, President Ulysses S. Grant approved the land patent. His acting vice president at the time was Senator T.W. Ferry (R-MI), who was E.P. Ferry's brother. The Interior Department issued the patent, dismissing the protestors' affidavits and other evidence.

The Marsac company began issuing lease, purchase, or vacate demands to inhabitants of the land at issue. In June 1877, Marsac manager and land agent E.W. Thayer became the target of what was called the "Red Hot Riot." Ten men led by Colonel John Nelson made a late-night vigilante visit to Thayer demanding that he sign a letter specifying lower prices than the company's offers. The men also demanded that Thayer leave town. One report of the altercation had Colonel Nelson laying hands on Thayer. The ten men were arrested, and seven of them were fined for their disturbance of the peace. The signed letter never surfaced.

Meanwhile, some residents took the Marsac group up on their offers. Then in 1880, Nims signed the remaining property over to E.P. Ferry.

The fix was in at the local level too. R.W. Chambers of the Ontario Mine originally spoke out against the land transaction. His opposition cooled when the Marsac group offered title to the Ontario Mill site at very reasonable terms. Colonel Nelson's ardor against the Marsac group also diminished when he was given title to plots of land he occupied.

The aforementioned John L. Street was recalcitrant and refused to pay Ferry for four lots, which Street said he acquired from the McHenry Company in 1874. In 1882, Ferry sued Street for possession of the land plus damages of $500 (about $12,500 in 2025 dollars).

Trial took place in November 1883. The court did not allow Street to argue that the original land patent was illegal, and subsequently ruled in favor of Ferry. The court directed Street to turn over the lots and pay damages and court costs.

Legal maneuvers ensued. Street appealed to the Territory's Supreme Court, but that body upheld the lower court's determination. Street then appealed in 1886 to the U.S. Supreme Court, but SCOTUS claimed lack of jurisdiction. It would not be the only SCOTUS trial to which Ferry was a party.

In parallel to these actions, Street reached out to the U.S. Attorney General in 1882. After conferring with the Land Office, the U.S. AG filed suit to annul Nims' patent. This trial took place in 1883 in Utah's Third District Court and was again decided in favor of Nims, Ferry, et al. The Territory's Supreme Court took a look and dismissed an appeal in 1888.

With options exhausted, the fight was over. In this real estate scheme, Ferry may have made about $32,400, or close to $800,000 in 2025 dollars. Presumably, these funds were plowed back into mining operations. The gains were obtained by sharp practice, and in Street's words, "a copper bottomed conscience" may have provided vital cash flow in Ferry's pursuit of a mining empire.

THE BIG WHITE BARN

Built in 1922, the beautiful structure on the west side of Route 224 is called the McPolin Barn.

The McPolins sold it to the Osguthorpes in 1947, so people sometimes call it the Osguthorpe Barn. In quieter days, as late as the early 1980s, the Osguthorpes' dairy herd was known to interrupt traffic as their cows crossed Route 224.

According to the Park City municipal website, the McPolins built the structure using recycled timber salvaged from an old mine tailings mill. They then fit the timbers together without using nails. Sounds like they had the same supply chain issues as contractors did during the pandemic. The barn is about 7,500 square feet in size.

The seventy acres surrounding the barn are the McPolin Farmland conservation easement, held by the wonderful Summit Land Conservancy land trust. As of this writing, Summit Land has more than 14,000 acres protected from development in Summit and surrounding counties. The land trust holds several easements, like McPolin, on behalf of Park City Municipal.

In the spring, you can frequently see nesting sandhill cranes and heron along the nearby stream. In the weeks before Halloween, there's an exhibit of colorful scarecrows along the paved bike path just uphill of the barn. In the winter, there's a delightful stretch of cross-country ski trails around the pastures. It is one of Park City's iconic views, and when driving by, you frequently see photographers striving to capture the image.

Sawmills and Stills: Thaynes Canyon Through the Years

Anyone who has recreated in Thaynes Canyon knows it is an active, well-traveled place. Turns out that's always been the case, with its history of mining, agriculture, lumber, the raising of thoroughbred horses and prize cows, and even the manufacture of bootleg whiskey.

The canyon's namesake, John Johnson Thayne, was born in Scotland in 1825. His family emigrated to Ontario, Canada when he was a child. Life grew hard when his father died shortly after their arrival. A family memoir states: "The family was left without much property or money, in a cold country. At times they were obliged to peel the bark from fences for fuel to keep warm."

Surviving these hard times, Thayne developed a head for business. He traveled widely to sell a glue he made for repairing china. A member of the LDS Church, Thayne met his wife-to-be Sidney Boyer on one such sales call, and upon marriage, the couple moved to Iowa in 1855. (Clearly she was stuck on the glue salesman.) There he made a good living running a sawmill, something he would do for most of his life.

In 1861, they moved to Utah and established a home in Salt Lake City's Sugar House neighborhood. At this time, Thayne entered the practice of polygamy by marrying Elizabeth Hunt, who had traveled in the same party of Saints from Iowa. Thayne had fourteen children by his two wives.

After the move to Salt Lake City, Thayne built a water-powered sawmill in Mill Creek Canyon and a steam-powered one in Park City's Thaynes Canyon area. Both operated until 1875. The exact location of the Thaynes Canyon mill is unknown, and there is mystery involved with it. The memoir continues: "Enemies or someone who was jealous burned one sawmill down and he lost most of his property."

The family then moved to Woodland, Utah, establishing another sawmill using the Mill Creek equipment. Thayne died in 1910 in Wellington, Utah.

In 1878, Civil War veteran William M. Ferry and his wife Jeannette arrived in Park City and bought 160 acres at the mouth of Thaynes Canyon. In 1890, they built a large wooden Victorian mansion filled with stained glass and other ornate touches. Upon the colonel's death in 1915, the Silver King Consolidated Mining Company purchased the home. U.S. Senator and mining magnate Thomas Kearns spent summers there, and raised thoroughbred horses, a common practice among his millionaire mining and railroad contemporaries such as George Hearst, James Ben Ali Haggin, and Charles Crocker. The mansion ultimately was moved to Park Meadows and is in private hands.

In 1894, P.J. Sullivan bought ranchland in Thaynes Canyon. Sullivan, known as the "milkman," raised dairy cows, and his wife Elizabeth continued operations upon his death in 1898. Apparently, milk was not the only drink available on the premises. In 1921, three men, one of whom was named Jack Sullivan, were arrested for operating an illegal whiskey still in the canyon. In 1924, another Sullivan (most likely Dan) was caught making moonshine in the vicinity.

Around 1930, the Sullivans sold the property to local mine manager Andrew Hurley, who built the 35-by-140-foot barn, now known as the Armstrong barn. Salt Lake City banker and mayor Herbert Snow then bought the ranch in 1934 and continued the dairy operations until his death in 1957. The ranch, called Snow's Summit Ranch, stayed in the family.

Snow's daughter Heloise married William Melbourne Armstrong. Their children all lived on the property at one time. Heloise's sons, Herbert "Herbie" Snow Armstrong and William Melbourne "Mel" Armstrong Jr., worked alongside their grandfather and took prize Guernsey milk cows to the Utah State Fair. Their stock won Grand Champion a number of times.

Herbie and Mel were instrumental in preserving much of the lands in Thaynes Canyon that were part of the original Snow's Summit Ranch. The November 2018 bond passed by Park City voters that preserved Treasure Hill also included funding for the Armstrong Snow Ranch Pastures. Herbie and Mel's wife Kerry Armstrong made a substantial contribution of value to ensure the pastures were protected. The iconic 1926-era dairy barn that Mel and Kerry restored in the late 1970s is protected under a conservation easement as well. The redoubtable Utah Open Lands (UOL) currently holds three easements preserving about 175 acres in the canyon.

The Armstrong name is honored in the eponymous trail in the canyon. An uphill bike trail, it was designed to lighten the load on the popular Spiro trail.

"The land at the mouth of Thaynes Canyon has been supporting and sustaining Park City for more than a century, both in terms of agriculture that has fed us and recreation that keeps us in touch with nature," says Wendy Fisher, UOL executive director. "The generosity of the Armstrong family continues to have a major impact on our community."

Entrepreneurism and the White Mule

During the years of national Prohibition (1920 to 1933), the entrepreneurial spirit to *make* spirits gripped Park City. Illegal stills abounded, producing "White Mule," a clear liquid with a kick. Many miscreants operated in the basements and back rooms of Old Town, Empire Canyon, Richardson Flats, Thaynes Canyon, and elsewhere. According to the Park Record, a fair amount of the product was destined for Park City's "soft drink" parlors.

While it is easy to romanticize the era and to view the scofflaws with bemusement, white mule could be devastating, like the fentanyl-laced street drugs of our time. Park City miner Jack Beakel, for example, died in a Salt Lake City lodging house after quaffing a bad batch of this firewater in May 1923. In January 1925, miners John Pezely and Dan Ryan died after partaking too much over the holidays. Sometimes the mule's kick was fatal!

Here are some of the entrepreneurial high points:

- Expanding the product line: September 1920 saw Park City barber Alex Hamlin pulled over in Parley's Canyon with three gallons of white mule in his suspiciously brand-new vehicle. His wife and children were also in the car. The Salt Lake sheriff impounded the vehicle, and Hamlin was released on $800 bail (almost $13,000 in 2025 dollars . . . multiply all the dollar figures below by sixteen to get current values). The article does not record any family tensions that may have ensued. It does imply Hamlin was selling the whiskey through his shop. Indeed, in a prior run-in, Hamlin deployed the "barbers use alcohol" defense in court.

- Foreign-born entrepreneurs: In October 1920, stills were uncovered on upper Main Street and in Empire Canyon. Newspaper accounts state both stills were operated by foreign nationals, who were listed in the police reports as John Doe and Richard Roe. Justice O'Neil imposed the maximum fine of $299. A night later, another raid caught Gus "The King of Sweden" Nielson, who had a still "consisting of an old dirty carbide can, a coil of pipe and a slop-bucket."

- Flood the market: A November 1920 raid on the Woodside Avenue home of Tony Levy uncovered a still, ten gallons of white mule, and two barrels of "dago red," a vintage of questionable provenance. The still was dismantled, the liquor confiscated, and the barrels busted open with the contents poured out.

- Quick pivot: In August 1921, Marshal St. Jeor ran into Joe McKoskey, who was suspected of having a still secreted in the surrounding hills. The marshal spotted a whiskey bottle in McKoskey's back pocket, and demanded it. This prompted McKoskey to pull his revolver and shove it in the marshal's belly. "Throw up your hands!" McKoskey growled. The marshal remarked cooly that he would not throw up his hands. McKoskey then demanded the marshal hand over his pistol. Again, St. Jeor demurred. When McKoskey grabbed for the marshal's pistol, St. Jeor quickly latched onto McKoskey's right hand and pressed down. McKoskey's revolver discharged and the bullet crashed through the bootlegger's knee, taking the fight out of him. Cool-headed work by the marshal!

- Women-owned businesses: In July 1922, Olga Hrvatin, a widow with five children, was arrested for having a still and liquor on her premises. Her husband had recently died and "undoubtedly she had been persuaded to distill moonshine for a living." She pled guilty and the judge only fined her fifty dollars "because of the little ones depending on her."

- Fail fast: In August 1924, Dan Sullivan outran the sheriff when a raid in Thaynes Canyon uncovered his outdoor manufacturing operation. The authorities confiscated the gear and "rotting corn" mash, which made the sheriff's office smell like a "decomposed limburger cheese joint . . . or worse." Sullivan evaded capture for a day. The question of appropriate food pairings was not discussed.
- Proprietary knowledge: In August 1925, a Denver-based federal agent made a clandestine visit to Park City without alerting local authorities. (Yes, at least one local cop was on the take.) The agent soon learned of a large 100-gallon still in a mill in Woodside Gulch. Only then did the agent alert the sheriff's office, and the bootleggers, George Siddoway and Vic Carlsen, were arrested.
- Executive leadership: In September 1925, a raid on a Norfolk Avenue home yielded a still, some moonshine, and fourteen barrels of precursor mash. House renter George Butterfield claimed he was just "in the employ of someone else," but the article does not shed further light. The article does happen to mention the landlord, Frank Lake, so readers could take the hint.
- Niche market: On a November 1926 day, John D. McDermont was caught in the act of passing moonshine to prisoners in the jail. The unlicensed catering cost him seventy-five dollars in fines.

These are the tales of some of the moonshiners who got caught. History shrouds the myriad stories of those who escaped the law's attention! But be assured, those uncaught entrepreneurs were active, because Park City was known throughout the region as a "wet" town.

THE EMPIRE CANYON LANDSLIDES

At the very top of Daly Avenue, well after it changes from paved to gravel, you can visit the Judge Tunnel, Judge Mining and Smelting Company building, Alliance mine structures, and an old storage bunker for explosives built into the hillside. This area was also the site of two landslides, in 1967 and 1969.

Daly Avenue and the dirt road that today passes by the base of Deer Valley's Lady Morgan lift used to be the Guardsman Pass Road, aka Route 224. In June 1967, melting snowpack saturated the ground and an estimated 100,000 tons of rock, mud, trees, power lines, and telephone poles slowly slid off the steep slope to the east. Pushing across Daly Avenue, the slide took with it the Judge Mines assay office, crushed a garage, and pushed a car toward the gully. The landslide dammed Poison Creek for a few hours, which called for the temporary evacuation of residents downstream.

Two years later in May 1969, the earth moved again in the same vicinity, and the scars of this slide remain for hikers and bikers to observe today. This landslide was larger and more dramatic, swiftly and loudly crashing down from the ridgeline hundreds of feet above, and moving house-sized boulders along the way. It stopped up the creek with a 400-foot-wide, 100-foot-tall berm, creating a temporary pond estimated to be sixty feet deep. Residents downstream again went on alert until the flooding danger passed.

After this event, two things were moved. One, the mine superintendent's house, built in 1907, was relocated in August 1969 to Snows Lane at the mouth of Thaynes Canyon after a seven-day trip down Daly Avenue, Main Street, and Route 224.

Two, the Guardsman Pass Road route was moved to Marsac Avenue and Ontario Canyon, where it remains today.

These events remind us that the canyons surrounding us are dynamic and ever-changing. Geologic time is slow, except when it isn't!

THREE HISTORIC AERIAL CRASHES

In November 1941, a twin-engine B-18 bomber making a night flight from Colorado to Salt Lake City encountered heavy weather and veered off its flight path. The combination of south winds up to fifty miles an hour, extreme turbulence, sleet, and the B-18's sluggish flying characteristics caused the seven airmen aboard to abandon ship over the Park City area.

Six of the seven were able to parachute out of the plane. Horrifically, the unpiloted plane looped around and cut across the glide path of the parachuters. Major R.E.L. Pirtle, commander of the 88th Squadron of the Seventh Bombardment group, was killed when the plane fouled his parachute.

The seventh airman, Sergeant Jack Duane Anderson, was unable to exit the severely buffeted aircraft and died when the B-18 struck dirt, bounced, and crashed on the side of Iron Mountain, near where the Mid-Mountain trail traverses the area. Bystanders on the ground spoke of a terrible roaring as the plane flew overhead, banked into the mountain, and burst into flames.

The five airmen who successfully parachuted landed in the Park Meadows area, which, at the time, provided a soft, muddy landing zone.

For more on this incident, visit *parkcityhistory.org/category/way-we-were/* and read the detailed accounts written by local history researchers David Nicholas and Steve Leatham.

In March 1969, a light plane with four people on board encountered engine trouble and made a hard landing on Park City Mountain Resort's Hidden Splendor trail, a most unusual way to experience the Greatest Snow on Earth™. The plane was wrecked, but thankfully, the plane's occupants and nearby skiers avoided any serious injuries. The pilot, Jack

Leavitt, and his three passengers were all Brigham Young University students. In emails and phone interviews, Leavitt said: "We took off from the Heber airport where the plane was stationed. The plane was owned by Grey's Lumber, my father's company. The plan was to fly to Salt Lake City, land, have a Coke and then return to Heber via Provo Canyon. While passing over the ski resort, the stall light illuminated. I followed my training and turned on the electric fuel pump and pulled the lever for carburetor heat.

"The stall light stayed illuminated and it became obvious we were losing power. To gain elevation, I turned north where the slope runs downhill. We were gliding at this point and there was no response from the carburetor heater nor the electric fuel pump. As it turned out the carburetor was almost closed with ice. I knew we were going down, so I picked an opening in the trees which turned out to be the Hidden Splendor ski run. There were no skiers on that run. It happened pretty fast."

Ski Patrol responded quickly, and treated the students for minor injuries and shock. In the week after the wreck, a helicopter made several trips to remove the plane's components from the ski trail. Leavitt remarked that he was at the stage where he was allowed to fly cross county solo. Without an airplane to use, he did not continue with training, though he did pursue a career in aerospace manufacturing.

In 1985, Park City Ski Area hosted the first of several International Ski and Snowboard Federation (FIS) world cup alpine events. The efforts of the resort's vice president of marketing, Craig Badami, were in large part responsible for bringing these events to the area. By November 1989, the resort had gained international recognition for their successful event management. Badami brought panache to Park City's slopes.

For the set-up and breakdown of the 1989 contest, which was shortened one day due to heavy snows, a six-passenger Alouette helicopter ferried some of the equipment up and down the race hill. According to local historian Larry Warren, Craig hopped on for a ride back up to the top of the race hill. "Five passengers and the pilot were aboard. Just after lifting off from the lower parking lot, the dangling cargo cable snagged a corner of a ski waxing trailer.

"The helicopter climbed until the cable grew taut. The sudden resistance yanked the ship sideways. Then the cable broke free of the trailer and slingshotted up into the rotor, shattering it. The Alouette fell hard onto First Time ski run in the Three Kings area."

Immediately, ski patrollers extracted and began treating the pilot and four of the passengers, all of whom were critically injured. Unfortunately, Craig Badami was killed on impact. "Grief dominated every aspect of Park City life that day, and for months after," Warren concludes.

In 1994, after a new trail called C.B.'s Run was cut, Nick Badami distributed his son's ashes over it. Ironically, the ceremony was done from a helicopter.

POLYGAMY

Out-of-state visitors to Utah often arrive with clichéd and outdated perceptions. They associate Utah with polygamy, specifically the practice of a husband taking more than one wife. Those perceptions are no longer accurate for the mainstream population of the state.

Certainly in the early decades of the LDS Church, plural marriage was accepted doctrine, and many of the Church's leaders practiced it. Our man Parley Pratt had a dozen plural wives. Brigham Young was joined to more than fifty women. (*The 19th Wife* by David Ebershoff is recommended fiction.)

The Federal government passed laws in the 1860s outlawing polygamy, and the U.S. Supreme Court upheld those laws in Reynolds v. United States in 1879. Reynolds argued the anti-polygamy laws violated his free speech. Why did this case go all the way to the Supreme Court? Anyone in any kind of long-term relationship knows there's only very, very careful speech in such relationships.

In 1890, Church president Wilford Woodruff issued a manifesto that incrementally moved the Church away from polygamy. This move broke the logjam against admitting the Utah Territory as a state, and Utah became the 45th state in 1896.

Is there polygamy in Utah? Yes, splinter sects that spun off the LDS Church still practice it, and it's estimated that 1 percent of the state's population is part of polygamist families. Basically most people ignore it, since a lot of these practitioners live in rural parts of the state.

Polygamy has a low profile in Summit County, but we did have a dramatic incident in January 1979. Polygamist John Singer was shot by law enforcement personnel on snowmobiles who surrounded him near his Marion, Utah, home. After a stake-out, they were there to arrest him for child neglect and contempt of court, stemming from his not adhering to provisions of a Certificate of Exemption for home schooling previously approved, then rescinded, by the school district. He pulled a handgun and an officer discharged a shotgun in his back when Singer appeared to take aim at another officer. Public reaction, at the time, focused more on the home schooling/personal freedom aspects of the Singer household than on his having two wives. The national coverage of the story did not put law enforcement in a good light.

A subsequent investigation by the Federal Department of Justice closed the case, ruling that Singer's civil rights had not been violated by law enforcement's actions. Hiring famous Wyoming lawyer Gary Spence, Singer's wife Vickie brought suit against the State. The case was dismissed, and after complex litigation, ultimately the U.S. Supreme Court refused to hear an appeal.

Side bar: When my wife and I announced our impending move from Northern California to Utah in 1997, my wife had a conversation with her Berkeley friends on the topic of "Utah? Why Utah?" My wife jokingly claimed she was bringing equal rights to Utah by demanding multiple husbands, maybe as many as four.

After a good belly laugh, the ladies tried to figure out what possible use the men could serve. They quickly agreed the first husband was for fun, the second one for money, and the third to fix everything and do yardwork. But they couldn't think of a use for a fourth husband until the mother of four boys said, "Oh that's easy. The fourth can follow everybody around the house putting down the toilet seats."

This was obviously before the advent of self-lowering toilet seats.

On a closing note: The Top of Main Brew Pub on Main Street (sadly closed in 2026) served Wasatch Brewery's Polygamy Porter. When that microbrew was first released, the marketing campaign was "Why have just one?"

PARK CITY PRESENT

Useful stuff for visitors and regulars alike to know.
Good coffee and good people make this community go round.

BEST PLACES TO GET BUSINESS DONE: MORNING EDITION

Most out-of-office business around here gets done in our coffee shops. The classic place to see, be seen, and hold a meeting used to be Park City Coffee Roasters at Kimball Junction. It's now a Bagel Den, and I'm told it is developing its own morning-meeting vibe.

The following are the best places for out-of-office business, in no particular order other than roughly north to south:

- Park City Bread & Bagel in Pinebrook is an easy drive from surrounding neighborhoods, making it a convenient spot for Snyderville Basin residents and commuters on the way to the Salt Lake Valley.
- Cupla has excellent pastries and coffee, and good space outdoors for private conversation. The only knock on meeting indoors there? The tables are tightly spaced.
- Hill's Kitchen is another great place for pastry and drinks, and the breakfast menu has some good protein options. As with Cupla, the space indoors is tight, plus the space outdoors is limited. Like Aristotle, embrace the peripatetic approach. Grab something to go and stroll on the bike trail.

- Barnes & Noble has a nice café space in their Kimball Junction store that opened late in 2024. There is pleasing artwork around some tables and laptop counter space.
- Hugo Coffee at the Visitor's Center in Kimball Junction has lots of light and air, good coffee and food, and enough spacing between the tables for relative intimacy indoors and out. And every day is "Bring your well-behaved dog to work" day!
- Garden Café at the Park City Nursery on Route 224. The air-circulation fans in the greenhouse can muffle any privileged conversation. The greenhouse itself is a balm on the February soul when Seasonal Affect Disorder is raging. The ham and cheese croissants are quite good.
- Five5eeds, in Snow Creek, has good eats in a rotating seasonal menu and a variety of seating options.
- Silver King, also in Snow Creek, is primarily a drive-through, but has a pleasant outdoor seating area in milder weather. The menu offers a more-than-decent chai, coffee, and good breakfast eats.
- The Daily Rise in the Park City Market is a third coffee place in Snow Creek (clearly a theme). Excellent coffee, but you have to improvise for table space elsewhere in and next to the market.
- Urban Sailor is a relatively new entrant (in the old Ritual Chocolate location) on Ironhorse Drive. Chill vibe and decent seating for getting together.
- Lucky Ones Coffee in Park City Library: good cause, good brews, decent opportunities for quiet conversation. Browse the stacks afterwards.
- Atticus Coffee & Teahouse on Main Street has a funky independent-bookstore layout, but you can usually find a quiet space mid-morning.

- Deer Valley Café allows you to sit out on the deck for plenty of privacy. Watch the ducks dabble on the pond and the stand-up paddleboard newbies struggle. Focus on the avocado toast, grilled cheese, or BLT! Or just a Deer Valley chocolate chip cookie.
- Buzz Café at the Montage is a bit of a drive, but you can find a private spot around the hotel lobby or out back near the pool. The morning buns are to die for.
- First Tracks Kaffe at the Stein Eriksen Lodge has superb pastries and a beautiful setting.

Is there a "Best Places to Get Business Done: Afternoon Edition?"

We can't recommend any business getting done in the afternoon in Park City. Whether it's the No-Name Saloon, High West Distillery, or the bar at the Pendry, you're not going to be in your most productive state if you are taking full advantage of everything these places have to offer, which is what you should be doing. Don't sign anything except the bar tab.

PLEASE AND THANK YOU: THE J-1 PICTURE

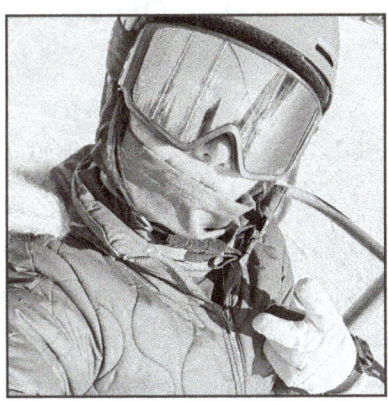

According to *travel.state.gov*, "Generally, a citizen of a foreign country who wishes to enter the United States must first obtain a visa, either a nonimmigrant visa for temporary stay, or an immigrant visa for permanent residence. Exchange visitor (J) visas are nonimmigrant visas for individuals who are approved to participate in exchange visitor programs in the United States."

The J-1 Visa enables foreign nationals to come to the U.S. to teach, study, conduct research, demonstrate special skills, or receive on-the-job training for periods ranging from a few weeks to several years. The J-1 program supports both winter and summer employment.

Without J-1 workers, Park City in the winter would come to a grinding halt. Roughly 10 percent of Deer Valley's workforce is made up of J-1 holders, according to resort spokespeople. Numerous restaurants on Main Street and elsewhere also employ J-1ers. The resorts and other businesses participate in the BridgeUSA Intern/Trainee program, which specializes in hospitality or culinary internships. These are generally six-month visits timed in such a way that many visa holders leave town by mid-March. This timing can prompt the resorts to limit terrain or put management out on the line loading lifts.

In the calendar year of 2023, some 298,858 people participated in the BridgeUSA program nationwide. Of them, 4,465 were in Utah. In the 84060 and 84098 zip codes, there were 1,984 J-1 holders (44 percent of Utah's total).

A good number of J-1s are well educated and come from affluent families. When you're about to sample a tasty appetizer at a nearby restaurant or boarding a chairlift, a simple "Please" and "Thank you" to the person helping you is sufficient, because they may have studied English for years in school. Unless you're fluent in Spanish or Portuguese, and can engage in an in-depth conversation, skip the "Gracias" and "Obrigado" and avoid the risk of condescension. Be grateful for the presence of these young people; they are doing our community a good turn.

A Refuge from Billboards

When you exit the Salt Lake City International Airport and navigate the freeways toward Park City, you're assaulted by a phalanx of billboards. The dramatic juxtaposition of the Salt Lake City skyline against the backdrop of the snow-covered Wasatch Range loses a lot of its visual power, given the clutter of ads for injury lawyers, auto dealers, and Chick-fil-A.

Once the freeway climbs out of the valley and into Parley's Canyon, there is relief. Salt Lake County and UDOT have managed to keep this section of highway billboard-free. The lack of odious outside promotions continues when you cross into Summit County, which also has remained billboard-free to a high degree.

There is a beautiful and concise phrase in Summit County Code (11-6-4: SIGNS) that goes like this: "Off Premises Signs Prohibited: No sign shall be erected or maintained on a parcel, lot or project area other than the specific lot or parcel on which the use or activity advertised on the sign is located."

The code also includes language that allows the county to remove billboards that have been abandoned for at least twelve months. Utah is one of the top states for total number of billboards, that is, one of the states with the most visual pollution. The Summit County regulations put our corner of Utah in the league with no-billboard states like Vermont, Washington, and Hawaii.

The Summit County Planning Commission has long held the line. For example, in 1977, it declined to meet with the Utah Association of Outdoor Advertisers to discuss a relaxation of billboard restrictions.

We're not entirely free of the blight. There are a couple of non-conforming displays scattered about. "Non-conforming" means they were in place prior to the establishment of the relevant county code.

One billboard is in Park City, on the east side of Park Avenue, just north of 10th Street. It's owned by Salt Lake City-based Outdoor 4th South LLC, which appears to be a subsidiary of Reagan Outdoor Advertising. The billboard has been around for a long time, as evidenced by city council action in 1975 and a complaint about it in the Park Record in June 1989. The billboard is probably old enough to qualify for the Historical Register.

Recently, the sign has advertised anything from Vail's Epic pass to McDonald's hamburgers. We imagine these advertisers are getting a sweet deal from owners to ensure that the sign does not get abandoned.

There is another sign in Kamas, on Route 248 near Main Street. Ironically, one of the advertisers on this two-sided structure is Summit County itself. One ad was for the Health Department (June 2024), and another for the Summit County Fair (August 2024). Why would the County, with its billboard-averse code, encourage the long-term viability of a non-conforming monstrosity by running an ad on it? "Health Department, meet Planning. Planning, meet Health."

This sign was also a sore point between the Kamas City Council and the State Legislature. Back in 2005, the city devised its first sign ordinance, and the language disallowed new billboards within city limits. Existing billboards were grandfathered in. At the time, this particular sign was located a few blocks north of its current location.

In 2009, the billboard-friendly State Legislature passed a law preventing communities from taking down billboards already in place and allowing their replacement within a mile of the sign's current location.

In 2017 at a city council meeting, Reagan Advertising requested to move the sign to its current location. Several city council members stated that they would not approve the request but the State Legislature had tied their hands. Begrudgingly, the council approved the move, expressing frustration all the while. Welcome to life under a supermajority, folks!

There's a third billboard, just as you drive off I-80 into Coalville, sponsored by the city and the Lions Club. Like Coalville itself, it feels like a slice of the 1950s.

Summit County did approve a large, temporary billboard near the Sheldon Richins Building in Kimball Junction during the 2002 Winter Olympics. The billboard advertised VISA, a major sponsor of the Games. According to former county council member Pat Cone, the County negotiated a package of 4,000 event tickets, which it distributed to county school districts. That's a decent exchange of value!

However, Utah's billboard industry writes a lot of checks to Utah's legislative and executive branches. They made an attempt in 2021 to override Summit County code. The bill failed, but no doubt, the fat cats will be at it again in future legislative sessions. The industry will use any wedge, such as the hosting of the 2034 Olympic Games, to urge the legislature to ignore local ordinances. Watch this space, as they say, and follow *scenicutah.org*, a Salt Lake City-based non-profit that fights visual blight.

SUPERMARKETS AND FARMERS MARKETS

Summit County is far from being a food desert. There are many fine venues you can visit to shop for fruits, vegetables, meats, fish, and sundries.

Where you shop is a Rorschach test of your values and personality. Here are some of the more popular and easy-to-locate grocery shopping experiences in Park City:

- Fresh Market in Park City: You're committed to a sustainable lifestyle, but hauling groceries on public transportation is just too much, despite its close accessibility and frequency. You'll drive one more time, and then take the bus next time. Really.

- The Market at Park City: If you've lived here awhile, you're still calling it Dan's, and with all the specialized chocolates, it's feeling more and more like Whole Foods. Nonetheless, it does do a good job highlighting local Park City and Utah products. The Market's proximity to the liquor store is an opportunity to chain errands and lower your carbon footprint while you raise your blood alcohol level.

- On Ironhorse Drive, you'll find the Good Earth Market. The limited floor space dictates a small selection of products, but the market states that they prohibit more than 100 chemicals, preservatives, and artificial ingredients found in foods at conventional stores. "Instead, we focus on foods that are clean, organic, and non-GMO with nothing artificial."

- Smith's (Kroger): You are there for the fuel points. Plus the tinfoil-wrapped breakfast burritos put you in touch with your family's working class roots. Decent produce selection, quality, and pricing here. The cheesemonger is top-notch. The coupon-savings game is easy to play.

- Walmart: Surprisingly good food variety and pricing, but the twinge you feel is guilt at giving quadzillionaires like the Walton Family some of your money, since they are just going to pour it into conservative political action committees. But stand back and observe like a foreign visitor. Walmart is all that is right and wrong about America, under one roof.

- Whole Foods: That twinge you feel is guilt at giving a gabillionaire like Jeff Bezos some of your money. Bezos is just going to pour it into some new $90 million home or putting the remaining small independent bookstores out of business. But the salad bar, the hot food bar, the lemon-and-garlic infused hummus shampoo! Where else can you find these things?

- Macey's Market Pinebrook: They reduced their square footage by 20 or 30 percent to make room for a much-needed Ace Hardware. Yet they don't seem to have reduced variety or quality. Brilliant! And take that, Home Depot!

- Food Town: Out in Kamas, Food Town is big and friendly and has all the food one could need, as well as a deli and camping/fishing supplies for your next trip to the Uinta Mountains. Industrious, and sometimes mischievous, local high school kids serve as checkers and baggers.

- Anaya's Market: Situated in Silver Creek, this is the place for Latin American foods and flavors. Good values in the bakery, meat department, and spice rack.

In terms of farmers markets and farm stands, the big wheel in town is the weekly summer Park City Farmers Market, currently happening Wednesdays in the parking lot near the First Time Lift at Park City Mountain. The asphalt vibe is more gritty than bucolic and can make it a bit toasty on warm days. Thankfully, it is one of those farmers markets where you actually have a wide choice of farm goods versus those farmers markets that are predominately scented candle vendors with a couple of sad little zucchini stands.

The Park City Farmers Market has its fair share of tie-dye fashions, leather goods, and hats, but it's also got an ample variety of locally sourced and produced fruits and vegetables, honey, and olive oil. And you have to love Volker's bakery, Freshies lobster rolls, Auntie Em's pies and cookies, and Wasatch wagyu beef jerky, to name a few of the specialty vendors.

Admittedly, you can see some of these same providers at the Park Silly Market during summer Sundays on Lower Main Street, but on Wednesdays at the Park City Farmers Market, you don't have to share the space with tens of thousands of sweltering Salt Lake Valley residents escaping the heat.

Another choice is Tagge's farmstand, which sets up in the parking lot of the Lutheran Church on Route 224 seven days a week. When the corn is fresh, it's darn good. Same with the peaches. There's a variety of fruit, including as many berries as you can possibly want. Try the mango salsa. Strike that, try all the salsas and relishes.

A third option is the Copper Moose farmstand near Willow Creek Park. It is almost too precious for words, but their effort is sincere. Got a lunch meeting? Grab a prepared salad from the fridge and sit at one of the shaded picnic tables. There's kombucha and kefir on draft. Plus you can get Auntie Em's pies without waiting in line!

CO-WORKING SPACES

Like a lot of western resorts in recent years, Park City is a "zoom town," attracting remote workers and entrepreneurs. The outdoor lifestyle makes our community appealing, but the cost of housing can limit work-from-home options. Broom closet office, anyone? During the COVID pandemic, remote workers made up 13.7 percent of Summit County's workforce. A lot of them have stuck around.

Working from home can become stale and unproductive with its lack of personal interaction. This leads people to look for co-working spaces, to combine office amenities and the creative spark that socializing brings.

The largest space in the area when it comes to co-working is Kiln in Kimball Junction. Kiln offers dedicated and non-dedicated workspaces, meeting rooms, educational programs, networking, and other services. Individuals and teams can rent dedicated office space as well. There are bike storage and ski lockers and a wellness program. Kiln has drop-in locations throughout Utah, Arizona, Oregon, Idaho, Colorado, and California. So it's kind of Planet Fitness for the entrepreneurial set.

Also in Kimball Junction is Assemble Park City, which has a sizeable footprint. The facility offers workstations, executive offices, conference rooms for hourly or daily rental, a business lounge, and membership events. If you are visiting the area and need a place to hold a one-off meeting, day-use rentals are available.

In the Prospector neighborhood is Elevated Workspace. Here you can find executive offices with shared meeting rooms, a kitchen, and other amenities in a LEED Gold-certified building.

Or you can shun the membership model, take the low-budget approach, and become a coffeehouse co-worker. Walk into Hugo Coffee and the Chamber Visitor Center, for example. You'll notice that in the lounge area, electrical outlets in the back (south) half of the floor are taped over. That's because the Chamber wants to preserve seating for out-of-town visitors and discourage "campers." If the outlets are available, the laptop lone rangers take over, grab a seat, order a single coffee, and hog the lounge space for hours at a time. With this in mind, the Chamber offers free Wi-Fi in the space, but it's limited to a two-hour timeframe every twelve hours.

No coffee shop in town is immune from the phenomenon of post-pandemic workspace pirates. If you are one of these people, you should have the decency to impose a latte-an-hour schedule on yourself, or do it the old fashioned way and go to the library. And earbuds or not, don't take a work call in any of these environments. Nobody wants to hear any of it.

Garbage and Recycling

Republic Services holds the contract for trash and recycling services in the county. Put your trash out weekly and your recycling every other week. Republic Services has specific schedule information on their website.

Recycling includes plastics (#1 through #7), metal cans, aluminum foil and foil pans, paper including magazines and newspapers, cardboard, and certain paper food containers such as juice boxes and cereal boxes. Things that shouldn't get tossed in the recycle bin include glass, plastic bags, plastic wrap, greasy food containers, construction debris, batteries, and Styrofoam.

The county operates the twenty-eight-acre Three Mile Landfill (near Rockport Reservoir), and it can take scrap metal, mattresses, construction waste, etc. for a modest fee. Free of charge, the landfill will take hazardous waste such as batteries, fertilizer, fire extinguishers, motor oil, etc. The thinking is that by not charging a fee, it will encourage people to bring their Roundup to be safely disposed.

Some interesting facts about the landfill (as of September 2024):

- The site accepts about 42,000 tons of waste a year, and another 16,000 tons a year at a "dry" landfill for construction site waste in Henefer. This works out to well more than a ton of waste per year per county resident. This is high by national standards, but in line with other tourist meccas. If your town appears in Condé Nast Traveler magazine on a regular basis, and attracts a lot of out-of-town visitors, you can pretty much double your waste stream.

- About 26 percent of the tonnage accepted at the Three Mile Landfill is food waste, which doesn't compact well and creates methane gas as it decomposes. There are encouraging efforts countywide to start collecting food waste to divert it from the trash heap. Check out Recycle Utah or the Park City Community Foundation's websites to sign up.
- About 5 percent of the waste stream is cardboard, and the landfill is getting pretty good at diverting that away to recycling services.
- The landfill does encourage people to reuse or recycle the plastic bags they get at the supermarket. When these come loose in the disposal process, they can fly away from the landfill, requiring expensive, time-consuming retrieval. The landfill's requests? Use fewer of the bags, use them in your wastebaskets around the home, or tie them in a knot before tossing them away.
- A fantastic non-profit, Recycle Utah, will accept glass, e-waste, Styrofoam, plastic bags, plastics, batteries, metals, bicycle tube tires, plant pots, paper, cardboard, and more at their facility, currently on Woodbine Way. They also manage a glass bin at the Jeremy Ranch Park-and-Ride.

This all reminds us: How hard is it to carry a bag or bin or box of glass from the back of your car to the Recycle Utah bins? When I was growing up, my siblings and I were required to clear the table after dinner and carry our plates, glasses, and cutlery to the kitchen.

"Don't be a lazy waiter," my mom would say, meaning, "don't try to carry too much in one go." Make two trips if you have to. Don't be a lazy waiter, and the rest of us won't have to navigate an Annie Lennox-inspired

"Walking on Broken Glass" path to the bin. Think of it as therapy. It's deeply satisfying to throw each bottle into the depths of the bin and hear the glass shatter.

You can also sign up for Momentum Recycling's monthly glass pick-up service. After a one-time twenty-five-dollar set-up fee, it's $12.50 a month (as of 2024).

The community grapevine has it that different neighborhoods have different tastes. Park Meadows generates lots of green-glass wine bottles. Old Town tends toward aluminum beer cans. Prospector likes its bottled-beer brown glass.

THRIFT STORES
AND OTHER BARGAIN HUNTING

The Park City area is the perfect confluence of high-net-worth homeowners and thrift stores ready to capitalize on high-net-worth homeowner boredom. When someone in the upper class grows tired of their current dining table or living room set, they off-load it to Habitat for Humanity's ReStore facility out by the Summit County Justice Center. Chances are the furniture has hardly a scratch on it. These pieces, coddled in second and third homes, are in great shape when they begin their second act. And ReStore prices the goods to move.

In addition, the ReStore facility has a wide selection of lighting, bedframes, bureaus, pictures, and more. There's also a selection of paint and some decent clothing to rummage through.

For a more traditional selection of gently used clothing, kitchenware, abundant appliances, and sporting gear, head to the Christian Center's facilities on Bonanza Drive and the Kimball Junction Outlet Malls. You can pick up a nearly new, thick winter vest or coat for a bargain. The Christian Center also runs a food bank, so your purchase of used clothing items helps the entire array of programs they offer.

Recycle Utah's warehouse in Park City proper provides an eclectic array of housewares and building materials at dirt cheap prices, plus recycled moving boxes and packing peanuts.

Right at Home Designs in the Bonanza neighborhood is another good source of high-quality consignment furniture and accessories.

A little farther afield, Heber City's St. Lawrence Thrift Store has an excellent, regularly refreshed selection of clothing, books, and home goods. And, of course, Deseret Industries and Goodwill, both with multiple locations in Salt Lake City, are good options. The selection of aloha shirts is typically worth the trip.

Of course, there are the usual line-ups of garage sales in the mild-weather months.

If you're looking to refresh or expand your winter gear, the ski swaps in the fall are a cost-saving opportunity. The Park City Ski Swap, one of the biggest in the western U.S., is typically held the first weekend in November. Hosted by the Park City Ski & Snowboard non-profit, it takes over the Basin Recreation Fieldhouse in Kimball Junction and has wall-to-wall boots, skis, snowboards, poles, headgear, goggles, and clothing. You can sell your used gear at the swap too.

Ski gear pricing in our retail stores like Jans and Cole Sport drops in April as they clear out inventory. You can also find year-round deals down in Salt Lake City at Level Nine Sports, which offers last year's equipment still in the wrapper.

9/11 AND THE ECKER HILL FLAG

Photo credit: Jim Ayers.

When near the Ecker Hill Middle School, look for the flag flying on a nearby peak. That's Ecker Hill itself, elevation 7,057 feet. The flag is an unofficial 9/11 memorial, and there's a story on how it came to be there.

On September 10, 2001, Dr. Scott Zuckerman and Dr. Julie Asch loaded their car to begin a move from New Jersey to Utah to start new jobs. After overnighting in a Pennsylvania hotel, they awoke to horrific images of the Twin Towers burning. "A horrible event, frozen in time, happening just as we were about to start a new chapter in our lives," Zuckerman says.

"Sometime later, I learned that Sal Gitto, a friend of mine and parent of one of my patients, was a 9/11 victim. It was really affecting. That personal connection intensified our grief."

Zuckerman and Asch settled in Pinebrook, but never had the opportunity to mourn with friends and family the loss of life. "We could see the top of Ecker Hill from our house. On the first anniversary of 9/11, we were sad. We decided to hike the hill and hang a U.S. flag on a piece of rebar we knew to be there," Zuckerman says.

They put the flag up in the cold rain after slogging through mud. "That little gesture was comforting and helped us mourn. Somehow it eased our sadness," he says.

Zuckerman has found other ways to process his grief from 9/11. He's written two non-fiction books, and the latest, called "Nothing Left to Prove, Nothing Left to Hide," has several key references to 9/11 and is dedicated to those who died that day.

Jim Ayers moved to the neighborhood in 2003. When he first learned of the flag, he hiked the hill. Despite Zuckerman's regular visits to the flag, that day, Ayers found it in tatters and touching the ground, due to recent high winds. "Well, this won't do," he thought.

Ayers owned a metal fabrication shop, and he fashioned ballast rings to weigh down and secure a metal flagpole he had obtained. The rings weighed more than seventy-five pounds each.

"In the fall, I hauled those rings up there. I would carry two at a time about fifty yards, put them down, walk back for another two, and hike them up to the first set, over and over. I ran out of light the first afternoon. The next day, I rounded up some buddies and we managed to get all the rings up there, raise the pole, and rehang the flag."

The ballast rings and the base of the pole are covered by rocks for further stability. The flag is not attached to a halyard, so it takes carrying a ladder up to swap out a flag, Ayers says. "I lived in Pinebrook until 2013, and I usually changed out the flag twice a year."

It wasn't until several years ago that Ayers learned the backstory of the flag. "I met Scott Zuckerman for coffee and we shared stories. It was great to learn the origin, and from then on, I made a point of sharing the story with people I met on hikes to the summit," Ayers says.

In 2018, Ayers' son Jackson, a Marine Poolee (a Marine term for those waiting to report to bootcamp), went with other poolees to the site for a flag-changing ceremony. The event was repeated the following year with another group waiting to ship out to bootcamp.

Ayers has since moved out of state, and now a small group of Pinebrook residents, some with military backgrounds, maintain the site on a volunteer basis. Solar lights have been installed for nighttime lighting, in an effort to observe flag etiquette.

Standing out against all the green foliage in the area, the flag serves as an aviation guide. The Hill Air Force Base squadron likes to use Ecker Hill to line up their annual Fourth of July fly-bys over Main Street. The flag also served as a vital visual waypoint for tanker bombers fighting the Parley's Canyon fire in August 2021.

Several years ago, Zuckerman posted about the flag's significance. "We've been moved by the response. People have expressed their gratitude and appreciate having a deeper understanding of why the flag is there. We're grateful that Jim Ayers erected a flagpole, and for all the people who have stepped in to maintain the flag," he says. "Those efforts have turned it into a community landmark."

The neighborhood group swaps out the flag around the Fourth of July and Veterans Day. Community members are encouraged to bring their children to these events. Check with the Pinebrook *Nextdoor.com* site for details. If you are hiking there and observe a maintenance need, you can send word via that site as well.

SKI TOWN LIFE AND DAY-TO-DAY STUFF

Chairlifts are just complex meat-delivery systems.
We can only hope the meat packets are self-aware
as they descend the slopes.

How to Get Your Pass Pulled at the Ski Resorts

The slopes have gotten more congested in recent seasons, and we're all guilty of glissading a little faster than we should in crowded alpine intersections.

Suppose you are flagged down by a ski patroller or other resort employee for playing things a little too fast and loose. Or worse, suppose you collide with another skier. What should be your reaction?

First be aware that the county has pertinent ordinances, namely 5-2-3: RECKLESS SKIING and 5-2-2: SKIING IN CLOSED AREAS. Okay, the actual text of these potentially fineable misdemeanors will have your eyes glazed over faster than the fine print in your monthly Verizon bill. The quick version:

- Don't duck that orange rope, ya idiot. That's avalanche terrain.
- Follow the Skier Responsibility Code. People downhill have the right of way, etc., etc.
- If you're involved in an accident, stick around, exchange contact information, and help if you can, short of moving an injured person before ski patrol arrives on scene.

- Apropos of a collision or other accident, if a resort employee (not limited to ski patrol) asks for your personal information, you are required to provide it. Don't get cute. That kind of behavior (such as giving a false cell phone number) doesn't sound very good to a judge and jury a couple of years down the line, should it come to that.
- Don't do a hit-and-run and leave the scene, or peel off after a furtive rope-ducking. Remember, resorts have many eyes, and ski patrollers have many radios. Radio transmissions go faster than skiers.
- And don't be a doofus and use vulgar language or spray snow on strangers.

When the jig is up, what do you do?

- One, apologize.
- Two, listen to the patroller's remarks, nod, and apologize again.
- Three, don't be a jerk. That's how you get your pass pulled.

Be especially careful when skiing blues and greens in the vicinity of ski school lessons. Remember the "Crazy Ivan" scene in *The Hunt for Red October*? That's where the Russian sub commander pulls a sudden figure eight move to see if anyone is following. I treat every ski instructor like a Russian sub commander. You never know when they are going to pull a sudden veer across the slopes.

All this reminds us of a story about Father Bob, who was the Catholic priest in town for many years. He also conducted the Sunday 2:00 p.m., ski-in/ski-out, interfaith service high up at Sunset Cabin on Deer Valley's Bald Mountain. Being a bit of a powder hound, Father Bob was known to duck ropes, much to the chagrin of Ski Patrol. Finally, some clever patrollers caught the officiant in the act of crossing the orange rope between Park City's McConkey's area and Deer Valley's Empire area.

"Father Bob, we're going to have to pull your pass for two weeks," said one of the patrollers on scene.

"But how am I going to get to Sunset Cabin to do the Sunday service?" Father Bob asked.

The patroller thought a moment, and said, "The Lord will provide."

One of the tasks that Deer Valley CEO Bob Wheaton took upon himself was to meet with anyone whose pass was pulled in recent days, to give that person a stern talking-to. When he came in the next morning and saw Father Bob's pass in the "naughty" pile, he thought, "I'm going to Hell."

The Lord, or at least Bob Wheaton, did provide two weeks of Sunday snowmobile transport for Father Bob. One can speculate that Father Bob's sermons in the coming weeks were on the topic of forgiveness and redemption. What is not in question is that Father Bob is a nice person and did not lip off to Ski Patrol. He was just a repeat offender.

By the way, Father Bob has a canine pet named Pilot. So clearly, God is his co-pilot, but Pilot is his dog.

NON-PROFITS

There are nearly 12,000 non-profit organizations registered in Utah. Summit County has around 380 of them. In the Park City area, there are roughly 130 substantively active ones.

More seem to pop up every day. All are ably supported by the Park City Community Foundation, which provides non-profit training and grants, and puts on the fun and exciting Live PC Give PC fundraiser each November.

If you're new to town and want to find non-profits supporting causes near and dear to you, *parkcitycf.org* has a searchable directory.

There are almost as many charitable organizations here as there are bartenders. Nonetheless, there may be room for another non-profit. My friend Sandra has a great idea for one she calls Deer Valley Seniors, and it sounds like a quintessential organization for our community.

"There are a lot of well-off older people around here who have to take a Required Minimum Distribution from their retirement accounts, and they are upset to find they have to pay taxes on those distributions.

"By donating to the DVS, they can get a Deer Valley seniors season ski pass, and a food per-diem. They just submit receipts for that carrot cake, which they would have been buying anyway, and take a tax deduction on the non-profit donation. My job as executive director would be to ski and manage some accounting. It's a win-win," Sandra says.

Deer Valley spokespeople were not available for comment on the idea.

LIBRARIES
(AND THE MINERS HOSPITAL GHOST)

Libraries? We love them all. The Summit County Library (four branches including Kimball Junction plus a bookmobile) is free to county residents and has an active roster of book discussions, film screenings, and more on a monthly basis.

The Park City Library is free to municipal residents, and has a collection and services that make it worth the investment for those of us living in the unincorporated parts of the county.

And heck yes, the Salt Lake City public library is an easy drive down the canyon and well worth the out-of-county fee to boot.

Back in the day, the Park City Library occupied a small space on Main Street, then moved to City Park, and moved again to the old high school on Park Avenue. These transitions are enmeshed with the story of an iconic Park City building, the Miners Hospital.

After the 1902 Daly West explosion that killed thirty-four miners, the state, the mining companies, fraternal organizations, and the Western

Federation of Miners Union #144 pooled their resources to build the Miners Hospital. The hospital, which opened in 1904, was originally located near what today is the Park City Mountain parking lot, on a plot of land donated by Eliza Nelson, daughter of Civil War veteran Colonel Nelson.

In the words of museum researcher Chris McLaws, "The Miners Hospital served Park City's medical needs for thirty years under the Union. In the 1930s it was sold and run as a private clinic. In the late 1960s and 1970s it functioned as a restaurant, bar, skier dorms, and a hostel.

"In the late 1970s plans were made to demolish the hospital and develop the land into a condominium unit, hotel and conference center. Citizens of Park City rallied together to save the hospital. It took two days to move the 400-ton building to its present location at City Park on Park Avenue. Voters approved a bond to turn the hospital into a public library."

Yes, it was a slow drive for a flatbed semi carrying the three-story brick building down to City Park, but the relocation was achieved with only minimal repair work needed.

This left the problem of transporting the book collection from the Main Street library. Residents rallied and formed a bucket brigade. The story goes that of all the volumes hand-passed that day, only one title went missing. The book? *The Joy of Sex.*

Books weren't the only things involved in all this to-ing and fro-ing. There are reports that the Miners Hospital, which is listed on state and national registries of historic places, is haunted by a rainslicker-clad ghost, possibly a past patient. A friend and longtime county resident Claire states, "I never saw 'Slicker' but I did hear him knocking on things inside the building. Sometimes I would knock back and we'd have conversations that way."

For a time, Claire worked in Human Resources for the city, and her office was in the basement of the Miners Hospital. "Normally HR is a complaint department, with staff showing up unannounced in your office, sitting down, and venting. I loved my office in the Miners Hospital because no one wanted to visit. What's in the basement of a hospital? The morgue."

As for the nature of Claire and Slicker's communications? She won't say. It's HR-confidential.

REALLY, GAS FIRE CIRCLES?

"Each day, Park City's resorts come alive with the warm glow of flickering flames. From rustic fire pits to elegant rivers of fire, these carefully crafted outdoor spaces offer more than just warmth; they become gathering points where stories are told, marshmallows are toasted, and memories are forged against the backdrop of Utah's breathtaking landscapes." So gushes an article on local fire features in the Spring 2024 edition of Home, a mountain lifestyle and real estate magazine published by the Park Record.

The article goes on to describe the flickering amenities at the St. Regis Deer Valley, Pendry Park City, and Goldener Hirsch. Fire features can also be found at the Stein Eriksen Lodge, Montage, Marriott Mountainside, and other high-end resort properties around town.

What the article doesn't mention is just how much greenhouse gas these artificial bonfires release on a daily basis, including on warm summer nights. According to researchers at the National Institute of Standards and Technology, the average patio heater generates 40,000 British Thermal Units (BTUs) of heat per hour. Over 24 hours, that releases about 130 pounds of carbon dioxide. The eternal flames and marshmallow melters at our hotels are likely burning more propane and natural gas than a residential deck heater, so the carbon dioxide outputs are likely higher.

In a town dependent on a recreational economy that is in turn dependent on reliable snowfall, do we really need to add to the local carbon footprint?

Furthermore, back in the mining days, the air near Main Street was smoke-filled, and respiratory ailments were the order of the day. Natural gas burns cleaner than wood and coal, but we're still a box canyon that can trap noxious fumes. Why add pollutants to the air we breathe?

There are more carbon-friendly practices. How about putting the gas fire pits and circles on timers so they are not running twenty-four-seven? How about a hiatus during the summer? How about battery-powered ranks of flickering electric candles or mood lighting combined with heating elements powered by solar panels? Or go old school . . . how about wool blankets for keeping warm?

We as a community can do better than give lip service to the concept of sustainability.

CLAM CHOWDER

There are a lot of restaurants in the Northeast and throughout the country that get away with serving a version of New England clam chowder that closely resembles spackling paste. We're talking bland, thick, potato-heavy bowls of blah.

With diligence, you can find some great clam chowders out there, like the bowls served up at Ken's Place on Pine Point Road in Scarborough, Maine, or Gilbert's Chowder House in Portland, Maine. You can find a similar level of excellence when you visit the Boston Harbor Marina or the Cove in Olympia, Washington. Those establishments offer well-seasoned, West-Coast takes on the classic dish.

What you don't expect is landlocked Utah to have any contenders in the "Best Clam Chowder" contest. Can you trust seafood in Utah? Well, as they say at the Blind Dog Restaurant sushi bar, "We're not on the ocean, but we have plenty of airplanes."

There happen to be a number of solid chowder competitors in the Beehive State. Friends swear by the offering put forth by downtown Salt Lake City's Market Street Grill. Another fine contender can be found at the soup counter in the Harmon's Grocery Store, also in downtown Salt Lake City. If my wife ever kicks me out of the house, I'm making a play for the Harmon's soup lady.

Another is the Bake Shop in Kimball Junction. Completely fresh ingredients, though not available every day. Their other soups are excellent as well, but mostly winter fare.

The fourth contender can be found at the Sticky Wicket Bar at Deer Valley's Silver Lake Lodge. The Sticky Wicket is a retro 1970s ski bar, complete with a shot-ski experience and "table keg" beer delivery. Vintage posters and memorabilia adorn on the walls and a rocking soundtrack blasts at all times.

It's a great place to wait out the holiday weekend traffic that can bring downtown Park City to stop-and-go stasis. The menu has a variety of ski bar bites, and the clam chowder is surprisingly well done for someplace more than 700 miles from the nearest ocean. Like the best clam chowders, the Sticky Wicket's version is not afraid of butter. Clog your arteries, not the streets!

High-Altitude Baking

It wouldn't be a vacation if you didn't bring your sourdough starter and bake a loaf in the VRBO you're staying in. It adds that homey smell to your temporary digs. Just be aware, the chemistry of baking changes as you gain elevation, and you're going to need to adjust proportions, baking times and temperatures accordingly.

As Food Nation states: "Baking is affected by high altitude because air pressure decreases the higher you go above sea level, and decreased pressure affects baking in some pretty profound ways. First of all, liquids evaporate more quickly due to low pressure, causing baked goods to dry out. Lower pressure also causes liquids to boil at a lower temperature than at sea level, causing baked goods to rise too quickly, often before they have properly set up, and then collapse. Finally, the gases produced by leavening agents (such as yeast, baking powder and baking soda) expand and react more quickly when the pressure is lower, creating tunnels and holes in batters and doughs, resulting in baked goods that lack structure and stability."

With ovens situated around 6,500 feet above sea level, Summit County presents some challenges. As mentioned above, doughs expand and lose moisture more quickly than at lower elevations. Moisture loss in turn affects how sugars in your recipe react, sometimes leading to structure weakness. When it comes to breads, yeasts are impacted by elevation as well.

Trial and error (mostly error) will guide your high-altitude learning process. Here are a few areas of experimentation:

- Turn the oven temperature up a little and shorten the cooking time. This will reduce moisture loss.
- For sweet items, dial down the amount of sugar you use by a tad.
- Add a few extra teaspoons of liquid to the recipe.
- For breads especially, add a few extra teaspoons of flour.

For exact amounts to experiment around, there are plenty of good guides online. Search for "high altitude baking tips" and find the analysis that appeals to you. Letty Flatt's "Chocolate Snowball" cookbook is another useful source. Or you can leave it to the pros and purchase comestibles from places like The Bake Shop, Auntie Em's Pies, Windy Ridge, the Deer Valley Café, Red Bicycle Bread, and the Montage.

Avalanche Routes

"I got smoke!"

A wisp of smoke wafts from the fuse stuck in the two-pound charge of plastic explosives. The patroller lobs it into the top of a chute.

"Thirty seconds . . . fifteen seconds!" another patroller with a stop-watch yells.

All of us watching quickly place our hands over our ears and open our mouths to reduce pressure on our Eustachian tubes.

KA-BLAM! Despite us standing thirty feet back from the top of the chute and the charge landing thirty feet down into the chute, the air pressure created by the blast thumps against our chests. If we hadn't done the "Hear no evil" move, it could have damaged our ear drums. The technical term of what we experienced is "brisance," meaning the shattering or crushing effect of an explosive.

The crew moves along the ridge to the next chute and repeats the bomb-throwing process. Two other procedures can be part of the avalanche mitigation effort. One, a patroller may "cut" the top of an avalanche path, traversing across the snow to get it to dislodge. Before the cut commences, several other patrollers communicate that they have "Got eyes on" and are ready to spot and rescue the cutting patroller should he or she be swept downhill in a slide.

Two, a patroller may ski to the top of a wind-created cornice and begin stomping and kicking it, in another deliberate attempt to dislodge a chunk of the overhang. Again, other patrollers watch the action closely, ready to provide assistance if the kicking patroller ends up plummeting into a chute on top of a refrigerator-sized chunk of ice or snow.

To the lay person watching these processes, there appear to be different levels of fun involved. Lobbing a two-pound load of pentaerythritol tetranitrate (PETN or PENTA) is big fun, especially when it causes a dangerous snowfield to shed its overnight load of fresh snow. Cutting? Maybe less fun. Stomping a cornice? Definitely not!

Oddly, Wikipedia says that PENTA is "also used as a vasodilator drug to treat certain heart conditions, such as for management of angina." That makes sense; once they figured out that nitroglycerin can be helpful for heart conditions, it was only a matter of time before they experimented with other explosives. New use for old dynamite?

I observed all these procedures in person, tape recorder in hand, while on assignment for a public radio science program. Utah is one of the premier centers of avalanche science in the world, and various mitigation techniques were developed or refined here over the decades. It was fascinating to see that science applied, plus I got to interview one of Deer Valley's avalanche dogs, Lila, on the air. One bark for yes, two for no.

Side note: Back in the mining days, the worker who carried the explosives out to the drillers was called the "powder monkey." What's the phrase for the patroller who carries all the explosives from the patrol shack out to the route? Chris Errkila, Deer Valley ski patrol director, remarks, "Oh, we call them rookies."

Absolutely untrue, but a great answer, nonetheless.

The Xbox Injury and KDS

At any ski resort, there is continual radio traffic going on in the background. Among other purposes, this traffic allows patrollers to respond to accidents quickly and maintenance teams to keep lifts running smoothly. Central to this radio traffic is the use of "10" codes, like "10-4" for "I understand." There's also some jargon that most resort clients might miss, even when they are riding a lift with a radio-equipped staffer.

Several years ago, on the day after Christmas, I was training a new mountain host at Deer Valley Resort. As we approached the bottom of the Silver Buck run, we spotted a pair of crossed skis—the industry-wide distress signal for a possible injury—on the bridge below the Banner run. There was a young boy sitting quietly on the snow with an adult nearby attending to him.

As we pulled up, the adult addressed us. "This is not my kid. He's complaining of leg pain. His mom is down there." He pointed a hundred yards down the run.

Normally I would have spent a moment talking to the child to determine what happened. However, it was a busy stretch of the run, and I felt some urgency to get resort resources rolling. I radioed the Flagstaff ski patrol shack, requesting a patroller to respond to a "possible 10-50," radio code for a potential injury. They acknowledged the request and a patroller was en route.

I turned to my fellow host and asked her to stay on scene and await the patroller's arrival. "I'll go talk to the mom," I said.

I slid up to the mother. Before I had even stopped moving, she demanded, "Is he crying?"

"No, ma'am but he's complaining of leg . . ."

"If he's not crying, he's not hurt," she interrupted. "I know what's going on. He got an Xbox for Christmas, and he wants to go back to the hotel and play with it."

Shortly thereafter, the patroller arrived and did a quick assessment of the young boy. It was apparently a miracle cure, because the child popped up, clipped into his skis, and made his way to his mom. I discretely left the scene as she began shaking her finger at him.

Later, I stopped by the Flagstaff ski patrol shack to apologize. "Sorry, I should have done due diligence before asking for your help. I should have radioed '. . . possible 10-50 KDS.'"

KDS is Deer Valley's radio code for "Kid Don't Ski." It indicates to patrol that it's a non-urgent situation. There are similar occasions when "ADS" is the radio call. That usually involves a tired adult who wants to head back to the hot tub. A resort guest overhearing a radio transmission using "KDS" or "ADS" would probably not think twice about it, and nobody's subject to embarrassment.

I'm not calling out Deer Valley here; I assume other resorts use the same or similar jargon.

SNOW PARK OBSERVATIONS

Deer Valley Resort's Snow Park Lodge got its name from a small, mostly-weekends ski area situated on the runs now called Wide West, Solid Muldoon, White Owl, and Lucky Bill. Bob Burns and Otto Carpenter ran the enterprise from 1946 to 1969, and they are memorialized by Deer Valley's Burns and Carpenter lifts and Ottobahn run.

Lift tickets were $2.50. Hamburgers twenty-five cents. Near today's overnight ski check facility, you can see some delightful old photos that show lift towers made of aspen trees. The chairlift was powered by an old pick-up engine.

When recovering from hip replacement surgery, this writer worked as a non-skiing mountain host, greeting guests "on the bricks" at Snow Park Lodge. What follows are some observations.

Carrying your skis: Before I started my assignment, Brian, a host who had done a similar injury-recovery stint, urged me to wear a helmet even though I wasn't going to be working on the snow. "Why?" I asked.

"Have you seen our guests and how they carry their skis?" he replied.

Less than half of our guests carry their skis vertically in the approved manner when heading to the slopes. Most carry their skis on their shoulders, putting the facial features of others at risk. Many are emulating Moe and Curly carrying two-by-six boards on a job site. Others are carrying multiple pairs of skis, with family trailing behind.

Litter: Snowfall is variable, but litterfall is constant. On at least four days of my bricks assignment, I picked up more than ninety pieces over a three-hour span. As my colleague Sam with the Ticket Office says, "We're a messy species."

Hand warmers account for a significant percentage of litter. I've learned they come in camo. Why the camouflage, when they are hidden inside gloves?

Is there a market for discarded scrunchies? It would be nice to monetize them. (Apparently one Deer Valley patroller has a giant ball representing thirty-five years of them.)

In the clean-up process, I found forty-six cents on the ground. That makes litter patrol one of the best performing parts of my investment portfolio in recent years.

Littering is a moral issue. The author Sebastian Junger writes: "When you throw trash on the ground, you apparently don't see yourself as truly belonging to the world that you're walking around in."

This is snow, that is pavement: Guests are improvisational. Sometimes they ski directly onto the bricks rather than risk stepping across the snow/pavement interface. They are also apt to adjust their bindings right on the pavement. This is different than the stone grind offered in our ski shops.

Guest demographics: Most, but not all, of Deer Valley's trail names come from old mining claims. It seems to me that we could honor our clientele appropriately with the addition of "Aging Playboy" and "Trophy Wife" to the map. They kind of sound like old claim names.

Best guest question I heard on my assignment: "We always ski Flagstaff first, then Bald Mountain. Is it okay to ski Bald Mountain first?"

Best guest comment: One guest waxed poetic on how wonderful the Ticket Test Station is. He needs to get out more.

Another great guest comment: Two fashionable ladies eye the "$5 wax" sign at the Snow Park overnight ski corral. "I guess that's for your skis," says one.

Fashion: What have we done as a civilization to deserve the return of ski suit "onesies"?

Like the cafés in Paris: If you wait long enough, everyone you know in the world will come up the stairs at Snow Park.

DIVINE GUIDANCE: SNOWBOARDS AT DEER VALLEY?

Will Deer Valley Resort ever allow snowboards? There are a couple of arguments in favor, and a big one against that happening.

The Military Installation Development Authority (MIDA), a State of Utah development entity behind the Falcon Hill Aerospace Research Park at Hill Air Force Base and the Military Recreation Area in Wasatch County, has spent a lot of money at Deer Valley's East Village, to ensure military personnel have access to winter recreation. Should MIDA insist, Alterra Mountain Company (Deer Valley's owner) might consider a change in policy, though no doubt the topic has come up repeatedly and Deer Valley has held firm.

Of more salience, within Alterra's own back office, the revenue maximizers continually assess the market. As Deer Valley's client base ages, the demographic trends might open a wedge for the "knuckledraggers." The quants are just looking to the bottom line, not to Deer Valley's four decades of skiing-only distinction.

On the other hand, this writer has it on the highest authority that Deer Valley will stay the course. In March 2018, while working a mountain host shift, I joined my LDS friend Kimberlee for a run. We boarded the Carpenter lift, along with a tall, distinguished-looking German man and his daughter. The man and his daughter conversed in German, and Kimberlee nudged me, whispering, "That's Elder Uchtdorf!"

A member of the Quorum of Twelve Apostles, Elder Uchtdorf is one of the top leaders of the LDS Church. An outgoing personality, he soon turned our way and began engaging his chair mates in conversation. Noting my Deer Valley uniform, he mentioned he was a long-time season passholder.

This was just a few weeks after Deer Valley had announced its sale to what would become Alterra. I mentioned that the host department was scheduled to take some of the new owners on mountain tours in a few weeks.

"Well, please convey to the new owners that Deer Valley should remain snowboarder-free," Elder Uchtdorf jokingly requested.

I thought for a moment and asked, "Of course, sir. Is that official Church policy?"

This earned me a sharp elbow in my side from Kimberlee.

With a smile and a laugh, Elder Uchtdorf replied, "Yes, it is."

So there you have it.

TRANSPORTATION

*We spend a lot of time in our cars.
That our vehicles are progressing toward sentience at a
faster pace than our drivers is a worrisome trend.*

PARLEY'S CANYON AND I-80

Interstate 80 (I-80) is integral to the Summit County experience. Even though most of the Parley's Canyon route lies in Salt Lake County, it's worth learning about the transportation history of the route.

When the Latter-day Saints came marching into Utah in 1847, they descended westward into the Salt Lake Valley by way of Big Mountain and Emigration Canyon. As my friend Steve says, "I always marvel at explorers' creativity when it came to naming. 'Gee, what should we call this great salt lake? Or this big mountain? Or these rocky mountains? Or this canyon we emigrated through? Anyone?'"

In July 1848, Parley Pratt and two companions scouted the next canyon south of Emigration for a possible road. Pratt was given permission from the Church in 1849 to build and operate the road as a private enterprise. The route followed what became known as Parley's Canyon eastward to Kimball Junction and beyond. Pratt named the route the "Golden Pass."

According to historian Don Strack: "Pratt collected a toll for the use of his road which consisted of fifty cents for each vehicle drawn by one animal; seventy-five cents for each one drawn by two animals; ten cents for each draft, saddle, or pack animal; five cents per head of loose stock; and a single cent for each head of sheep."

The toll station was near Suicide Rock (where I-80 and I-215 split). Pratt stated in his autobiography that he made about $1,500 in tolls in 1850 (about $60,000 in 2025 dollars). It's estimated that 6,000 people used the route that year.

Pratt sold the Golden Pass operation in 1851, and a stagecoach station was built at Mountain Dell and run by Ephraim Hanks around 1858. The Postal Service began using it for mail service, including the Pony Express, in 1860.

By 1866, the road was showing wear and tear, and the territorial legislature passed a bill that funded road maintenance between Salt Lake City and Wanship for $6,000, which in today's dollars (about $120,000) would cover a fraction of the road cones the Utah Department of Transportation (UDOT) loses every year. To defray costs, toll stations were placed near Lambs Canyon and Wanship. The Lambs Canyon toll booth may have been situated to capture traffic from a competing upper canyon route through Toll Canyon (near Summit Park).

With the advent of the transcontinental railroad in 1869, horse and wagon traffic on the Parley's route declined. Conversely, with the Union Pacific charging exorbitant rates, coal mined in Coalville was regularly transported to Salt Lake City by wagon on the road.

Railroads

Park City was once a rail town, with lines and spurs. Now we're a ski town, with congested roads. What would all of us give today for efficient rail transport to and from our resort bases? Look at Europe. Utah will not be a truly worldclass ski destination until we figure out this railroad stuff. There's got to be a way, up Parley's or the Cottonwoods.

In the 1870s and early 1880s, there were a number of unsuccessful attempts to raise funds for a railroad up Parley's. The different efforts didn't pencil out enough to generate significant construction. (We're facing similar discussions today.)

Finally, in the 1890 timeframe, one of Brigham Young's sons, John, built the Salt Lake and Eastern Railway. It was a narrow-gauge affair that ultimately, after some financial reorganization and a name change to the Utah Central, made it all the way to Park City.

Its uphill freight consisted primarily of supplies for Park City and its mines, and its downhill cargo consisted of mine concentrates, sandstone, and ice from ice ponds in Gorgoza and Kimball Junction. One can still see the remnants of sandstone quarries in Gorgoza, Pinebrook, Round Valley, Quarry Mountain, and elsewhere in the area.

The Utah Central's tracks reached Park City proper in the midst of a worldwide drop in silver prices. This prompted another reorganization, and the line was sold to the Rio Grande Western Railway in 1893.

The Rio Grande (which became the Denver and Rio Grande Railroad in 1908) resurveyed the Parley's line, moderated the grade (or steepness), built a 1,100-foot tunnel at what's now Summit Park, and converted the track to standard gauge. The Denver and Rio Grande ceased operations in 1946.

When you drive west on I-80, you can still see the railroad grade on the hillside north and west of Lambs Canyon. In Kimball Junction, you can also follow the line south through the Swaner Preserve.

Building the Highway

The Lincoln Highway, from the East Coast to San Francisco, was an "improved" route first designated in 1913. In 1919, then Lieutenant Colonel Dwight D. Eisenhower led a convoy of some eighty vehicles on the route to test road conditions and military readiness. The highway passed right in front of the Kimball Hotel Stage Stop in Kimball Junction. "Improved" meant mostly gravel road surfaces, which often turned into a muddy gumbo. The convoy included its own tow truck but also had to rely on local farmers to drag stuck vehicles out of the mire. When Eisenhower became President, his experiences prompted the launch of the National Interstate Highway System, which ultimately led to our current multilane I-80 asphalt route.

The dirt-road route saw increasing traffic in the 1920s as Americans put more gasoline-powered vehicles on the road. In 1927, a daily average of 1,018 vehicles transited to and from Salt Lake City via Parley's Canyon. These days, it seems like there's an average of 1,018 Amazon Prime vans on the route daily.

Over the subsequent decades, the road, which was known originally as Highway 40, saw regrading, oiling, paving, and other improvements. A good portion of the route followed the old narrow-gauge railway line. Nonetheless, the curves and grades, especially in the lower part of the canyon, were challenging, and it was regarded as a dangerous road.

In 1955, construction began on a four-lane, limited-access road. Blasting and other work in the lower canyon kept the route closed for a full year, with traffic rerouted to Emigration Canyon. The mid-1960s saw more work, and I-80 as we know it emerged from major construction projects that culminated in 1973.

In 2025, UDOT reports that I-80 in Parley's Canyon saw a daily average of 57,000 vehicles. It's estimated that 22 percent of the vehicles were heading to Evanston, Wyoming liquor stores.

DRIVING IN SNOW

Those killjoys in khaki, the Utah Highway Patrol, have published an excellent set of recommendations regarding winter driving. The tips make perfect sense, but they take all the fun out of driving. Despite our qualms about the fun meter, here is a recap of the main points:

Slow Down: "People driving too fast is the main cause of crashes in winter." That may entail leaving five minutes earlier for your destination than you would when the roads are clear. It definitely means driving a few miles an hour slower when it's storming out there.

Speed Limits: The more snow there is on the road, the more MPH below the posted limit you should travel. Pro tip: the posted speed limit is for dry, ideal conditions. Use your judgment, or that of someone more sage than you.

Quick = Slick: Avoid abrupt starts, stops, and turns. "Accelerate slowly, brake gently and don't turn quickly."

Space, the Final Frontier: Give the car ahead of you plenty of room since you'll need more space to stop when conditions are challenging.

The Lane-change, Berm-banger: Take care when changing lanes. Snow can build up in ridges between lanes and cause your vehicle to go off course. Minimize this risk by reducing the number of times you swap lanes.

Four-wheel and AWD Invincibility: If you feel a sense of security from having four-wheel or all-wheel drive, know that these features help with traction but not with stopping or turning. Slowing down is still your best defense.

Snow Tires: Four good snow tires on a four-wheel or all-wheel drive beat four "all season" tires on a four-wheel or all-wheel drive. This is due to the mix of different, cold-resistant rubber compounds in the tires.

Ice, Ice, Baby: Icy roads represent the top weather-related danger in the country, accounting for nearly 2,000 deaths annually. Most of these occur when the vehicle is going more than forty-five miles per hour, regardless of the vehicle or tire type.

A Bridge Too Far: Bridges freeze before the rest of the route. Be careful on overpasses.

Snowplows: We could write an entire vignette on snowplows alone. You're safer behind them. Don't try to pass them. They are designed to throw tons of snow off the roadway. They could launch your Subaru like a hockey stick hitting a soda pop can. Pro tip: Follow UDOT's Instagram site at *@utahtransportation*. Pretty funny shiz going down there all the time.

Easy Peasy: If you start to skid, lay off the gas and turn toward where you want to go.

High Visibility: Pretty high on the "duh" factor—keep your windshields and lights clear. And speaking of headlights, your high beams can create more reflection, especially off of heavy snowfall, which can leave you with less time to react, so if it's actively snowing, stick to your regular lights.

Cruising for a Bruising: As a general rule, don't use cruise control in winter conditions. Think of your drive as a *pas de deux* with the prima ballerina. Stay focused and engaged. She demands it.

Driving School: Utah Motor Sports out in Erda (near Tooele) offers a winter driving school. Or you can fly to Norway and take part in Volvo's driving course.

Lastly, of course, buckle up for safety, carry emergency supplies, and if you can, just stay home and wait out the storm.

JUST WHAT ARE THOSE TRUCKS HAULING?

Utah Department of Transportation statistics tell us that roughly one out of every ten vehicles traveling over Parley's Summit on I-80 is a "combo" truck, such as a semi or oil tanker. The highway is basically the Intermountain West's aorta for commercial traffic. U.S. Route 40 is not far behind.

What are those trucks carrying? Anything and everything. That includes a lot of chemicals that the County's Emergency Management staff and firefighters lovingly refer to as "Methyl Ethyl Kill'em Alls."

Despite the skills of these drivers, some are inevitably involved in accidents. According to the State Geographic Information Datasource (SGID), there have been about 100 reported hazmat incidents in Summit County involving vehicles from 1994 to 2022. This seems low, but at the very least, the reports give insights into the kind of cargo and chaos at hand.

Diesel spills were cited in more than half of the incidents, with most under 100 gallons and a couple exceeding 250 gallons. At least eighteen involved relatively small spills of hydraulic fluid, five of gasoline, and four of motor oil. So far, so good.

Things get interesting as you go down the list and find two spills involving jet fuel, one at 2,500 and another at 3,000. Apologies for those readers who struggled to get a C in Chemistry, but other notable incidents include:

- 3,100 gallons of emulsified asphalt
- Battery acid from seventeen pallets of new car batteries (I-84)
- Unstated amount of bleach about 150 feet from the Weber River (I-80)
- Heptane and hypochlorite solution (I-80)
- A leaking drum of nitric phosphoric acid (I-80)
- 600 gallons of paint (I-80)
- 42,770 pounds of antimicrobial peracetic acid (I-80)
- 3,000 gallons of propane
- 25,000 pounds of quick lime (calcium hydroxide) in a six-foot wide, one-mile-long, one-inch-deep band down Bitner Road
- A twenty-foot-by-twenty-foot, six-inch-deep spill of a white substance that was subsequently spread 100 yards by people DRIVING THROUGH IT. Luckily, it turned out to be sodium bicarbonate (baking soda) but geez, people, why take the chance?
- 2,790 gallons of sodium hydroxide (I-80)

The hazmat database is not all-encompassing, and the accidents keep coming:

- In June 2022, a truck rolled over on I-80 near U.S. Route 40, and released millions of bees from the 200 hives it was carrying.
- In May 2024, a semi rolled over at Milepost 160 on I-80 and spilled 5,000 gallons of milk in a dairy disaster. Unfortunately, the accident injured the driver and closed both lanes.

- In June 2024, another truck went wheels up in the same area, spilling thousands of onions onto I-80.

What one can gather is that if we wait long enough, several trucks will collide, creating a massive Greek salad big enough to feed the entire county, though the oil used may not be the most palatable.

In May 2024, a truck hauling three vehicles experienced wheel-bearing failure near Milepost 185 of I-80. A crash ensued and the three cars and the truck itself were consumed in a fire. Two of the hauled vehicles were electric, and the North Summit Fire District had a nasty time with exploding EV batteries that started two small brushfires nearby.

Additionally, Summit Park residents will remember a dreadful collision between two semis on I-80 at Parley's Summit on a snowy night in February 2017. One of the trucks was carrying oil. A huge fireball ensued, and one driver was killed. The highway was shut as the responders battled blizzard conditions.

This brings to mind all the tankers rolling from the Vernal area every hour of the day and night, hauling what's described as "highly paraffinic oil" or "waxy crude" to be processed in North Salt Lake. According to the Kem C. Gardner Policy Institute, about 300 insulated double tanker trucks travel from the Uinta Basin daily. If the truckers are delayed much beyond their usual drive time, their cargo can cool to the point (around 100 degrees Fahrenheit) that the liquid assumes a shoe-polish-like consistency. The drivers are motivated to reach their destinations, so again, give them a wide berth and do not make sudden moves in front of them. A full tanker can weigh as much as twenty-five tons and hasn't got the stopping distance or maneuverability of that Lexus you drive.

To entertain the family on long drives, you can play "Hazmat Bingo" using the red and orange Department of Transportation placards the trucks display. Orange designates explosives, while red designates flammable materials. Code 1267 is "crude oil."

Dodge Camper and Tesla Slalom

Living in Park City calls for driving I-80 through Parley's Canyon on a regular basis. Normally this is a fast, efficient, and scenic drive to and from the Salt Lake Valley. While there's apt to be a lot of truck traffic to consider, those drivers are professionals and generally the least of your problems. For the most part, the daily commuters know what they are doing, too. The latest available census data from 2022 shows 16,038 employees from outside of Summit County drive here for work, while 11,829 county residents commute to the valley and elsewhere.

Weather can be a factor particularly in winter. In heavy snows, sensible people slow down (or stay home) to mitigate a handful of potentially white-knuckle drives during ski season.

During summer, new risks, and new sports, arise. If you find yourself eastbound the afternoon before a holiday weekend, or westbound at the end of the holiday, you will experience "Dodge Camper," as a mass migration to and from campgrounds in the Uintas clogs the highway. This sport involves maneuvering around recreational vehicles (RVs) that suddenly pull into the middle lane to avoid even slower RVs and semis. "Look far ahead and anticipate" is our best advice. And according to the rules of the game, the use of blinkers is optional for any RV driver, so assume nothing.

In recent years, another sport has emerged, and sometimes you will find yourself playing both games at once. This sport is "Tesla Slalom." It involves getting the bejesus scared out of you when a Tesla driver appears out of nowhere from any lane to cut in front of you as they zig-zag around every vehicle in sight, as if those other vehicles are slalom gates. Other entrants may participate, particularly Ford F-250s, Audis, and Porsches. Play this game enough times, and you're allowed to rebrand the old Porsche joke.

Q. What's the difference between a Tesla [Porsche] and a porcupine?

A. With a porcupine, the pricks are on the outside.

[Apologies to Jennifer Marie, a long-time Tesla driver who observes all traffic laws and only guns it when it's safe to do so.]

A Prime Place to Get a Traffic Ticket

The sheriff's department and the Utah Highway Patrol love to go "fishing" on Route 224. The officers look for people making unwise use of the shared turn lane in the middle of the route or the bus lane on the right, both as you're heading north into Kimball Junction.

According to the Utah Drivers Handbook, "When making a left turn from a shared turn lane, you may only enter the lane more than 500 feet prior to turning if the last vehicle is more than 500 feet from the intersection." In other words, unless the traffic turning left at the traffic light at Olympic Parkway is backed up, you shouldn't merge into the shared lane until 500 feet from the intersection. That's roughly five telephone poles of spacing from the intersection, which is a lot closer than you may have thought. If you start merging over at Bear Cub Dr., you're risking a ticket.

The officers are especially concerned with drivers merging into the shared lane and racing by the stop-and-go traffic, only to rear-end somebody who starts to merge closer to the intersection.

The bus lane on the right heading north on Route 224 is prime ticketing territory as well. Here the signage is very clear. All along the road as you leave Park City are warnings to keep the bus lane free of traffic. The

"Bus Lane Ends" sign is very close to the intersection, just a few yards from where the righthand turn lane appears. This doesn't stop people from merging into the bus lane half a mile back, right by the "Bus Lane Only" sign near the little white barn. We understand the need to pick up the to-go order from Maxwell's while it's still warm, but cool your jets, people!

Also, a new seven-mile Bus Rapid Transit lane is under construction (as of 2026). That will alter traffic patterns further, so pay attention.

An in-town hot spot for a speeding ticket is the stretch of Marsac Avenue immediately above the roundabout. It's a twenty-five-mile-per-hour zone that's often interpreted loosely by residents and visitors alike. At commute hours or on busy weekend days, there's often a cop posted near the stop sign about a quarter mile uphill from City Hall. Deer Valley Drive between the roundabout and the Deer Valley Café is another likely spot. Slow your roll on these stretches.

Stop Signs and Wheaton Way

Step-Toe-On-Pedal. You may have noticed that drivers in Park City regard stop signs as a suggestion, not a mandate. The stop sign near Bartolo's in Newpark is one example. Drivers, bikers, and walkers, beware.

A corollary behavior is drivers treating yellow-changing-to-red lights as optional stopping opportunities; speeding up is the more prevalent approach. These behaviors are not unique to Summit County, rather they are another sign of the decline of American Civilization.

There is one possible, unofficial exception, this being the stop sign at the top of Wheaton Way (formerly Guardsman Connection) where it meets Royal Street. Under ice-and-snow conditions, if you come to a complete stop here, your vehicle may spin out or even begin to backslide into the car behind you. Slowly and steadily rolling through this intersection may actually prove to be a gesture done to create the greatest good for the greatest number. The drivers behind slowly crawling up the bobsled run that is Wheaton Way will thank you. The hapless driver of the bald-tired Camry that spun out to the side while trying to get to their housekeeping shift at the Chateaux will thank you.

Please note: Don't present this passage to the judge in traffic court in hopes that a dramatic reading will get you out of a ticket.

THE SALT LAKE CITY INTERNATIONAL AIRPORT AND WALKATHON

Proximity to a major airport is one of Park City's selling points.

There's a statue on Temple Square in downtown Salt Lake City that honors the Saints who pushed handcarts thousands of miles on their journeys to Utah. The privations they suffered were astounding. There is no truth to the rumor that the statue commemorates the first passengers flying out of the B gates at the refurbished Salt Lake City International Airport. As much as we all moan and complain, SLC doesn't even crack the top five airports nationally when it comes to long walks between gates. DFW, DEN, IAD, PIT, and MCO all have longer ones. The addition of the Central Tunnel to SLC's B gates in October 2024 further reduces our ability to whine.

We probably have better cause to grouse about having to bounce between different floors upon check-in. However, once you get past security, SLC is visually appealing and has a good variety of retail establishments to visit.

Of high importance is SLC Airport's ranking in 7th place for on-time flight departures worldwide. In 2025, 85 percent of flights lifted off within 15 minutes of the stated schedule, just ahead of Copenhagen. Unfortunately, you have to pay for it. SLC ranks high on the list of "most expensive airports to fly from."

A less celebrated aspect of SLC is the light rail connection from downtown Salt Lake City. If you're one of the many Summit County residents who works downtown, the ability to park at work, pay a couple of bucks to ride TRAX, and skip parking at the airport is well worth the effort. It does not take significantly longer than parking at the airport and waiting for the parking shuttle.

With the advent of the High Valley Transit 107 bus from Kimball Junction to Salt Lake City's Central Station, a few hardy souls have connected to the TRAX airport line there, so it is possible to get from Summit County to SLC using only public transit.

If you don't like SLC, try PVU. From Main Street, Park City, Provo's airport is an hour-and-seven-minute drive versus forty-seven minutes to SLC, and its long-term parking is right across the street from the terminal. PVU's route selections have been expanding over recent years, often with lower fares than comparable routes out of SLC. If you like going to Disneyland or Disneyworld, check it out.

On balance, we don't have a lot to complain about when it comes to SLC. Have you flown in and out of SEA lately?

CIVICS AND POLITICS

*While Summit County is a small blue island in a sea of red,
we share concerns like the rest of the state about schools,
crime, taxes, development, and more.*

SCHOOLS

The best way to learn about the schools in Park City is to talk to current parents. You'll get an earful. There are any number of issues that the Park City School District (PCSD) faces, and criticism of our local administration has long been an all-season sport around here. Contaminated soils near schools and insufficient protections for diverse students are some recent issues, and annual budgets seem to have prioritized everything except the classroom itself.

On the plus side, local voters and residents consistently support school funding, both in bonds on the ballot and donations to the Park City Education Foundation. Be assured that PCSD is considered one of the top districts in the entire state, and high-ranking colleges across the country give applicants from PCSD due consideration. For the 2025–2026 school year, the U.S. News and World Report ranked Park City High School as the number-five public high school in Utah and in the top 4 percent of public high schools nationwide.

The State's 2023 to 2024 "school report card" indicates that the district is "commendable" because a higher-than-average percentage of students scored proficient or above in statewide English, math, and science assessments. In addition, 82 percent of district students go on to enroll in universities, colleges, or trade and vocational schools.

In 2025, a Kem C. Gardner Policy Institute report indicated that the District has the highest rate of third grade student literacy in the state, at 70 percent. Overall, only 50 percent of Utah third graders demonstrate proficiency.

The Park City School District has four elementary schools: Parley's Park, McPolin, Jeremy Ranch, and Trailside. Trailside Elementary was ranked tenth in the state (out of 950 schools in the category), according to a 2024 report from the Utah Board of Education. As of the summer of 2025, students from these four elementaries will head to the sixth-to-eighth-grade Ecker Hill Middle School and the ninth-to-twelfth-grade Park City High School. A complex bus system services all these locations, though there is a multitude of micro-buses (usually an SUV piloted by parents) that jam up the roads every school morning and afternoon.

In addition to the Park City School District, Summit County also has the North Summit School District (Coalville) and the South Summit School District (Kamas). Notable private schools include Park City Day School (Pinebrook), Weilenmann School of Discovery (Summit Park), and the Winter Sports School (Silver Springs).

Of course, every day you'll see other buses loading up in various parking lots around town and heading to the Salt Lake Valley to private schools like Rowland-Hall, Waterford, and Judge Memorial. So there is a segment of our demographic that has the means and motivation to avoid the public school track. Our State Legislature has been making this path easier in recent years with the introduction of a voucher program. "Choice" is code for moving money from the masses to the upper class.

Compared to other states, Utah has a dismal ranking (last place as of this writing) when it comes to per-pupil K–12 spending. The other hitch in the legislature's approach is that voucher students need not take annual assessment tests as their public school peers must. We have no standardized measure to determine if the voucher program improves academic progress. This is not a slam on excellent schools like Rowland-Hall,

Waterford, or Judge Memorial, but rather a question about the qualifications of others in the more than four hundred schools and providers in the "Utah Fits All" program.

The first year of the voucher program saw participating families receiving reimbursement for ski passes, bicycles, and other questionable purchases. We're all for healthy lifestyles, but the program underwent some needed restructuring in year two.

The long-term ramifications of the voucher program statewide may be seen in the austerity experiment Kansas conducted more than a decade ago. Who knows? Maybe in ten years, Park City High will still be in the top five statewide, but Utah's overall rankings may have diminished on the national scale. It's all relative, right?

CRIME

Crimegrade.org states that a crime occurs on average every eight hours and fifty-four minutes in Summit County. This is about the same frequency as a Summit County resident gets a realtor license.

Summit County has a crime rate of 22.87 incidents per 1,000 people per year. This puts us in the seventy-fourth percentile nationally. In other words, we're safer than 74 percent of the rest of the country, give or take a fentanyl-enhanced cocktail or two.

In terms of vehicle theft and other property crimes, we get high marks from the website, with 0.87 incidents per 1,000 people per year. Stopping to scrape the ice off a windshield is a real party breaker for car thieves. Nonetheless, some good-hearted fellow residents make it easy by leaving keys in their cars when parked in their driveways.

Overall property crime sees 10.67 incidents per 1,000 people per year, good enough for an A- rating. Smash and grab heists at trail heads, in shopping center parking lots, and even in residential neighborhoods are not uncommon. So is rummaging through unlocked or open garages. Why is this a thing, people?

Identity theft has a low rate, but it seems to be the next big thing. Currently, we see 0.2 incidents per 1,000 people per year.

Beside identity theft, the Sheriff's office regularly issues public service announcements warning us of the latest scam. A couple of good ones include: Someone purporting to be from the Sheriff's office calling you to say that you owe thousands of dollars in fines, and . . . oh yeah, can you cash it out in gift cards? Or someone anxiously asking, in a supermarket parking lot, to borrow your phone to make an emergency call, and then draining your too-easily-accessed Venmo or Zelle account in seconds.

A quick scan of the police and sheriff blotters in the Park Record show a propensity for our residents to have one too many drinks before getting behind the wheel. In addition to closing time, law enforcement officers regard the early commute hours as a time of watchfulness. People who have overserved themselves get up and head to work while their blood alcohol levels are still above the State's .05 percent level.

While draconian in nature, the .05 law, which was passed in 2018, appears to have a positive impact. According to the National Highway Traffic Safety Administration (NHTSA), when vehicle miles travelled are considered, the fatal crash rate reduction from 2016 to 2019 in Utah was 19.8 percent, and the fatality rate reduction was 18.3 percent. In comparison, the rest of the country showed a 5.6 percent crash rate reduction and 5.9 percent fatality rate reduction over the same time frame. This is another call to take our lovely, free public transit when you're pub-crawling on Main Street.

As a side note, Summit County has a dubious honor when it comes to young people and alcohol. A 2023 state survey of students in grades six to twelve found that Utah has the lowest underage drinking rate in the country. That's all well and good; however, Summit County has the highest rate in the state. Some 55 percent of Summit County twelfth graders have consumed alcohol compared to 18 percent statewide.

What's behind this? It could be the affluence of our community and "rich kids with nothing to do." It could also be due to our having a lower percentage of teetotaling LDS families here, or simply parents allowing "supervised" drinking in the home. Regardless of the causes, given the effects of alcohol on maturing brains, parents are encouraged to discuss the topic with their kids while they are still in grammar school and potentially listening to you.

PARK CITY MAYORS

The position of Mayor of Park City is not an overly dominant one in terms of its relationship with the rest of the City Council. The mayor presides at the City Council meetings and only votes in the event of a tie.

As the chief articulator of Park City's vision, goals, and planning, the mayor does hold a lot of power to shape public opinion and municipal priorities, not just in city boundaries but also throughout Summit County and regionally.

New residents of the Park City zip code 84098 are sometimes surprised to learn that they cannot vote for the Park City mayor. That right is reserved for those in 84060. The 84098-ers can vote for the Summit County Council.

For some recent history and context, the following is some information on six recent Park City mayors, including, as of this writing, the current Mayor Ryan Dickey.

After stints on the city Planning Commission and City Council, Brad Olch served as mayor from 1990 to 2002. He was heavily involved in the winning bid and subsequent planning for the 2002 Winter Olympic Games. Other priorities in his tenure were the city's water system, the resort economy, and business on Main Street. Olch, city manager Tom Bakeley, and Myles Rademon were among those who really got the ball rolling on open space preservation.

Dana Williams took office in 2002 after diverse career experience that included farming, running a bar, and involvement in the Citizens Allied for Responsible Growth (CARG) non-profit, where Williams was instrumental in protecting open space, such as the Empire Canyon easement. Open space and historical preservation, water quality, and affordable housing were some of his priorities, and his administration earned praise for keeping the city coffers full and on-budget. He navigated negotiations with developers to keep Quinn's Junction from becoming Kimball Junction Lite.

Jack Thomas became Mayor in 2014 and his term was marked by the community tensions and complexities incurred with the sale of Park City Mountain Resort to Vail Corporation. He also focused attention on the increasing economic disparity of the community driven by growth. The Bonanza Flat open space acquisition was completed in his term.

After working with Main Street businesses and serving on the City Council, Andy Beerman started his mayoral duties in 2018. His strategy was to slow the roll on development. His term was marked by the Treasure Hill open space acquisition, the city's COVID response, and a controversy over social justice murals on Main Street. We can thank him for succinctly capturing Park City's appeal and advantages when he stated, "Take a step back and realize we live other people's dreams. Tolerating a degree of tourism affords Parkites amazing amenities and a low tax rate. A healthy economy also gives us the tools to address many of our challenges, and we should stop viewing ourselves as victims."

Park City's first female mayor, Nann Worel is a native of Seattle who moved full-time to Park City in 2008. With experience on the Park City Planning Commission, she made updating the city's General Plan (a multi-year process) a priority. On her watch, 430 acres were preserved as open space, and the 3Kings Water Treatment Plant was completed. The Snow Park development was a major area of concern and focus, as well as planning for the 2034 Winter Olympics.

Interested in changing perceptions about Park City, she was quoted in Park City Magazine, saying: "We can't solve the issues that are facing our community if we try to do it within the city limits alone. Our traffic problems don't stop and start at the White Barn. What happens within the city certainly affects our neighbors . . . . At times in the past, Park City has been perceived as arrogant and not willing to work with others. That's changing. That's got to change. We've got to be out there saying, 'I want to work with you. How can we change this together?'"

After a recount showing a mere seven-vote margin, Ryan Dickey became Park City's latest mayor. Like a number of his predecessors, he spent time on the City Council. His background also includes stints on the Snyderville Basin Planning Commission and the Snyderville Basin Water Reclamation District board. As of this writing, he has hired a new city manager and is prioritizing work on Bonanza Park and state Route 248. Planning for the 2034 Olympics looms large as well in his concerns.

TAXATION AND BUDGETS

Utahns have it pretty easy when it comes to taxes. Utah consistently ranks fairly high for its tax climate, according to the Tax Foundation's annual state listing. The listing takes into account the blend of income, sales, property, and other taxes. We rank close to some of those flashy states that are without state income tax, because our total blended load is not particularly onerous in the relative scheme of things. The State does tax Social Security payments but otherwise is fairly balanced in its approach.

Per the 2025 report: "Flat state-level individual and corporate income tax rates of 4.5 percent (with no local income taxes), imposed on reasonably broad bases, combine with extremely low real property taxes and a regionally competitive sales tax to produce a favorable overall tax climate, which is reflected in the state's favorable Index rank. Lawmakers have consistently trimmed state income tax rates as the state continues to experience strong revenue collections."

Summit County is a small but productive cash cow for the state budget. In 2020, residents filed 21,664 tax returns with an average adjusted gross income of $177,986. The county's average state income tax liability was $8,138, top in the state. The next closest county, Morgan, had average state income tax liability of $5,083.

Statewide, there were 1,354,946 returns, with average adjusted gross income of $78,213 and state income tax liability of $3,254. The suspicion is that we in Summit County contribute more to the state's general fund than we receive back from it. Contact your legislator. Oh, that's right, they are unlikely to respond.

Sales tax is a little less rosy. Park City's sales tax is 9.55 percent, a slight increase in the last year. The county's rate also rose slightly to 8.75 percent, and the Snyderville Basin Transit District's is 9.05 percent. The city and transit district rates generate funds to cover the cost of the bus systems.

When it comes to property tax, Summit County, with 1.2 percent of the state's population, accounts for 4.7 percent of the tax burden ($199 million out of $4.2 billion). This includes assessments for the county, cities, schools, and special districts. Luxury living has its price.

If you own a second home here, you'll feel the pinch of property tax. It's almost double the rate paid for primary residences. One way around this is to rent out your basement, so you can attest that your property is at least somebody's primary residence. That kind of maneuver helps our housing crisis, and, of course, it's in keeping with the Great American Tradition of avoiding (not evading) taxes.

Please note that the information in this section is not intended as legal, financial, or tax advice, blah, blah, blah. Seek the opinions of professionals, blah, blah, blah. Your mileage may vary. To state the obvious, this entire publication is a cover-to-cover opportunity for me to make wry observations on topics I have no business touching upon. You've been warned.

An interesting sidenote on the city and county budgets: Park City spins its higher sales tax revenue up into a $98.5 million budget (FY2026), while Summit County's is at the $100.5 million level for a larger population base. Entertaining all those skiers, snowboarders, and pickleball players adds up!

Of further interest, at $129 million, the Wasatch County 2026 budget is higher than Summit County's for a lower population base of about 39,000. Heber City's 2026 budget is approximately $89 million.

GERRYMANDERING — A LIBERAL'S LAMENT

Along with Salt Lake County, Summit County is one of the few Democrat Party strongholds in blood-red Utah. So what does the State Legislature do? Slice us up like a Davanza's pizza pie.

Summit is a mid-sized county as the state goes, yet it requires coverage by two state representatives and two state senators, and some of our representatives are truly bad-idea generators. Our state senators are merely complicit. In our experience, few of them return emails when they see the 84098 or 84060 zip codes. In fairness, a friend states that they received a response from Senator Mike Lee (federal level), but it was essentially a form letter rebuke.

The gerrymandering dilutes the resident Dems with staunch Republicans from Morgan, Wasatch, and other conservative counties.

Beside the geographic delineations, many Utah legislators have ties to real estate development. To emphasize this point, the Legislature on a regular basis presses their thumb down hard on Summit County, such as approving the ability of the town of Hideout (Wasatch County) to annex land in Summit County, or the creation of a brand-new transit district in Kimball Junction to take land-use decisions out of the hands of the County in favor of a major real estate developer. County council district machinations and Browns Canyon developments are icing on the cake.

Utah has a Republican super-majority, meaning anything that the American Legislative Exchange Council (ALEC) wants is what will go. This can lead to a lot of pass-then-fix legislation. Without sufficient due diligence, a bad bill is passed and then has to be repaired in the next session.

Luckily, the Utah State Legislature is only in session for a forty-five-day period early in the year. Former Salt Lake County mayor Peter Caroon (D) has described this as "the forty-five-day hostage crisis."

The super-majority mindset can get wearisome even for fellow Republicans. One can read in a 2024 Salt Lake Tribune article about a transgender-blocking bathroom bill: "I recognize that many Utahns feel trampled by an invasive and overly aggressive Legislature that too often fails to seek input from those most affected," state auditor John Dougall, a Republican, said in his statement. "Constituents unhappy with this Statute will not effect change by misdirecting their anger toward the [Auditor's] Office and its dedicated employees. The Legislature crafted these public policies, and only the Legislature can revise them."

Auditor "Frugal" Dougall is beyond staunch, so this is saying something.

The point of this section is to warn our liberal newcomers to buckle up. We're not in the People's Republic of Berkeley anymore.

We are happy to note that in 2024, the Utah Supreme Court unanimously ruled that the legislative map, devised by the overreaching State Legislature in 2025 in response to the Proposition 4 citizens' initiative in 2018, abrogates the will of the people. The case was sent back to a lower court, which ruled that the hastily drafted and disingenuously written Amendment D (set for the November 2024 election and intended to overturn Prop 4) was void. The Legislature appealed, and the state Supremes upheld the lower court decision.

The Legislature then made further moves to make a contortionist proud, including an out-of-state-funded, multi-million-dollar signature-gathering effort to place an initiative on the 2026 ballot to strike down Prop 4, which started the whole new district map fuss.

Still with me? It gets better, in a hoist-with-his-own-petard kind of way. In years past, the Legislature put such heavy guardrails on putting initiatives on the ballot, the signature-gathering effort fell short by a handful of signatures in two Senate districts.

So there's hope that Salt Lake County, at least, may in the future elect a federal representative who more accurately reflects the leanings of that county's voters.

Don't get your hopes up if you are a latte-sipping, tree-hugging, scone-nibbling liberal! Despite the courts, I have every confidence the Legislature will come up with creative new ways to thwart the will of the people. As U.S. Senator from Utah Mike Lee says, we're a republic, not a democracy, after all!

THE NEWS FIX

In Summit County, a variety of news outlets inform our public discourse. On paper, on air, and online are all options.

The Park Record is a twice-weekly print publication with a robust online presence. When you throw in the University of Utah's newspaper archives, you can find Park Record articles going back to 1880. It is Utah's oldest, continuously published non-daily newspaper. You can sign up for a daily email blast, and keep an eye out for its yearly "Mile Post" magazine, which serves as a de facto community report card. The weekly columns by Tom Clyde have been an inspiration for *The People's Guide*.

KPCW is our local radio station serving Summit and Wasatch Counties. It broadcasts on 91.7 FM, 88.1 FM, and 91.9 FM, and has a daily email blast plus a twenty-four-seven digital streaming website and mobile app. Untold tragedies have been averted thanks to KPCW's "Lost and Found" service, and the station's fund drives highlight many of our worthy non-profits. Regular shows, such as "Cool Science Radio" and "Mountain Money," are worth a listen. And pray for any poor public servant in the crosshairs of senior news director Leslie Thatcher. On air and online, KPCW offers a significant amount of Spanish-language content.

TownLift is a locally-owned outlet focused on news "affecting everyday life in Park City." Its small team of reporters relies on community input in the form of news tips, story ideas, local events, and cool photos and videos, which gives its feed a crowdsourced feel. It delivers a daily email blast.

All three of these news providers love to be the first to publish a scoop. As a result, we have a healthy and competitive news ecosystem in Summit County.

We used to have our own TV station, PCTV, but it closed in 2022.

Lastly, Summit County is within the ambits of the Deseret News and the Salt Lake Tribune. The first is owned by the LDS Church, and the second had its origins a century ago as an anti-Mormon publication. These factors continue to play out in how statewide stories and opinion pieces are treated in their pages. You've been forewarned.

WEALTH AND REAL ESTATE IN PARK CITY

When Thorstein Veblen coined the term "conspicuous consumption" in his 1899 work, The Theory of the Leisure Class, surely he had Park City in mind. We love to show off our clothes, cars, recreational gear, and, most of all, our real estate.

Air Quality and Where to Live

Look at the old photos of Park City's mining heydays. There are few trees to be seen on any of the hillsides. Mines and mills had a large appetite for wood, using it to shore up underground workings and to burn for running steam engines. Coal, much of it low-quality stuff from Coalville, was also used to power machines, run trains, and heat homes. The resulting air pollution in Park City's box canyon was harsh. The marvelous *Diggings and Doings in Park City* tells of the need to bring your laundry in from the line if wet weather was in the forecast. Otherwise, the acid rain would burn holes in the clothing.

Air quality was a factor that drove rich people like Thomas Kearns of the Silver King Coalition Mine and the Silver Queen herself (Susanna Bransford Emery Holmes Delitch Engalitcheff) to build or buy elegant mansions on South Temple Avenue in Salt Lake City.

Nowadays, things have reversed. The air quality in Salt Lake City is some of the worst in the world, thanks to its desert dust, its bowl-like qualities (hemmed in as it is by the Oquirrh and Wasatch Mountain ranges), and the modern addition of a large number of cars, factories, and homes. As a result, the millionaires and billionaires are building or buying in Park City, where the air is relatively cleaner.

It also seems to my historically minded friends that the billionaires building massive homes on the hillsides above Main Street could do the community a favor by sinking their construction funds into mine structure rehabilitation. For the same millions they are spending now, they could restore and convert the decaying four-story Silver King Coalition Mill (just downhill from the base of the Bonanza chairlift) into a private residence. It even had a big pool, used to concentrate ore through the water-and-soap-based flotation method, that could be unearthed and retrofitted for lap swimming. History is reclaimed, and the ability to show off to your other billionaire friends is retained!

THE SKIING/REAL ESTATE INTERFACE

Out-of-towners and folks from the Salt Lake Valley who normally ski Big and Little Cottonwood Canyons often remark on the amount of development near our ski slopes. The proximate cause is that the Wasatch Back's extensive mining operations evolved into private land holdings that are a lot easier to develop than publicly owned lands, such as the U.S. Forest Service's holdings in the west side of the mountain range, closer to Salt Lake City.

The Park City area is an ongoing, in-vivo experiment in combining skiing and snowboarding with real estate. The results are mixed.

The Red Cloud development on Flagstaff Mountain, Deer Crest on Little Baldy, the Colony at the Canyons Village, and the granddaddy, Bald Eagle in Deer Valley, all platted out dirt for massive houses. This, in turn, affected the design of the adjoining trail systems. All have required roadways that would make a contortionist proud, as well as expensive bridge and tunnel infrastructure that has affected snow quality.

Take the Little Baldy area for example. The Jordanelle Run is narrow, squeezed in by the venture capitalist "cottages" on either side. This makes it intimidating for a good portion of the skiing public. It's got beautiful views but you're too busy to enjoy them, what with looking over your shoulder for the next Alberto Tomba imitator. Jordanelle's bridges don't hold snow very well, and that, with its narrowness, makes it a pain in the neck for snowmakers and snowcat operators. From an operational standpoint, it is high maintenance.

Next door to the Jordanelle Run is the Mountaineer Run. Here you experience variable snow when you pass under an overpass. Your skis can slow or speed up unexpectedly depending on weather conditions, and in a weird optical illusion, you feel like you have to duck when you descend under the roadway.

On the other side of the ledger are the Park City side of Vail Park City and the Bald Mountain, Empire, and Lady Morgan sections of Deer Valley. These peaks are free of roads and second homes. The skiing and riding experience is truer to the pure possibilities of the terrain and snow.

While the concentration of hotels, retail, and residences arising at the Deer Valley East Village brings its own growth headaches and strains on Wasatch County infrastructure, Extell is to be commended for placing 3,500 acres of the upper hillsides under conservation easement. The skiing experience will take precedence over building more 10,000-square-foot treehouses for the One Percent. For a real estate development company to come to this decision is remarkable.

Pro Tip: If for some unknown reason, you are purchasing "rack rate" tickets at Deer Valley versus taking advantage of Ikon discounts, be sure to buy your tickets in Wasatch County to take advantage of lower sales taxes. Save two bucks on a 300 dollar pass!

THE FOUR SEASONS

Summit County excels when it comes to having distinct seasons. None of that "California mild" for us. Like an alpine peak, our temperature bell curve has true prominence. The seasons also drive our relationship with life at home.

Spring: Welcome to mud season. Early on, the trails are too wet to bike or hike. So most of our population heads to Moab, the rest to Baja. Cabo is Parque Ciudad Sur. Or Punta Mita if you need a gate attendant and a butler.

Checklist: Switch out your winter tires for your summer ones. Turn off the gutter heat tape. Clean your gutters. Wash your windows. "Summerize" your snowblower for off-season storage in the back of the garage. Put the patio furniture out. Change the batteries in your smoke detectors. Uncover and clean the gas grill. Reshuffle your storage space as you switch from winter gear to biking gear. This latter process can be complicated by a) the widening overlap between snow-sport and biking seasons, and b) whether you have a two-car, one-car, or no-car garage. A no-car garage is a garage too full of stuff for parking a vehicle, and a reason there are numerous self-storage businesses out near Route 40.

Summer: Park City is an adult summer camp. We are truly blessed to live here with temperate weather and lots of activities. Please note that summer has winter pretensions from time to time. It's not unusual to experience snow in June, July, and September. Only August seems to dodge the dustings.

Checklist: Use your patio furniture and grill! Goof off and go biking instead of washing windows and cleaning gutters (which you neglected to do in the spring). Do some yard work. Check the real estate listings to see if the market is up. Pay the utility bill; it's higher than usual, since you forget to turn off the gutter heat tape. Run your snowblower for five minutes, to keep its juices flowing, since you forgot to "summerize" it.

Fall: Crisp mornings and visually stunning hillsides highlight the autumn months. The restaurants tempt us with two-for-one deals. Hiking and biking conditions are superlative.

Checklist: Think about getting your winter gear tuned. Clean the windows again, thanks to the dust-infused thunderstorms we get. Change the batteries in the beeping smoke detectors since you didn't get around to this chore in the spring. Have some fabulous barbeques during "Indian Summer" and "Fake-out Fall." Delay swapping your summer tires for winter ones since the weather is so nice. Keep your bike handy for just one more week of riding.

Winter: It's our alpha season, but that doesn't mean you should drive like an apex predator. Leave an extra five minutes early and slow down along the way.

Checklist: Okay, really. Change those tires and put away the bikes. Get the skis and snowboards tuned. Turn on the heat tape. Put the snowblower and shovels in accessible places in the garage. Start thinking charcuterie board versus barbeque.

It is a truism in Summit County that those of us who moved here "came for the winters and stayed for the summers." Be sure to enjoy all the seasons, and when you are tackling all these household chores, it helps to blast some Vivaldi on your sound system.

SUBSIDENCE VERSUS SINKHOLE

My friend Todd, past president of the Park City Board of Realtors and a broker with Keller Williams, respectfully asks that all parties refer to any disturbance in the soil related to Park City's mining past as a "subsidence."

The term "sinkhole" is not to the liking of our friends in the real estate world of Summit County (at least on the seller's side). The description can have a deleterious effect on property value. "Collapse" is another term that our broker friends shun.

Estimates are that there were 300 active mines and 1,200 miles of tunnels and shafts in the Park City area. Every couple of years or so, the workings of an old mine subside. This is especially true after a high-snowfall winter that saturates the soil when the melt starts in the spring. Some notable ones in the past decades include the Bogan Mine on Park City's Claimjumper run, a shaft off the Rail Trail, and the American Flag Mine in Empire Canyon. Filling the American Flag's 1,100-foot shaft took 4,200 cubic yards of dirt, or about 350 dump trucks' worth.

Perhaps our most notable subsidence was the partial collapse of the eighty-five-foot-tall, eighty-ton Daly West steel headframe into a 2,100-foot shaft in May 2015. A headframe is the structure at the top of a mine hoist, or mine shaft elevator. No one was harmed, and no other structures (looking at you, Montage) were damaged in this subsidence.

This relic was the rallying point for the Friends of Ski Mountain Mining History, which fundraised to have the headframe re-erected in June 2022. The headframe was moved uphill, away from the mine shaft, to avoid future disturbances.

At the junction of Deer Valley's Custer and Webster runs, there is a nice little track of moguls one can enjoy. This Mountain Host no longer takes this particular path. In May 2014, the Daly #2 shaft, located under the mogul field, opened up. Some friends and I hiked there, peered down into the deep, dark hole, tossed a few rocks in, and shuddered to think what might have happened had the shaft collapsed during the ski season, which had ended just a few weeks before.

Over the next few weeks, the gaping hole was filled in, but it was a vivid reminder to me that we are hiking, biking, and skiing over the geologic equivalent of Swiss cheese. Back full circle to real estate, please note that Utah real estate laws are friendlier to sellers than, say, those of California. Signing off on disclosures in California will give you carpal tunnel syndrome. Signing off in Utah? Zip, zap, and you're done. Before you sign the paperwork when buying a Utah house, make sure the sellers disclose minor details like, "Oh, yeah. There was a mine under this property."

THE TIME TO WEALTH DISCLOSURE WITH A SIDE HELPING OF DIVERSITY

Back in the day, you could tell when somebody had made it in Park City when they repainted their house a bright color. To show you were a successful miner, you didn't settle for cheap white paint. You shelled out some coin and added bright tints. Hence all of our brightly colored miners shacks along Park Avenue. Things are a little more complicated these days.

When you start conversing with a new acquaintance, how quickly do they reveal their level of affluence? This phenomenon, called the Time to Wealth Disclosure (TWD), is not exclusive to Park City, but Parkites' TWDs are up with the best of them nationwide.

In Park City, the TWD occurs most frequently in casual conversations on chairlifts. "We just got back from skiing at Chamonix last week . . ."

Or "We've had our winery in Oregon for the last six years, but I spend the winter here so I consider myself a local . . ."

Or "I'm thinking of upgrading to the next Gulfstream. A six-seater is a little tight."

Since a chairlift ride is generally under six minutes, that's a robust TWD.

And among our wealthy, there may be a Time to Awkward Disclosure (TAD) factor as well. It was on a recent chairlift ride that the topic of diversity came up. I was riding up the Northside Express with a mergers-and-acquisitions professional who was on a host-guided tour of Deer Valley Resort. A single rider joined us, and in the course of conversation, the singleton noted he had done deals with the professional's firm.

The conversation turned to Deer Valley's positives. "I love the grooming here. I love the friendly staff," the single rider stated. "And I love the diversity. You have hedge fund managers, private equity guys, venture capitalists, family offices, M&A guys like yourself, all in one spot! You can get deals done."

Given that the State Legislature has recently banned pride flags in state offices and dismantled Diversity, Equity, and Inclusion programs at higher education institutions, this definition of diversity is sadly appropriate.

NIMBY and BANANA and CAVE

Park City and Summit County are home to a fair number of residents who exhibit three levels of anti-growth—verging on anti-change—sentiment:

One: NIMBY or Not In My Back Yard

Two: BANANA or Build Absolutely Nothing Anywhere Near Anything

Three: CAVE or Citizens Against Virtually Everything

There aren't strict delineations between these three states; there's overlap and shading from one to the next. But the underlying tune that's playing is Groucho's song in the film *Horsefeathers*: "Whatever It Is, I'm Against It!"

We recently learned of a variation of NIMBY, having to do with the controlled burns Park City was conducting on Treasure Hill. As the city started burning slash piles, which is an accepted process to reduce wildfire risk, some residents contacted the mayor, fearing that the trees had absorbed lead and other potentially dangerous minerals left over from mining days. They were concerned the smoke was supercharged with toxins. The city hired a consultant, who concluded there was no such risk. The city resumed the controlled burns late in 2024. In this case, NIMBY may mean Not In My Bonfire, Y'all.

WATER AND WEATHER

We live in a semi-arid environment.
The longer you visit or live here, the less likely you are
to take water and climate for granted.

WHERE DOES OUR WATER COME FROM?

Our water ultimately comes from rain and snowmelt, which feed wells, aquifers, and nearby streams. Like a lot of Utah, Summit County has balkanized water delivery and water treatment systems. There are multiple players involved in providing clean water to residents and removing sewage after use.

For a municipality its size, Park City has one of the most complex and highly engineered water systems in the nation. According to Park City Municipal, the city's system has three water treatment plants: Quinn's Junction Water Treatment Plant, Spiro Water Treatment Plant, and 3Kings Water Treatment Plant, which has been recently upgraded.

The district is serviced by sixteen water storage reservoirs with a maximum capacity of 14.6 million gallons of water. There are eight culinary water sources: three deep wells, one spring, two tunnels, Rockport Reservoir, and one imported source (Jordanelle Special Service District).

The complex water distribution system that the City maintains includes 140 miles of water pipeline, forty-three pressure zones, twenty tanks, sixteen pump stations, and forty-nine pressure-reducing stations.

Pressure zones? Pressure reduction? Are we talking Pilates, yoga, deep massage, or what?

The district uses almost 70 percent of the total summer consumption for irrigation of lawns and golf courses. Snowmaking makes a big dent (in the neighborhood of 20 percent) in the early winter months.

Given that 45 percent of the City's water comes from 100-year-old mining drain tunnels, the output can contain significant traces of lead, antimony, zinc, thallium, and other elements. Dilution, filtering, and chemical treatments are the order of the day. Lead? Yep, that's a definite concern. Zinc? Wait, isn't that a common supplement? Antimony? Isn't that what you pay after a particularly nasty divorce? It's all very confusing, and best left to the engineers.

Also providing water service is the Mountain Regional Water Special Service District, which Summit County created in 2000 to regionalize service in Snyderville Basin. Standing this entity up took the consolidation of several failing water companies. The district serves some 5,000 customers in a twenty-six-square-mile service area. It delivers about 10.5 million gallons on peak days, and about 6,000 acre-feet annually. It's got a water treatment plant that can treat four million gallons per day, and more than 200 miles of pipe. It's got twenty-four storage reservoirs that handle 10.7 million gallons of water, which is about fifteen average "district days" of volume. It also serves more than 1,500 fire hydrants.

Private players remain, such as the Summit Water Distribution Co., which primarily serves the Snyderville Basin area.

How about sewage treatment? To paraphrase Nick Badami, Park City is where the affluent meet the effluent. The main player is the Snyderville Basin Water Reclamation District, which calculates usage in terms of a Residential Equivalent (RE). One RE is equal to 320 gallons of generated wastewater per day (about what you get from a single three-bedroom house). From 1990 to 2023, demand for wastewater service has grown from 4,415 REs in 1990 to 28,453 REs, a 6.4X growth rate. Today, the district has a service area of approximately 102 square miles with a collection network of some 308 miles of pipeline, two reclamation facilities, one trunkline support facility, and ten pump stations.

The Reclamation District has a couple of hot buttons. One is the so-called flushable wipe. This personal hygiene convenience does not break down like toilet paper. Flushable wipes can aggregate in the system's pipes and treatment plants and cause expensive downtime and repairs. Don't use them, or if you do, pretend you're overseas, and dispose of them in the trash, not down the toilet.

The other hot button is the practice of pouring grease, fats, cooking oils, and dental floss down the drain. These, too, can clump up the works. To quote the district's website: "Greases and oils from cooking combine with the assortment of chemicals in your plumbing and the public sewer system (fatty acids combining with calcium common in sewer water) to form a waxy, soapy compound. Those fatty blobs stick to the walls of your home plumbing, lateral and public sewer pipes, sometimes referred to as 'fatbergs.'"

Instead, the district recommends collecting the gunk in a cup or can, letting it cool, and disposing of it in the trash. (Didn't we learn this decades ago?) Let the fatberg become Republic Services and the county landfill's problem, right? Even better, the Park City Community Foundation and Momentum Recycling have created a food waste disposal program to handle this issue and reduce methane emissions from the landfill.

As a side note, in 2025, the State Legislature enacted a statewide ban on putting fluoride in drinking water, making us the first state to do so, despite decades of evidence for the benefits of doing so and no significant public support for the ban. Maybe in a future session, they can enact a statewide ban on "dirty soda" shops (a Utah invention) to offset their deleterious actions.

THE MIGHTY WEBER

The Weber River offers whitewater fun a mere half-hour from Park City, near the town of Henefer. There are several competent professional outfitters you can avail yourself of, or you can do it yourself. Best practice: Take a professionally-led ride, then DIY!

Rule #1: Wear a life vest. The State of Utah is known to have staff at put-in especially on busy summer weekends. Their rangers will give you a stern talking to or possibly a fine if you try to embark without a life vest. And if you're floating in an inner tube, you're definitely going to need it.

In terms of difficulty, the "Mighty Weber" river is a Class II level experience. There are about four moves over four-plus miles that you need to make: Rock Garden, the railroad "limbo" bridge, Killer Pillars, and just above take-out, Taggart Falls. If you don't pay attention at these spots, you're apt to take an unscheduled adventure swim. The rest of the course is a low-stress, enjoyable float around easy-to-miss rocks and shrubbery, mixed in with a few splashy waves. Halfway down, you get a primo view of Devil's Slide, a fascinating limestone formation on river left.

There is no permit required to float the Henefer stretch. The whole scene on summer weekends can be a mash-up of "Animal House" meets "The African Queen." You'll be sharing the stream with a high number of Hacklebarnies (river rafting technical jargon referring to people who are ill-prepared in terms of gear and cognitive powers). A best practice is to run the Weber on weekdays, or if you must run it on Saturday or Sunday, put-in before 9:00 a.m. or after 4:00 p.m.

Regardless of when you run it, you will encounter an array of watercraft that include unicorn and swan floaties, as well as Walmart-sourced "rafts" that are as durable as moldy shower curtains. The banks of the Weber are littered with forlorn, multi-colored, post-puncture wrecks, especially downstream of Rock Garden.

There is also a fair amount of alcohol in use, though the aforementioned rangers take a dim view, especially if the drinkers are underaged. Nonetheless, a fair amount of cheap beer makes it past the watchful eyes of the State, and in the downstream carnage, there is an opportunity for those of us in sturdier and more maneuverable inflatable kayaks to exercise our salvage rights. One person's flip becomes another's fliptop.

In 2024, the Department of Wildlife Resources instituted a ten-dollar parking fee for the Henefer put-in on Fridays, Saturdays, Sundays, holidays, and other peak demand periods. The fee is fifteen dollars for vehicles with eight or more passengers. To the extent that this fee mitigates crowding on the river, this is a good thing.

No one will confuse the Weber with, say, Idaho's Middle Fork of the Salmon 100-mile wilderness run. But the Weber has a delightful bounce, and where else can you float under a train bridge while a line of freight cars rattles overhead?

As a reward, treat yourself afterward to a burger at Taggart's Grill on the north side of I-84 at the take-out. The grill is in Morgan County, but it gets an honorary Summit County burger pass.

JORDANELLE RESERVOIR

As a desert state, Utah is not known for an abundance of navigable waters. Park City is lucky to be situated close to Jordanelle Reservoir, which is located in Wasatch County. Opened in 1995, the 3,300-acre reservoir is in the Provo River watershed, and upon completion, it inundated three small farming towns, namely Hailstone, Keetley, and Jordanelle. This is in contrast with most Utah farming towns, like Heber City and Midway, which are becoming inundated in asphalt.

The busiest and most developed part of the Jordanelle is the Hailstone area, right off U.S. Route 40's Mayflower exit. The area has a large eight-lane boat ramp and full-service marina among other amenities. The marina rents boats, jet skis, kayaks, stand-up paddle boards (SUP) and those crazy "hydroflight" flydive rigs. With a large, wake-free area, Hailstone is a very popular SUP area.

Rock Cliffs is quieter, has nature trails, and offers excellent bird watching. Tucked into a narrow arm of the reservoir, this part of the Jordanelle is a relatively wind-protected place for kayaking.

At the north end of the reservoir, Ross Creek is quieter still, with a non-motorized boat ramp and access to the Perimeter Trail.

As a state park, Jordanelle Reservoir charges a day-use fee. As of this writing, it is between fifteen and twenty dollars per vehicle (up to eight passengers) depending on the access point. There is also a five-dollar fee for using the Perimeter Trail. There are more than 200 overnight camp-sites, with fees ranging from twenty to thirty dollars.

The International Dark-Sky Association designated Jordanelle State Park as an international dark sky park in 2021. The association better come back in 2031 to review the designation, given the vast number of residences being built around its shores.

Jordanelle is home base for the Park City Sailing association, which has lessons, races, boat rentals, a junior program, an adaptive program, and "Women & Wind," among other offerings. The youth program is well regarded and has put athletes on the podium in national regattas. In 2024, Park City High School sailor Calvin Marsh was admitted to the United States Merchant Marine Academy to compete at the collegiate level!

Who knew that training at altitude (elevation 6,188 feet) could help your sailing skills?

Lake Effect, Pineapple Express, and the Powder Buoy

When a storm from the west plows into the 11,000-foot wall of the Wasatch Range, the air mass pushes upward, cools, and snow begins to fall. The clouds must lighten their load of moisture as they move east. Depending on the wind direction, this can pay dividends for the ski resorts east and southeast of the lake. "Orographic lift" is a primary reason places like Alta (with a 546-inch annual average snowfall) receive significantly more than Park City (287-inch average).

Lake effect—the process by which storms pick up moisture from the Great Salt Lake—is another factor, adding 5–10 percent more snowfall to the front side of the Wasatch, according to Jim Steenburgh, professor of atmospheric science at the University of Utah (aka @professorpowder).

The tables are turned when our side of the Wasatch is hit with a storm coming up from the south or southwest. These "Pineapple Express" storms are usually warmer and wetter than our typical Utah storm, but by coming in the back door, they favor the Wasatch Back with big dumps. We may not get the dry, light powder from such storms, but these weather events are great for building the snow base. From a New England or Pacific Northwest perspective, a Pineapple Express brings heavenly conditions.

How do you know when to schedule your bout of powder flu? How do you know what's coming in advance of your ski vacation? A fun and diverting way is to follow the Powder Buoy online at *powderbuoy.com* or on your favorite doom-scrolling application.

The basic idea involves some National Oceanic and Atmospheric Administration (NOAA) weather buoys that are floating out by the island of Kauai. When these buoys "pop" (register significant increases in wave height), it means two things: one, there's going to be great surfing in a day or two in the Hawaiian Islands, and two, there may be a powder-rich snowstorm in the Wasatch about two weeks later.

The correlation is pretty darn high . . . about 80 percent most years. Yeah, buoy! But Steenburgh reserves judgment as he teaches his students, "All generalizations are wrong."

The long-term concern, of course, is what happens to the lake effect when the lake dries up? Furthermore, playa dust from cracked dry alkaline mud causes snowpack to melt more quickly in the spring. The combination will impact our future snowpacks.

Sung to the "Bad Boys" theme: Whatcha gonna do when the lake runs dry? Sit on the bank and watch the ski bums cry.

But don't despair. More on this topic in the "Salt Flat City" section later on.

Aspens in the Fall

A great joy hereabouts is the fall foliage.

Folks visiting Park City from the East Coast can be excused for thinking our aspen trees are related to birch trees. Despite the similarities in the color of their barks and the brilliant yellows they both exhibit in the fall, these trees are in different families. Aspen are in the poplar or willow family (Populus) while the classic New England white or paper birch trees belong to the birch family (Betulaceae).

The species name of the aspen is tremuloides, and it's known as the trembling or quaking aspen. When the wind picks up, the leaves create a lovely susurration. The Ute legend has it that the Great Spirit visited earth during a special full moon. All flora and fauna trembled with the deity's approach, except for the aspen. Maddened by this show of pride and disrespect, the Great Spirit decreed, from that day forth, aspen leaves would tremble whenever anyone looked upon them.

As nights lengthen in the fall, this triggers the change of foliage in the hills of Summit County. It would be great if the oaks, maple, and aspen would coordinate more closely, but as it is, the oaks and maples tend to change in early and mid-September, while the aspen colors peak in late

September and early October. For this reason, Utah's foliage is an eight on the New England scale of ten.

Photosynthesis slows with the shorter days and angled sunlight. The green chlorophyll in leaves is reduced and in aspen, a yellow tint (xanthophylls) predominates, though sometimes some trees take on an orange hue (carotenoid). While sunlight is the major factor, temperature, soil moisture, and plant health can impact foliage timing. Warm, sunny days with cool (above freezing) nights are the best lead-up to a visual feast on the hillsides.

Another factor is that aspen propagate via cloning. Individual trees share a root system, and a grove may represent a single organism. The collective root system sends up "volunteers" to propagate, which is just more evidence that volunteerism is strong in our community and that we're all connected. In scientific terms, these "volunteers" are called ramets, which would make a great Wordle word. Foliage timing can be relatively consistent among the individual trees in a cloned grove.

A fun road trip is to visit the Pando Grove in Fishlake National Forest, about 200 miles south of Park City. The grove's clone with its 47,000 ramets may be the heaviest organism on Earth, though envious Colorado scientists dispute this.

Aspens are relatively fire-resistant and can provide "succession forests" that allow conifers to grow. That's why you'll often see mixed hillsides of aspen and conifers.

One other notable feature of aspen trees beside the vibrant fall colors is the "pistol grip" shape at the base of some trunks. Since these curves generally point downhill from where the tree emerges from the soil, it may be due to slow, downhill pressure from winter snows. (To an extent, snow can demonstrate plasticity, flowing under the influence of gravity.) Some believe the shapes are caused by soil creep, but how does soil creep uphill?

WAIT, WHAT?
THEY CAN MAKE SNOW ABOVE FREEZING?

Okay, at the risk of making your head hurt, we're going to review some terms you may have last encountered in Physics 101. These terms have a bearing on one of the activities that keeps this town rolling, that is, snowmaking.

- Dry Bulb Temperature: This is the number normally associated with air temperature. It's the ambient temperature, and it's measured using a thermometer that is not affected by the amount of moisture or water vapor in the local atmosphere.

- Wet Bulb Temperature: Meteorologists like to wrap damp cloth around thermometers to see the effects of humidity. Evaporation of moisture from the damp cloth causes the wet bulb thermometer to register a lower temperature than a dry bulb thermometer. The drier the air, the more moisture will evaporate from the damp cloth, and the lower the wet bulb temperature reading will be.

- Dew Point Temperature: This is the temperature at which moisture in the atmosphere condenses, forming dew. As the temperature rises, more moisture can be contained in the atmosphere, and dew formation ceases.

As a general rule, the lower the wet bulb temperature, the better the quality of the snow produced by current snowmaking technology. A light, dry snow can be produced in the wet bulb range of nineteen to twenty-six degrees Fahrenheit. In a pinch, a denser, heavier snow can be produced in the wet bulb range of twenty-seven to thirty-seven degrees Fahrenheit.

So yes, the dry bulb temperature may be above freezing, but if the relative humidity is roughly 50 percent, the snowmaking apparatus (guns, sticks, and fans) can produce something that's skiable.

In fact, a denser production is often preferred for building a snow base that will last into April.

Now, luckily in Utah, we have a dry climate, so in December and January, when the big snowmaking push occurs, our snowmakers are dealing with relatively low humidity levels and low dry bulb temperatures. Our crews have more favorable conditions than, say, the crews at Wachusett Mountain in central Massachusetts.

Our resorts employ dozens of snow artists who use compressed air and water to create the big hump-backed "whales" of snow you see on early season slopes. These whales are then the object of another set of artists, those who drive ten-ton paintbrushes called snowcats.

Deer Valley Resort and Park City Mountain are big customers of the Park City Municipal's Water District. There's no truth to the rumor that Deer Valley only uses Perrier in their snowmaking pipes.

THE RISK OF WILDFIRE

It's not all gin and bananas here. There's a graph of "Hazards Compared" in the 2022 Pre-Disaster Mitigation Plan for Summit, Utah, and Wasatch Counties that categorizes the major risks for Summit County. The x-axis (left to right) shows severity from negligible to limited to critical to catastrophic. The y-axis (bottom to top) shows probability from unlikely, possible, likely, to highly likely.

Winter weather, avalanches, flood, drought, lightning, and wind are all accounted for in the chart. Earthquake even has a spot. But fire is the hazard that the graph puts the highest and farthest to the right. It's a likely risk that can have critical severity.

The U.S. Forest Service calls out Summit County as a high-risk area on its "Wildfire Risk to Communities" website. In terms of percentiles, Coalville has a very high risk of wildfire, higher than 90 percent of communities in the U.S. The town of Kamas weighs in at 92 percent, Park City at 94 percent, and Snyderville Basin at 95 percent. The Summit Park neighborhood tops out at an astounding 98 percent risk. In other words, we're the communities that experts are thinking about when they use the term "wildland urban interface."

Like *This is Spinal Tap*, the counties' Pre-Disaster Mitigation plan uses a scale up to eleven, and its risk assessment varies from the Forest Service's in a few particulars. The Promontory and Jeremy Ranch neighborhoods both are rated eleven, while Solamere and the Aerie hit ten. Summit Park earns a nine, since it has a Community Wildfire Protection Plan developed in concert with Utah's Department of Forestry, Fire, and State Lands, and also has had controlled burns for several years. The Colony is also a nine. Eastern Summit County communities such as Peoa, Coalville, Kamas, and Francis are rated fives and sixes.

The county faces considerable fire danger every summer and fall. Twice in recent decades, fires in Parley's Canyon have prompted evacuation orders for Summit Park, and in the second instance, Pinebrook. In 2013, a fast-moving wildfire near Rockport Reservoir destroyed more than a dozen homes and outbuildings. More and more neighborhoods that are similarly threatened are seeing a rise in fire insurance in recent years.

There's a certain amount of unreal thinking here in our community. We are in the crosshairs when it comes to wildfire. Since we as a people seem to do a poor job of limiting development in areas subject to fire danger, we need to adopt other ways to mitigate risk, such as underbrush/tree fuel management, prescribed burns, hardening buildings against fire with appropriate siding and roofing materials, vent covers to prevent embers entering the home, maintaining an emergency water supply and appropriate water pressures, using appropriate plantings around homes, and much more.

Our endangered neighborhoods are seeing increases in fire insurance as insurers recalibrate the risks of climate change. Full cancellation is not far behind. Homeowner Associations (HOAs) may find themselves in the self-insurance business, collecting and doling out the funds that insurance companies would take in days past, as long as they can work out that sticky stuff, like banks requiring insurance policies on mortgaged properties. Or it may be an opportunity for non-admitted (very lightly regulated) insurance companies. The State, loath as it will be to do so, will have to step in, and has done so to a limited extent.

In 2025 and 2026, the State Legislature passed and modified bills to stand up the Wildfire Preparedness Program. Starting in 2027, home-owners in high-risk areas will need to contribute to a statewide fund. The fees, ranging from twenty dollars to one hundred dollars a year, will fund wildfire risk assessment and mitigation. It's too early to determine if this approach will be effective, but let's give points to lawmakers for pay-ing attention to an important issue as opposed to wasting time on street name and rainbow flag policies.

One other aspect of wildfire is even harder to control. Fires in Utah and elsewhere in the western U.S. have impacted our air quality and clouded our views in recent years. According to one study, the annual average U.S. acreage burned by wildfire has doubled in the past twen-ty years. Wasatch County got a big dose in 2024 with the 33,000-acre Yellow Lake Fire.

The particulate matter and toxic substances in the smoke from these fires can affect children, seniors, and people with asthma and other health issues. By 2050, wildfire smoke could cause up to 27,800 U.S. deaths per year, according to the National Bureau of Economic Research.

Summit County has long been a refuge from the air pollution that plagues the Salt Lake Valley, but when the bad air encompasses all of our region, there's no place to escape.

RECREATION, HEALTH, AND WELLBEING AT HIGH ALTITUDE

A normal community has a triangle-shaped population distribution that starts with a wide base of slugs, then a smaller cohort of actives, then good athletes, then a tiny cap of top-level athletes. Summit County's "athletic triangle" has a smaller base, steeper inclination, and a generous cap of world-class competitors. And how we behave in our athletic pursuits has a big impact on quality of life here.

TEN SECONDS OF KINDNESS: TRAIL ETIQUETTE

With 400 miles of multipurpose trails in Summit County, trail etiquette is foundational to civilized behavior. The National Park Service (NPS) has a good guide to proper trail-user behavior. Some general rules include:

- Hikers and, to an extent, bikers coming uphill have right of way.
- Bikers yield to hikers, horses, and other pack stock (looking at you, llamas).
- Hikers yield to horses and other pack stock.
- Everybody yields to moose. (I made that part up, but the NPS probably concurs.) In general, don't bug the wildlife. Back away slowly.
- Stay off muddy trails so you don't cause damaging erosion. The website *pctrails.org* is a good resource for checking current trail conditions.

With its predominant mountain biking scene, Park City has some fine print to modify the NPS guidelines. Here, for example, it is good form for hikers to step aside when mountain bikers are approaching.

Though technically you have right of way, it may be easier for you to move to the side of the trail so the bikers don't have to stop or dismount. This is not a hard and fast rule, rather a gesture of what the Mountain Trails non-profit calls "ten seconds of kindness."

According to former executive director Charlie Sturgis, that means, "Slow down, smile, be safe. That's all it takes. You can take that to almost any place in the world, and any situation, and probably go, 'Oh. Okay, yeah, that works.'"

Bikers, in turn, are welcome to slow down or even stop and allow hikers to move past. When bikers actually do this, it melts the hearts of the walkers like nothing else. See, everybody can get along!

Encouraging words and "Thank you" and "Have a nice day" or "Have a nice walk/ride" from all parties also exemplify good form. This is not hard stuff, people.

Bear in mind that a trail like Mid-Mountain, which reaches from Pinebrook all the way to Deer Valley's Little Baldy Peak, can see lots of traffic (tens of thousands?) throughout the summer. Go early in the morning or late in the afternoon and avoid high-congestion times like holiday weekends.

While you're at it, don't forget to pick up the pieces of trash and micro-trash. Take a bag on your hikes and make a game of trying to fill it up. You'll be surprised how easy it is to do, and you get the added exercise of bending over to pick stuff up. "Whose job is it to pick up litter at Disneyland? Everyone's!"

Paddleboarding and Mussels

Paddleboarding is the pickleball of aquatic sports. Really, to an old whitewater river guide, those boards could use a little more giddy-up. Admittedly, the sport does provide a good workout, and can get you out to some beautiful places.

There are some good paddleboarding spots with spectacular scenery in Summit and Wasatch Counties, like Jordanelle, Deer Creek, Echo, Rockport, Smith & Morehouse, Mirror Lake, and Washington Lake to name a few. In town, the snowmaking ponds near the Deer Valley Café offer another venue, albeit one that is rich in duck muck.

Please note that the Utah Department of Natural Resources has put in place an online course on mussel awareness for all private boaters (e.g. not watercraft renters). This means anyone who launches a boat or any other watercraft in Utah—whether they are a resident or non-resident, whether the watercraft is motorized or human-powered (such as a paddleboard), or whether the body of water you're visiting has mussels or not. Only Lake Powell is known to have mussels at this point.

The awareness course and the fees levied on any motorized users are designed to fight the spread of the quagga and zebra mussels, which are invasive species that can cause a lot of harm, including:

- Plugging water lines, even large-diameter ones.

- Gumming up water delivery systems, costing millions of dollars annually to keep the pipes free, which can result in higher utility bills.
- Removing plankton from the water, which hurts fish species.
- Damaging motorized boat engine cooling systems.
- Dying in large numbers, causing a stink and leaving sharp shells of dead mussels that can cut your feet as you walk along the beaches.

The course is quick and easy, and you learn cool new phrases like "byssal threads" to weave into the conversations that usually start with, "But it's great for the core."

A closing public service announcement: Utah's lakes are warming and experiencing more frequent and larger algae blooms. These can be toxic to humans and dogs, so it's best to avoid recreating near these outbreaks.

Mountain Biking and Other Mayhem

The Park City area is blessed with a plethora of fantastic non-profits, and one of the best is Mountain Trails, founded in 1993. Thanks to their efforts, those of our recreation districts, and wide community support, the area now boasts more than 400 miles of non-motorized trails, one of the most extensive continuous trail systems in the nation. This puts us in the same conversation as mountain biking "death by Go-Pro" meccas like Moab, Utah and Grand Junction, Colorado.

Deer Valley and Vail Park City both offer lift-served mountain biking in the summer. This allows you to fulfill all your "Mad Max" cosplay fantasies. Strap on the leather and shoulder pads, wicked helmet and shin guards, and have at it, screaming down Tidal Wave and other white-knuckle trails.

There are a number of fun and free group mountain biking experiences and lessons (co-ed and female only), orchestrated by Woodward Park City, White Pine Touring, Jans Mountain Outfitters, and others. Paid lesson programs abound at the resorts, the businesses above, and other places.

Lessons and group ride introductions to local terrain are highly rec-ommended, for as the Instagram meme says, "Mountain biking is a great way to meet potential dates. Usually medics."

One study reports that the sport incurs 16.8 injuries per 1,000 hours of exposure. That's more than triple the 5.5 injuries per 1,000 hours expe-rienced in amateur soccer (National Institutes of Health).

The same study indicates that when mountain bike riders are going cross-country, 0.4 riders are injured per 100 hours. When the riders are downhill racing, like you essentially do when you're using one of the lift-served flow trails at our resorts, the incidence rate rises to 4.3 riders injured per 100 hours. Ask our buddy John K. from Cleveland . . . about his forearm . . . on Tidal Wave.

It's important to put the injury rate of mountain biking in juxtaposi-tion with other sports. For example, according to the National Ski Areas Association, skiers face an injury rate of 2.5 per 1,000 skier visits, and snowboarders face a rate of 3.9 per 1,000 snowboarder visits. (If you've had the buffet at the Stein Eriksen Lodge, your hours of skiing per visit will be drastically reduced as you digest. Be safe, have seconds!)

Some stats from other sports follow, with your correspondent's com-mentary added to assist a weighing of the evidence, since these are not apples to apples:

- Horseback riding has a head injury rate of 46.2 percent among participants. Lesson? Don't be rich.
- In 2022, 230,506 people visited hospital emergency rooms after being injured while skateboarding or using scooters and hoverboards. Beware of sports that have coined the term "swell-bow" (for swollen elbow).
- BASE jumping has an annual fatality rate of approximately 0.04 percent per jump (forty deaths per 100,000 jumps). This sounds improbably reassuring. Skydiving sees one fatality per 200,000

jumpers, or .0005 percent. However, both these sports have an overly optimistic relationship with gravity.

- A study of men's collegiate hockey showed an estimated injury risk of 7.6 per 1,000 athlete exposures. If you're dating a hockey player, you should be concerned about other exposures.
- Crossfit's injury rate is 20 percent. Physical therapy clinics consider Crossfit a "feeder program."
- One in 500,000 bungee jumps is fatal. The person holding your beer has a similar risk of being hit by a meteorite.
- In researching this section, I learned there are firefighting SPORTS? What? Running up burning stairwells?!?

The real question is when to put away your mountain bike and take up a truly risky sport like pickleball, another physical therapy feeder program!

One other aside regarding snow sports: Your perceptions are wrong.

It's not the headbangers with the slouchy pants. The National Ski Areas Association (NSAA) compiles two fact sheets after each ski season. One reveals the number of on-mountain fatalities and the other the number of catastrophic injuries, defined as "life-altering injuries" such as paralysis. Of the thirty-five people who died at NSAA ski areas in the 2023 to 2024 season, thirty were male and twenty-eight of them were on skis. Of the forty-nine catastrophic injuries, forty-one were male and thirty-four were skiers. The majority of both incidents occurred on intermediate terrain.

Here's the twist: Most of the on-mountain fatalities during the 2023 to 2024 season happened to people who were between the ages of fifty-one and sixty. So while the stereotype is that the young-gun snowboarders hucking cliffs and going way too fast are paying the ultimate price, in reality, it's the middle-aged guys on two planks sliding on groomed blues. Just ask our buddy John K. from Cleveland . . . about his clavicle . . . on Tycoon.

E-Biking on Streets and Singletrack Trails

The vitriol of tennis versus pickleball is one thing. The debate between e-bikers versus the rest of the pedal pack may surpass the nets-and-chardonnay kerfuffle in terms of amplitude in community rage. E-bikes weigh between forty and eighty pounds and pack a much bigger punch than a 0.78-to-0.93-ounce pickleball. A pickleball accident is typically a turned ankle. An e-bike accident can lead to death.

This writer is torn on the question of making more of our trail system accessible to e-bikes. Being a senior myself, I appreciate the proviso allowing sixty-five-plus folks to e-bike on singletrack trails, which are defined as being the approximate width of a single bike. Whether I will ever do so is an entirely different question. I like my collarbones the way they are.

E-bikes are convenient and non-taxing. The fact that they don't burn as many calories as non-motorized bicycles does not particularly worry me. You might actually ride a longer route on an e-bike, making the difference in calorie burn negligible. Traditional bikers will try to shame e-bikers, but obloquy and calumny will not break the resolve of the electric set. E-bikes are damn fun, and to the extent they get people off their couches and outdoors, they are a positive element in our community.

On the other hand, they are ripe for abuse. Any two-wheeler can damage a muddy trail; a heavy e-bike can really mess things up. And with only common sense and a concern for fellow trail users to govern their speed, the artificially fast nature of e-bikes can lead to some scary and dangerous encounters around blind corners.

We're also seeing the wholesale adoption of e-bikes by the younger set, that is, kids who don't have their driver licenses yet. Go on *Nextdoor. com*, and hourly you are beset with messages about e-biking youngsters barreling through intersections, not wearing helmets, endangering themselves and others. Hard to say this, but it may take a severe accident to get parents engaged in teaching their kids the rules of the road. It's not happening to date, despite some language in Utah state law around Class I, II, and III e-bikes. To review the latest state legislation:

- Class I = Pedal-assist, no throttle, runs up to 20 MPH. No license or insurance required.
- Class II = Pedal-assist with throttle, runs up to 20 MPH. No license or insurance required.
- Class III = Pedal-assist, runs up to 28 MPH.

Age restrictions: Helmets are required for those under twenty-one years of age operating an e-bike. Nobody under sixteen can operate a Class III e-bike. Anybody under fifteen on a Class I or II e-bike needs to be accompanied by a parent or guardian, or complete a safety training course for certification. Anyone under eight is not allowed to operate any kind of e-bike in the public space.

There are e-bikes that don't conform with the three classes in the market. These e-motorcycles generally have foot pegs instead of pedals and can reach speeds of 30 to 60 MPH. They are not legal on public roads, sidewalks, or bike paths unless properly registered. They must be operated in line with state motor vehicle or off-highway vehicle laws. The 2026 legislation gives police and sheriffs more tools for enforcement of all these vehicle types, including citations and impoundment.

E-bikes have the look of inevitability. In 2022, 1.1 million e-bikes were sold in the U.S., four times the number sold in 2019. This question of balancing trail access will bedevil us for years to come. As it currently stands, I do think e-bikes are better suited for commuting on paved, high-visibility trails versus recreating on mountainous singletracks.

As a side note, the Summit County Bikeshare program is the poor man's e-bike. These pedal-assist bikes are located at strategic locations in Park City and the Snyderville Basin. An annual pass is modest, and individual rides are about four dollars. These bikes are not designed for singletrack, and are best used on the paved paths around the county. The program experienced 23,000 rides in 2025. Give 'em a spin!

THE RAIL TRAIL

One of our area's beloved multi-use paths is the Historic Union Pacific Rail Trail, a relatively gentle path (some of it paved, but mostly gravel) that extends twenty-eight miles from Bonanza Drive in Park City all the way out to Echo. Be assured, there is a headwind both directions.

The trail averages a sweet 2 percent grade, with a maximum of 3 percent. The Park City end is at about 6,900 feet in elevation, while the Echo end is about 5,280 feet. Many the family fight erupts on the first climb back to Park City. Prospector residents can attest.

The trail is proof that Park City was a railroad town back in the day. The history behind the creation of a rail line between the mines of Park City and the Union Pacific's Echo railyard is a story of fits and starts. First, in 1869, the Coalville-Echo Railroad company was organized to haul coal from Coalville mines to the main line at Echo. The company ran out of iron rails. Two years later, the Summit County Railroad Company formed and continued to wobble through several years of supply chain issues. The narrow-gauge line began formal operations in 1873.

The Union Pacific made more money shipping coal from Evanston, Wyoming, and effectively froze out the Summit County operators. UP purchased the line in 1877, and began converting and expanding it to standard gauge. That line extended to Park City by 1880.

Ultimately, in 1989, UP abandoned the railroad line. The railroad, along with the Division of Parks and Recreation and A&K Railroad Materials, launched plans to turn the abandoned railroad corridor into a non-motorized recreational trail. The Historic Union Pacific Rail Trail State Park was dedicated in 1992. It is the first non-motorized rail trail in Utah.

If you tackle this route, make sure to bring plenty of fluids. The opportunities to top off your water bottle are few and far between. It's about fifteen miles from Park City to Wanship (where there is a small convenience store) and then another eight to Coalville (which has some markets). You're in dry and hot sagebrush country for much of the time, so plan accordingly.

For bonus points, check out the beautifully restored Union Pacific train station which stands at its original location in Park City at the intersection of Main Street and Heber Avenue. This used to be the Zoom Restaurant located at 660 Main Street. Owned by actor Robert Redford, Zoom opened in 1995 and was part of his Sundance Resort Group. A Park City staple for twenty-two years, Zoom unexpectedly closed in 2017 as a result of a lease and landlord dispute.

Bonanza Flat

In historical terms, Bonanza Flat wasn't a bonanza, and in hiking and biking terms, it sure ain't flat. This 1,500-plus-acre plot of open space is located near Guardsman Pass and was purchased by Park City Municipal in 2017. Utah Open Lands holds the easement.

An early mining claim was the Jones Bonanza. One of the Jones brothers was hauling lumber to sell to the Park City mines. The log he was dragging got snagged in the boulders, and when Jones took a prybar to it, he broke off part of a rock. It revealed galena ore, dramatically altering Jones' career trajectory. Despite this promising beginning and the best efforts of mining experts like John Daly, few of the mines in Bonanza Flat amounted to much.

Given its proximity to Big Cottonwood Canyon, Bonanza Flat has become a prime summer recreation area for Salt Lake Valley residents in addition to the expected numbers coming from Summit County. The recreation pressure is high and rising. Parking can be an issue, and in the summer months, the city has added paid parking kiosks and runs a shuttle to ease congestion. Like a lot of our outdoor assets, it's best avoided on weekends.

Perhaps the most popular and heavily trafficked trail is the one to Bloods Lake. How did it get its name? Some students of local history point to Henry H. Blood, seventh Governor of Utah. His administration coincided with the Great Depression. However, "Blood's Lake" appears on an 1893 mining claim map produced by Robert Gorlinski, a Salt Lake lithographer, forty years before the Governor's administration.

A more likely candidate for the lake's name is George D. Blood, a well-regarded geologist and mining engineer who worked at Park City's Ontario and Marsac mills plus Silver King Coalition, Daly-Judge, and Park Utah mines in the late 1800s and early 1900s. But note, there's no definitive record from that time of how the lake was named.

People who hike to Bloods Lake in the early summer say it should be so named for the swarms of mosquitos encountered there. Or if you're hiking with kids, feel free to take liberties and make up a gripping tale of murder or mayhem to keep them focused on staying on the trail!

Please also stay focused on minimizing your impact on Bloods Lake. It is a direct drinking water source for the nearby Girl Scout camp. Leave no trace and take the following steps with your dogs:

- No dogs in Bloods Lake
- Keep dogs on leash (as per Wasatch County Code)
- Clean up after your dogs, per Poop Fairy information discussed elsewhere.

THE ATMOSPHERE, ALTITUDE SICKNESS, AND TEAM MELANOMA

Newcomers here may feel winded climbing a flight of stairs. Rest assured, each breath you take is still 21 percent oxygen molecules, just like in Central Park, Miami Beach, or Dodger Stadium. What you have is a density problem.

Air loses density as it gains altitude. At higher altitudes, there is less air pushing down from above, and gravity is marginally weaker. At 9,000 feet, air pressure in millibars is about a third less than at sea level. This means there are fewer molecules—oxygen, nitrogen, etc.—in a given volume of air. Your "effective oxygen" per breath is equivalent to 15 percent versus sea level's 21 percent. A hard-charging run down Jupiter Bowl (10,000 feet) starts in 14 percent territory. No wonder you're gulping like a guppy when you get to the bottom.

The good news is—at least in the summer—that your golf ball will fly farther in the thin air. Unfortunately, this includes sliced shots.

Utah's dry climate, and the tendency to respirate more to make up for lower oxygen intake, can lead to dehydration.

Rule One: When you get to town, hydrate early and often. This can mitigate headaches.

Rule Two: If you can spend a night in Salt Lake City (around 4,200 feet in elevation) before you head up to the Stein Eriksen Lodge (8,100 feet), your body will have a better chance to acclimate. Once you do get to Stein's, ask staff to show you how to operate your in-room humidifier. (There's a reason they are perennial contenders for the World Ski Awards "Best U.S. Ski Hotel" designation.)

Rules Three and Four: Grab a nap, get a good night's sleep, take it slow the first day at altitude. Go easy on the alcohol at the start of your trip. So much for tapping Stein Eriksen's million-dollar-inventory wine cellar right off the bat.

Rule Five: A blood-thinning baby aspirin before bedtime may help you sleep better (but check with your doctor since studies of aspirin usage are all over the map).

These rules are a statement of an ideal world. If you're here for a business conference, bachelorette party, or high school reunion (and you moved to sea level after high school), you ought to be able to follow Rule One, but good luck with the rest of them. Regardless, your body will adjust on its own in about three to five days . . . just in time to head back to the airport.

And speaking of the consequences of a thin atmosphere, welcome to Summit County. Congratulations! You're on the starting varsity squad of Utah's "Team Melanoma."

Utah loves to tout its accolades, especially on the economic front. "Best State for This and That," depending on the priorities an evaluating organization puts in place. Right-to-work state? The American Legislative Exchange Council (ALEC) says to go to the front of the line, union buster!

Utah also leads the nation in melanoma rate. While melanoma accounts for 1 percent of skin cancers nationwide, that 1 percent is deadly, according to the American Cancer Society.

The national average from 2016 to 2020 is 22.5 cases per 100,000 people. Utah is the frontrunning overachiever at 40.8 cases. Furthermore, consistency is the mark of a true champion. Utah has held the melanoma title for fourteen of the last fifteen years, according to the Centers for Disease Control (CDC).

Okay, the state has a predominantly white population. Heck, those LDS missionaries convinced a lot of Scandinavians to move here. And high altitude counteracts the protective effects of ozone. So cut us some slack.

The best practice in high-altitude Summit County is to use copious amounts of high-SPF sunscreen when you head outdoors. Lather up, people!

Hospitals, Clinics, and Senior Care

Be happy to know that our community is not a healthcare desert. If you are in need of a twenty-four-hour emergency room, Intermountain Healthcare's Park City Hospital is the local option. It is near State Route 248 and U.S. Route 40. In addition to an emergency room with Level III Trauma capabilities, it is well known for its orthopedic surgery and maternity care capabilities. Patients staying overnight in the thirty-seven-bed facility might as well be staying at the Montage, it feels that well-appointed. The facility's nickname is the Posh-pital.

The other big healthcare system in Utah, the University of Utah, has an urgent care facility in Kimball Junction. Called the Redstone Health Center, its normal hours are Monday to Friday from 7:00 a.m. to 7:00 p.m, and 8:00 a.m. to 7:00 p.m. Saturday and Sunday.

Also in Kimball Junction is Stat+MD. Their hours vary day to day so check online for the schedule.

Park City Instacare, located on Sidewinder Drive, offers urgent care seven days a week from 8:00 a.m. to 7:00 p.m.

The People's Health Clinic, at Quinn's Junction near the Park City Hospital, is a volunteer-driven, community-supported, non-profit clinic providing high-quality, no cost healthcare to uninsured residents of Summit and Wasatch Counties in Utah. It is open Monday through Thursday from 8:00 a.m. to 5:00 p.m., Fridays from 8:00 a.m. to 1:00

p.m., and closed on weekends. It is a great cause to support with your charitable donations.

The Coalville and Kamas Health Centers offer a range of services. Coalville hours are Monday through Friday from 9:00 a.m. to 5:00 p.m., and 9:00 a.m. to 12:00 p.m. on Saturdays. Kamas hours are Monday through Friday from 8:30 a.m. to 8:00 p.m., and 8:30 a.m. to 5:00 p.m. on Saturdays.

Days and hours of operation of all these locations may vary by season, so check online before visiting any of these facilities.

Side notes: On Tuesday evenings during the summer, Deer Valley offers twilight mountain biking. Our clinics and the local fire stations always gear up for these nights. It's a lift-served experiment in Darwinian principles.

And don't go to the historic Miners Hospital for medical care. It last served patients in the 1950s.

While we have ample medical resources, Summit County is not well provided with senior care facilities. According to the U.S. Census, about 15.6 percent of Summit County's population is sixty-five years or older. Statewide, seniors make up about 12 percent, understandable since Utah is considered the country's youngest state demographically speaking. Nationwide, seniors account for 17.3 percent of the population.

Summit County's senior population is fast-growing. It increased 139 percent between 2010 and 2022. We also outlast most places: At 85.5 years, our life expectancy exceeds both Utah and the U.S., both of which come in at lower than eighty years.

When it comes to independent living communities, assisted living, memory care assisted living, and hospice care, Summit County is a resource-thin environment. The lion's share of these services is available down the hill in Salt Lake County.

With that said, the Park City Senior Center is an excellent non-profit offering fitness classes, lectures, coffee klatches and other activities for local seniors.

GYMS, SPAS, AND SPORTS PROGRAMS

Western Summit County boasts a plethora of gyms and fitness centers. This is not surprising, given that Northwell Health's 2023 study put us as the number-eleven most physically active county in the U.S., out of about 3,200 contenders.

On the public side, the two main fitness centers are the Basin Recreation Fieldhouse and the Park City Municipal Athletic & Recreation Center (PC MARC). For those of us who just plug and plod away, these are perfectly fine options with a decent array of equipment and classes. Basin Rec has a nice twice-a-week program with bounce houses and run-around space for toddlers. "Looking for a way to tire your kiddos out before naptime?" is how Toddler Time is promoted.

There is a public swimming facility, the Park City Aquatic Center, at Ecker Hill Middle School. It offers open and lap swimming, water aerobics, swim classes, and more. The Basin Recreation Fieldhouse also offers a lap pool.

In Kamas, the South Summit Aquatic and Fitness Center includes leisure and lap pools, slides and water features, well-equipped weight and cardio rooms, basketball courts, and more.

On the private side, the biggest player for year-round gym and pool fun is the Silver Mountain Sports Club & Spa, but there is a range of smaller and more specialized fitness providers such as Orangetheory Fitness, F45 Training, Pure Barre, various Pilates and yoga studios and even the Park City Boxing Club. What's not to "lycra" with this much choice? Align Spa in the Prospector neighborhood offers specials for locals.

Heber City has several establishments including Anytime Fitness, the Fit Stop Health Club, and Iron Backs Gym.

In terms of spas, just follow that waft of sandalwood incense to the nearest purveyor. The fancy hotels like Stein Eriksen Lodge, the Montage, St. Regis, and Hotel Park City have longstanding services, and there are lots of smaller, independent options throughout Park City and the Snyderville Basin. The hotels springing up in Deer Valley East are adding to the local choices.

One should not be surprised by the number and specialization of these services in our community. We're a fit (bordering on vain) demographic, and our visitors have the appropriate spending limits on their credit cards to keep the massage oil warming around the clock.

On the younger demographic side, our access to world-class winter sports resorts and facilities, our relative prosperity, and a plethora of youth development programs all provide athletic avenues for youth. If your child has the least inclination, introduce them to Nordic jumping! We need a competitive team in 2034 and Park City is the best place in the country to start that journey. We're also one of the best places in the world to train for bobsled, luge, and skeleton.

Traditional sports are also well represented here. Our children have opportunities to excel in track and field, soccer, tennis, hockey, golf, mountain biking, and more. As a lacrosse official for twenty-eight seasons, I'm happy to report that both the local boys and girls programs consistently produce skilled players and competitive teams, and the programs have secured a sizeable number of state championships.

Avoiding Organ Recitals

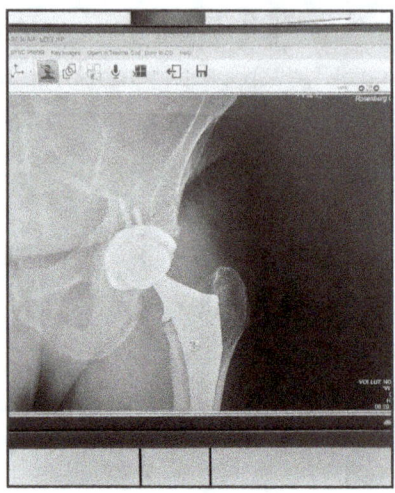

There are phases in life where all you talk about is your kids, or new house, or travels. When people of a mature age get together socially, or encounter friends while running errands, they can fall into the conversational habit of talking about recent ailments. This activity is called an "organ recital."

In Park City, this behavior is not restricted by age, because at any given moment, a lot of us are recovering from sports-related injuries. You need to arm yourself with some polite conversational gambits to extract yourself from the medical minutiae. Remember: "Get over yourself" is not a fruitful way to end a chat. Here are some scenarios to keep in mind:

Anterior Cruciate Ligaments (ACL): Live in Park City long enough and you're going to blow your knee out. It's slightly less common than catching the flu. The best way to keep the conversation short is to express sympathy, note how skilled our local orthopedic surgeons and physical therapists are, and most importantly, resist the temptation to discuss your own joint pain or past ACLs.

Broken Collarbones: Following closely on the Quotidian Scale to ACLs are broken collarbones, a common outcome of mountain or road biking. The same conversational rules apply; express sympathy, make a general observation, and don't reciprocate with your own experiences.

Hip Replacement Surgery: This procedure seems daunting. Afterall, the hip is a big piece of machinery in our bodies. The truth is modern medicine has this operation dialed in, and most recoveries are remarkably low on pain and fast on the resumption of normal activities. There's really not a lot of drama involved. Conversations about the topic inevitably devolve to the statement, "I wish I had done it sooner." As soon as you hear that phrase, you are free to initiate disengagement protocols. Telling the hip replacee that they look great and are moving well usually takes enough wind out of the sails to move ahead with your day. They can't argue, and their narrative loses momentum.

Knee Replacement and Shoulder Surgeries: Unlike the prior procedures discussed, these operations entail long, painful and genuinely tedious recoveries. The post-op conversations that trap you can be described in similar terms. You're not getting out of one of these monologues without making repeated sympathetic murmurs.

A best practice? Take a page from commercial river rafting. Longtime river guides speak of being buttonholed by a guest at camp and getting stuck in the "babble eddy." Guides have a secret signal to alert their crew members that they need rescuing so they can resume preparing dinner. "Hey, excuse me, sir. Mike, can you help me with the Dutch oven? Sorry to interrupt."

You and your spouse or significant other need to agree on a similar signal. If your partner sees from across the room that you are, say, gently pinching your earlobe, he or she should swoop in, grab you by the elbow, apologize to your interlocutor, and steer you across the room to such-and-such who has a question about this-and-that.

Sometimes these gambits fail to lessen the length and durability of someone's ability to talk about their ills. In these cases, drastic measures are called for. You may be forced to play the Tedium Card, and change the topic. "Can you kneel comfortably yet? I'm wondering how that would affect gardening. Have I told you about my tomato plants?"

Worst case, you can change the topic to your Carv or Strava subscription. You'll see a flicker of panic in the eyes of the person you've been talking to, as they suddenly search for a way to disengage. Problem solved!

LIQUOR
AND CHURCHES

In Utah, these topics go hand-in-hand.

Churches, Synagogues, and Other Places of Worship

Members of The Church of Jesus Christ of Latter-day Saints compose 36 percent of Summit County's population, making the county the least Mormon in the state. Overall, Utah's LDS population is about 60 percent of residents.

According to the church's website (*newsroom.churchofjesuschrist.org/*): "Each member belongs to a ward or branch. The lay leader of a ward is called a bishop. He is a member of the congregation who has been asked to serve as a volunteer in this position. Members of a ward worship together on Sundays and hold activities during the week."

Several wards are administered under what's called a stake, similar to a Catholic diocese. The leader of a stake is called the stake president. (My friend Jennifer Marie says that when she first moved here, a Mormon acquaintance asked her which "steakhouse" she belonged to. "Ruth's Chris? Butchers? I was so confused!")

There are eight wards in western Summit County and they share four meeting houses: one at Jeremy Ranch, another south of I-80 near Ecker Hill Middle School, one in Park City proper near the high school, and one in the Trailside neighborhood. Anybody is welcome to visit a meeting house. Non-members of the church cannot visit Mormon temples. The nearest temple is in Salt Lake City (Ground Zero) with another one on its way in Heber City.

When it comes to other Christian denominations, Summit County has a diverse range including Catholic, Presbyterian, Episcopal, Lutheran, Methodist, Baptist and various evangelical churches. This diversity is a testament to Park City's mining past, which attracted workers from around the world.

The St. Mary of the Assumption Church, part of the Catholic diocese of Salt Lake City, is the oldest church in Summit County. A small structure near Main St., it was built in 1881 to serve the predominately Catholic miners from Ireland who had flocked to town. The structure is on the National Register of Historic Places. Catholic services are now held at the beautiful, modern St. Mary's Church, near the big white barn on Route 224.

There are currently nine Jewish congregations in Utah, some as far south as St. George, and two of them are in the Park City area. Chabad Lubavitch of Park City is an orthodox congregation, and Temple Har Shalom is reform.

This reminds me of a story that a friend of my wife told us years ago. When Temple Har Shalom was being built on Route 224, there was a sign on the main road which said, "Coming Soon – Temple Har Shalom."

My wife's friend and her young grade-school daughter were driving by. The daughter looked up and said, "Oh, great. *That's* all we need."

The mom had a sudden quiet panic attack that she was raising an antisemite. "Honey, what do you mean?"

"All we need is another hair salon."

Our Jewish friends who are here in town on ski vacations can avail themselves of Shabbat services at the Sunset Cabin on Deer Valley's Bald Mountain at 2:00 p.m. on most Fridays during the ski season. (There's an interfaith Christian service on Sundays at 2:00 p.m. too.)

Vail Park City also offers kosher dining and services at the Silverado Lodge (Canyons side). Check the resort websites for details on these offerings.

Summit County currently has no mosques, but information about the Islamic community in Utah is available at *utislamiccenter.org*. In addition, there are several Buddhist temples in the Salt Lake Valley. Use your favorite search engine to find out more.

Despite Utah's reputation and reality as an LDS epicenter, residents and visitors alike have a wide choice of places to worship.

Utah Liquor Laws and the Pricing Gambit

The Department of Alcoholic Beverage Services (DABS) is an odd duck. Utah prides itself as a business-friendly state with a light hand when it comes to regulations that degrade the workings of the free market. Yet the State is happy to maintain a monopoly when it comes to selling beer, wine, and liquor. Sure, you can get a 5-percent-by-volume beer in the supermarket. Want to consume anything stronger? With a few minor exceptions, you have to purchase it in a state-run liquor store.

Part of this stems from the state's culture, which arises from the teachings of The Church of Jesus Christ of Latter-day Saints. The LDS Church is not a fan of alcoholic beverages. In fact, up until a few years ago, DABS was called DABC for "Department of Alcoholic Beverage Control." Emphasis on "control."

It also stems from the ginormous amounts of money the state generates from monopolistic sales. The mark-up is huge. Let's say a manufacturer ships a case of whipped-cream vodka to the State distribution warehouse with a "landed cost" of 100 dollars per case. When the State puts those bottles on display in a DABS outlet, they get to mark it up to

$188.50. (This is a hypothetical example for ease of calculation. No case of good vodka is going to cost that little, and really, who wants to drink whipped-cream vodka anyway?)

In any event, from whiskey to wine, the State levies an 88.5 percent surcharge, day-in and day-out with no competitive forces at work, such as are in play in states where liquor sales are handled by the private sector. On "heavy" beer, the Utah mark-up is 66.5 percent . . . what a deal! There's also a beer tax of $13.10 per 31-gallon barrel of imported or in-state manufactured beer.

Oh, then you get to tack on state sales tax, so it's a double-whammy on every purchase.

In fiscal year 2025, DABS managed statewide sales of $551.35 million and returned $204.5 million to state coffers. Or about $155 in sales per resident, with a per-capita return to the state of about fifty-eight dollars. While that's a drop in the wine barrel of a $31 billion state budget, that's a pretty hefty sin tax on residents unaffiliated with the LDS Church, or for that matter, on LDS members buying a little hootch on the side. You can see why the normally highly conservative Legislature is hooked on the cash infusion that socialized alcohol sales brings about. (In fairness, Brigham Young had few issues with selling "Valley Tan" to non-believers passing through Utah. Mark Twain called it a kind of whiskey or "a first cousin to it.")

When you go into a state liquor store, you'll notice the advertisement-free environment. With sharp eyes, you might be able to read the little info cards tacked below some of the wines and spirits. You might even notice some selections on sale, which is due either to the specific beverage getting phased out or the local brand representative trying to drum up sales so the beverage doesn't get phased out in the near future.

Did you read about an intriguing new vintage in the latest edition of Wine Spectator? Don't hold your breath. It may take months, if ever, for it to appear on the shelves. The State's monopoly means they don't have to be particularly customer-focused.

With all that said, treat the employees of these liquor stores with kindness and respect. They aren't all that well paid, and they have to ask for identification from everyone who walks up to the check-out station. No exceptions. That means you, Santa! Furthermore, a recent state law requires all bars and restaurants to card everyone who asks for an alcoholic beverage.

Since the mining days, Park City has been known as a drinking town, and today is no different. Park City's main liquor store, DABS #38 on Snow Creek Drive, has a wide selection, and is the number two highest-volume outlet in the entire state. Unlike most DABS stores in the state, it closes at 10:00 p.m. rather than 7:00 p.m. DABS #37, in Kimball Junction, moves enough product to rank number four in the state, with a slightly smaller, but still decent, selection (also with a 10:00 p.m. close). DABS #36 is a seemingly small shop on Swede Alley, with a limited but adequate selection (8:00 p.m. close). Despite its tiny footprint, it ranks number ten in the state in sales volume, out of 51 DABS stores statewide. Heber City has the decently-stocked DABS #43 store for Wasatch County imbibers.

All of these stores are closed on Sundays. Avoid them all on Friday afternoons or the day before federal and state holidays. The check-out lines stretch out. A best practice? Do your booze shopping at 11:00 a.m. on any weekday. You'll breeze in and out.

Remember those goofy little exceptions I mentioned earlier? A small number of retail or lodging establishments can sell a limited supply of stronger stuff. The Market & Liquor Store on Canyons Resort Drive is an example. Consider these establishments as "In case of emergency, break glass" options, without, of course, breaking any glass, please.

Our Kamas friends Hope and Sandy recommend Kamas Liquor & Wine near Food Town. It has a reasonable selection, friendly service, and you never have to wait in line to check out.

Of general interest: the DABS annual report lists top sellers state-wide. The distilled spirits category accounts for 60 percent of sales, with Tito's Handmade Vodka leading the charge. Wine accounts for 33 percent, with Lamarca Prosecco and Veuve Clicquot Brut Yellow Label on top. "Heavy" beer is 5 percent of sales, with two double IPAs, Templin Ferda and Squatters Hop Rising, as the top sellers. Flavored malt beverages and cider are 1 percent of sales apiece.

A point of order: Adam, a friend and local lawyer and wine aficionado, is adamant about one aspect of liquor store etiquette. "If you find a wine you like, DON'T buy all the bottles in the display rack. Utah is a regulated state, and we may not get more for weeks."

Utah's monopoly ends at the Wyoming border. There's Evanston, Wyoming, sixty-four miles away with a sales tax rate of 6 percent versus Park City's 9.55 percent. You can see why the stores there do a booming business in . . . ah . . . lottery tickets. Yeah, that's the "ticket."

The trip to Evanston is also an excuse to drive through the dramatic red rock scenery of Echo Canyon.

PINTS FOR THE PEOPLE

Utah's liquor laws are infamously quirky. No one knows this better than local producers and purveyors of the spirited stuff, and we can be thankful that they soldier on every day. Park City and the surrounding areas have several noteworthy breweries, distilleries, and a winery.

The High West Saloon & Distillery on Park Avenue is located in the charming and historic National Garage building. You can enjoy tours, food, and flights here, or visit their big operation out in Wanship. Constellation Brands bought High West in 2016, and early investors did quite well. Other than dropping the very drinkable Silver Whiskey, Constellation hasn't messed with High West too much. The Silver Whiskey is out of production, but legend has it some bars still have a bottle or two stashed.

Alpine Distillery Social Aid & Pleasure Club takes up a basement space on Main Street. Calling themselves "flavorists," they produce a range of spirits that give High West a run for their money and your tastebuds. Alpine has won numerous national and international awards, and they frequently rank near the top of the Park City Cocktail Contest, an annual throwdown among the bartenders at top haunts. For groups with a little more liquidity and a couple hours to kill, the Gin Crafting experience is where the master distillers walk you through the science behind the botanicals and let you make your own custom blend.

Old Town Cellars buys high-quality grapes from around the county and blends red, white, and Rosé wines right on Main St. You can enjoy them at their bar and lounge.

Red Rock Brewing, another stalwart of the Utah scene, opened their Kimball Junction location in 2003. How did they get the names of their flagship IPAs past the DABS committee? Elephino/Fukiphino!?! Red Rock made it easy to remember by nestling themselves into the RedSTONE development, home to other fabulous fare such as Sushi Blue, 11 Hauz Jamaican Cuisine, and Hearth & Hill Kitchen. They also operate a "speakeasy lite" for your après-appetizer thirst-quenching needs. It doesn't hurt that your correspondent's primary residence has been with-in ~~staggering~~ walking distance for several years.

Offset Bier is a relative newcomer located off Bonanza Drive, but is already making a name for themselves. Offset aims for more tradition-al old-world beers that would warm the German miners' hearts. Try the pretzels as a side. The location is somewhat less walkable than the others mentioned in this chapter, but that's what our frequent and efficient tran-sit system is for.

Park City Brewing is located in Kimball Junction. As they state: "Park City Brewing was founded in 2013 by a group of guys who loved beer. What started as a hobby turned into a booming business—but it turns out selling beer isn't for the faint of heart. There were some growing pains, some mistakes were made, and in 2020, a new group who wanted to keep the beer flowing took over. The people bringing Park City Brewing back are all locals who live, work, ski (and drink) here. We're making beer that represents Park City culture and history—and that's just damn good, wherever you live."

Your correspondent's son Danny has articulated the "Brewery Rule" which posits: If a brewery is named after the city in which it is located, it will either have amazing beer because the brewers are too focused on their craft to bother with clever names, or the beer will be somewhat forgettable because the brewers aren't putting any effort into making a name for themselves, regardless of their pride for where they're coming from. I think this hypothesis might be a little harsh, and I have happily downed a few pints of PCB Pale with no complaint. Danny would also like to add that the only part of the Rule that always applies is that sometimes the Rule doesn't apply.

Heber Valley Brewing gets an honorable mention as a fine brewery in neighboring Wasatch County. It's producing beverages with unique flavors.

Finally, Dendric Estate is for those seeking fruitier fare. It's a high-altitude cidery/vineyard in neighboring Kamas that offers something akin to dry sparkling wine. Danny, who assisted on this chapter, notes that the Salt Lake Valley is home to some excellent cideries and cider bars, found here: *ciderguide.com/cider-maps/united-states/utah-cider-map-directory.*

Side Bar 1

There's no shortage of scandal in the history of Park City. All that seems to change are available methods and means by which misappropriations are made. Technology has just made fraud more efficient; there's a reason Kickstarter has their disclaimer: "We aren't the ones taking your money and can't help you if this thing you're backing never happens."

In July 2024, a Snyderville Basin man went to prison for misappropriating $1.7 million of investor funds in Mine Shaft Brewing. The Security and Exchange Commission (SEC) stated that the man told investors that "approximately 70 percent of invested funds would be used to acquire brewery and restaurant equipment and to purchase a building or make improvements to an existing building, with the remaining 30 percent of invested funds used for inventory and other Mine Shaft business expenses."

Instead, as alleged, the perpetrator used his personal Limited Liability Corporation as a pass through to pay his personal expenses, including restitution to victims from his prior securities fraud scheme. Mine Shaft investors, hoping to replicate the returns of early backers of High West, got . . . well . . . shafted. Due diligence, people!

Side Bar 2

For nearly a decade. we've engaged in a massive drinking game with Breckenridge, Colorado, in an annual challenge. During the 2024 record-breaking Main Street Shotski event, people lined up on Main Street with shot-glass-holding skis bolted together end to end to form a chain 1,385 imbibers strong. Breckenridge took the title back in December 2024, with 1,401 participants. In October 2025, Park City reclaimed it with 1,410 participants. However, there's an asterisk. In March 2025, Mont Orford Ski Resort in Quebec blew the doors off with a 1,460-participant shotski. Where did they come from? Where will this end? Do they raise money for non-profits like ours does? Maybe not. *Zut alors*!

What each shot glass is filled with is up to the participant, and, knowing Utah, there's probably plenty of folks opting for a virgin drink, so we may have to concede "total proofed ounces consumed" to our rivals (though remember we have great transit available if you choose to pre- or post-game). Regardless of the outcome, our local businesses are the winners.

CRITTERS

From the domesticated to the wild,
animals enhance our lives here every day.
Except ticks. Nobody likes ticks.

BARK CITY

Seemingly, there are as many dogs as people in Summit County. It's legitimate to say that you live in "Bark City." Oddly, Summit County Animal Control indicates that, as of 2024, there are actually only 988 registered canines that live fulltime in the county. About thirty-nine percent live in the 84098 zip code, and about 14 percent in 84060. Animal Control also states there are ninety-nine dogs registered elsewhere in the U.S. that live somewhere in Summit County more than thirty days a year. Most of these are Pomeranians from Manhattan Beach.

We had other questions for Animal Control, but because they have changed tracking systems in recent years, they weren't able to provide all the data asked for in my Government Records and Management Act (GRAMA) request. Yes, to obtain the data in paragraph one required the filing of a GRAMA request, essentially the same process used by the federal Freedom of Information Act. Our County regards the privacy of our pooches as sacrosanct. In their defense, Animal Control provided the information within a week of request, and did so without complaint.

The 988 registered dogs number puts our "dogs per capita" ratio at about 2.3 percent, which seems really low, given that the World Population Review puts the "dogs per capita" ratio nationally at 19.1 percent. Is this community overrun with "illegal alien" dogs? Do we need to build a wall?

Some of our dog-owning friends point out that those 988 registered dogs are probably the ones that neighbors complained about, prompting the owners to get the paperwork done with Animal Control. Failure to register your dog is a fifty-dollar fine; most citations are for dogs running at large at $150 a pop (or a poop?).

Regardless of whatever the real numbers are, we're certainly enthusiastic about canines, but we're not as "wacka-poodle" as those folks in Boulder, Colorado. That city has ten businesses that can perform dog acupuncture versus three in Park City. (An edge for Boulder in the Sundance Film Festival bidding?) And in Boulder since July 2000, city ordinances use the term "guardian" as opposed to "owner."

We do have four dog parks in the area where you can let your pet off leash. The first to be officially designated is at the Quinn's Junction athletic complex, thanks to the efforts of Ian Weinman and his dad, Rich Wyman. A second is at Willow Creek, a third at the Run-Amok dog park and trail, and the fourth is a de facto one near the City Library. The first two have fun features, the third is a more natural forty-three-acre hillside setting with a dog-friendly hiking path, and the fourth is a big, open frolic field.

We do also enjoy a "Howl-o-ween" on Main Street every October. The street is closed to traffic, and dogs parade in costume. Kids are secondary.

Summit County Code requires dogs to be leashed or otherwise controlled (e.g., e-collar) when not on the owner's property. For owners using electronic leads, it is expected that they carry a regular leash with them in case of need (such as low batteries).

In practice, like the Pirate's Code, on-leash appears to be more of a guideline than a rule. Some areas are fairly compliant. For example, the paved Redstone walking and biking path sees about 80 percent use of leashes. (That figure includes those two little Scotties getting a ride in a covered pushcart.) The gravel path north of Willow Creek Park and parallel to Split Rail Lane has at best a 50 percent compliance with the leash law. Mid-Mountain and other trails see much lower percentages of on-leash dogs. This can be a prime stressor for moose, deer, and other wildlife.

In other words, there is a considerable amount of winking at the regulations and letting our four-footed loved ones run unrestrained. Nonetheless, there are unofficial rules that most dog owners abide by:

- First of all, use common sense. For example, when you arrive at the trailhead, don't immediately let your dog out of the vehicle to run wild. This is also when your dog is apt to defecate, and we don't need to see or smell that.
- Further, don't let your dog loose on a congested trail that you share with other users such as bikers and parents pushing baby strollers.
- Train your pup. There are no bad dogs, only bad owners.
- Move to the opposite side of the path as other dogs and dog owners approach. Keep your dog close to you.
- Leash up your dog if others who are approaching have their dogs on leash.
- Know your dog's personality and avoid situations that stress the dog. Communicate clearly with other dog owners if your dog is apt to react aggressively when meeting new dogs.
- Don't assume you can pat or feed someone else's dog. Ask first. Tell your kids to do the same. If you visit Kate and Todd Fischer's Silver Star Ski and Sport, their bulldog wears a sign that reads "Do not feed me" while it free-ranges around a nearby restaurant.
- And of highest importance, remember to pick up after your pet and dispose of the waste properly. Avoid the temptation to leave bagged poop, no matter how neatly tied, for the Poop Fairy to carry away. Because, after all, there is no Poop Fairy, and those bags really don't biodegrade anytime soon.

As a side note, not all of our multiuse trails are open to dogs. For example, Deer Valley asks, for the safety of all trail users, that hikers and bikers not bring their pets on their hikes and bike rides on resort property.

Please note: This publication is not advocating the flaunting of county code, rather it is merely describing the typical state of things. If your unleashed Bernese Mountain Dogs intimidate the billionaire next door, then of course you are in the wrong and you should keep them on the leash lest they wag or lick someone to death.

Moose, Elk, and the Occasional Bear

The moose is Park City's spirit animal, and the school mascot for McPolin Elementary (the in-town elementary school).

Utah moose belong to the Shiras subspecies (Alces alces shirasi), the smallest of the continent's four moose subspecies. Bulls in Utah generally weigh about 1,000 pounds, compared to 1,600 pounds for Alaskan bulls. Give all the sub-species space. When being stomped by a 1,000-pounder or a 1,600-pounder, the difference in the experience is subtle.

According to the Utah Division of Wildlife Resources, moose moved into Utah from Idaho and Wyoming, and the first recorded sighting of a moose in Utah was in 1906 or 1907. In recent years, the statewide population has maintained at around 2,600 moose.

Utah represents one of the southernmost naturally occurring moose ranges in North America, with some moose living as far south as Wayne County near Capitol Reef National Park. Is this a case of Bergmann's Law, in which animals tend to have larger bodies the farther north they live, in order to better retain heat?

According to Utah State University researchers, twinning is a sign of a healthy moose population. If that's the case, then Summit Park, Pinebrook, and Jeremy Ranch are A+ territory. For years, mama moose have been producing multiple offspring on a regular basis in those neighborhoods. Bonanza Flat is another prime area of moose habitat.

If you live in moose terrain, resist the temptation to put out bales of hay or salt licks for them. Their digestive systems adjust seasonally to different food sources, and providing non-seasonal fare can actually damage their systems. Plus, they don't need more reasons to visit your neighborhood. It's best they stay in more remote territory.

If you encounter a moose, especially a cow with a calf, back away slowly and quietly. Males in the rut season (September to October) are also pretty testy and should be given wide berth. If you can get behind something, like a tree or boulder, do so.

Years ago, my wife encountered a bull on a Summit Park trail, and when it lowered its head, she stepped back off the trail into the four-foot space between two spruce trees. The moose then ambled along, ignoring her. He would have had to use some tricky antler English to get at her.

If you are lucky enough to snap a moose photo worth posting on social media, please do not include specific information (verbal or visual) about the location where the photo was taken. The State issues just over a hundred moose hunting permits annually. Hunters sometimes follow social media accounts to cull location information. Let's let hunters track their prey the old-fashioned way, without online assistance.

The Rocky Mountain elk (Cervus elaphus nelsoni) typically live between 6,000 and 10,000 feet of elevation.

You often see elk herds around the Jeremy Ranch golf course, Round Valley, Quarry Mountain, McPolin Barn, Swaner Nature Preserve, Silver Creek, and occasionally on State Routes 224 and 248, in the most scenic traffic slowdowns possible.

The animals are sizeable. Males average 700 pounds and females 500 pounds. Big males can reach 1,100 pounds. Typically, they stand four and a half to five feet at the shoulder. Their coats are light brown, and their head, neck, and legs are darker. The rumps are cream colored. They favor aspen groves during the summer months, both for the forage and the shelter.

Early September to mid-October is the rut, the animal's mating season. In the fall, bulls tend to gather "harems" of a dozen or so cows, and defend them from other males. This polygamist approach may account for why the tradition-minded Legislature designated elk as Utah's official state animal in 1971. Females give birth in late spring or early summer.

Ungulates like elk and moose do not change their migratory habits and routes just because humans build roads in the way. The non-profit Save People Save Wildlife has designated the stretch of State Route 224 near the McPolin Barn as a "wildlife slaughter row" and public transit vehicles as "wildlife assault buses." The speed limit here is forty-five miles per hour and it does make a difference. Slow down, and you'll be able to adjust. Don't turn your SUV into an asphalt-to-elk guided missile.

There are a few black bears (Ursus americanus) in our area, but they are a rare sight. They occasionally raid trash and bird feeders. One has been spotted fairly regularly around the Armstrong Trail. Another, with an obviously discerning palate, was caught on camera raiding the trash bin in the Stein Eriksen Lodge parking garage several years ago. In June 2014, a 250-pounder crossed City Park, then loped past the Burger King and onto the municipal golf course. "Would you like fries with that garbage can?"

Black bears forage on plants, insects, small mammals, and deer if they can catch one. Attacks on humans are rare, and mostly happen in national park campgrounds. In fact, the National Park Service advises talking calmly to the bear, to let the animal know you are human and not prey. The NPS does not specify if "Hey, Boo-Boo!" is an effective communication tactic. In any event, back away slowly, waving your arms to make yourself look larger.

RATTLESNAKES AND TICKS IN PARK CITY?

Hikers new to the area often ask about the risk of encountering biting critters, in particular rattlesnakes and ticks.

The presence of rattlesnakes in the high hills of Summit County is pretty rare, but not impossible. In general, Utah's Great Basin rattler (Crotalus oreganus lutosus) is not a concern when you're exploring our back country. The species is more common in the hotter foothills of the Wasatch Front, so plan accordingly when you're hiking to the Living Room above the University of Utah.

As the climate warms, the Great Basin rattler is apt to migrate up into our mountains. For example, there have been reported sightings on the Jordanelle Reservoir Perimeter Trail. You are far more likely to see benign, non-venomous garter snakes and rubber boas (yes, a species, not a toy).

Based on slightly modified information from the Sonoma Ecology Center in California, you can further isolate yourself from the threat of "buzzworms" by taking the following steps:

- Don't be young and male. Fifty-five percent of bite victims are men between the ages of seventeen and twenty-seven.
- Don't try to pester, pick up, or take a selfie with the snake. Eighty-five percent of bites are on the hand or fingers.

- Moderation in all things. Twenty-eight percent of bite victims are intoxicated at the time.

Based on these guidelines, it's a good thing rattlesnakes don't like spring skiing. Otherwise, the demographic doing afternoon laps on the 9990 chairlift would be decimated in a matter of hours.

If you are visiting or moving from a part of the country that has high risks of Lyme Disease, take heart. In Utah, the only human-attaching tick that can transmit Lyme disease is the Western Black-Legged Tick, and the chances of encountering one that is capable of infecting you with Lyme Disease are very, very low. Utah State University (USU) researchers looked around and only found this particular tick in Tooele, Millard, and Washington Counties, and not one of those ticks was Lyme'd up.

The tick that is most likely to attach itself to you or your pet in Utah is the Rocky Mountain Wood Tick. It doesn't carry Lyme Disease. It can potentially transmit other nasties, including something called tick paralysis, but the risk levels are entirely manageable. (That's paralysis for the human, not the tick.)

USU researchers state the most common tick-transmitted disease here is Colorado Tick Fever (thanks, Colorado) and the next is Rocky Mountain Spotted Fever. On average across all of Utah, one to two Colorado Tick Fever cases are reported annually and an average of one Rocky Mountain Spotted Fever case is reported every five years.

Inexplicably, according to the Centers for Disease Control (CDC), there is a higher rate of exposure for Rocky Mountain Spotted Fever in the Southern Atlantic states. We don't have very good gumbo, so it balances out.

Rest assured that some benighted employees of the Utah Department of Health & Human Services (DHHS) conduct regular "tick drags" in Summit County and elsewhere around the state. This entails two to four DHHS employees going to a designated drag site and hauling a white cloth around for thirty-minute increments. "Drags are checked every twenty-five steps to ensure any captured ticks do not fall off of the drag. Ticks are collected from the drag and placed in labeled tubes for further analysis."

So, your current job could be worse.

The other takeaway is tick prevention. USU has some good resources on dressing for success prior to venturing out, using sprays, and then conducting proper post-recreation tick checks. Preferably you perform the tick check in the shower with a willing partner, though that technique is not specifically endorsed by USU. If you do get bitten by a tick, check with your medical provider for follow-up care.

If you ever find yourself on one of Deer Valley's history hikes led by your writer, rest assured that any ticks along the trail will latch onto me, not you. In my younger days, I fancied I was a chick magnet, but nowadays I'm just a tick magnet.

One other likely risk on our trails is flora not fauna. Poison ivy (Toxicodendron rydbergii) can grow at relatively high elevations, typically in shady areas. It rarely exceeds four feet in height. As you learned at summer camp: "Leaves of three, let it be."

If you think you rubbed against some, give that area of your skin a good washing with cold water and baking soda. If itching starts, cortisone creams and calamine lotion can help.

Sandhill Cranes, Magpies, and Mountain Bluebirds

Summit County is one of the best places in the country to see a large and interesting bird, the sandhill crane (Antigone canadensis). One of the best places to see them in Summit County is the Swaner Preserve. Totaling 1,200 acres, Swaner Preserve has two sections. The 350-acre Northern Section encompasses sagebrush-covered hillsides, and offers ten miles of public access trails. Roam to your heart's content here.

The Southern Section is 800 acres of grass and wetlands, and to protect sensitive habitat, unsupervised public access is not allowed. A lovely outing is to join one of the Saturday morning guided nature walks onto this part of the Preserve. A moonlit snowshoe trek is another option.

The star of the show is the sandhill crane. At nearly four feet, it's tall, has a distinctive red crown, and when mating, it's an elegant dancer. The crane's coiled trachea helps it produce a low, vibrating call, kind of an oboe to a loon's clarinet. It migrates to Summit County from its winter home in New Mexico and Texas, sometimes as early as February, then returning in the fall. The crane is an omnivore, and you will realize the bird descended from dinosaurs if you ever see one spear and gobble up a rodent.

It mates for life, and the domesticity is on display on the Swaner EcoCenter's "crane cam." The video feed is focused on one returning pair's nest in the swampy rushes near the center. For the birder crowd, it's like a daily soap opera. The hatchlings are called colts, presumably for their long legs.

On the guided walks, you might visit one of the several small ponds in the preserve, and these are teeming with mallards, kingfishers, cinnamon teals, and even the occasional white pelican. Overhead there are owls and raptors, and in the brush, you can sometimes see the curved-bill glossy ibis or even—wait for it—snipes.

Another way to experience the preserve is to volunteer to pull invasive weeds, or help build or repair beaver dam analogs (BDAs). BDAs are structures woven of willow branches and other materials. They slow streamflow to emulate the benefits of beaver dams. Bring your mud boots.

Some of these outings are capped off with a beer or two on the EcoCenter's deck, and are well worth the sweat equity.

Those of us who live here full- or part-time can grow inured to the sight of magpies (Pica hudsonia). Long elegant tails, patterned feathers that are white and blue. Wait, no, the iridescent feathers are black. No, they're blue. Who can tell?

The birds are beautiful, ho hum. With fresh eyes, visitors find them striking, and they are in good company doing so. The journals of Lewis and Clark describe the bird in detail, and some of the writings note how magpies would hop into the party's tents to steal morsels of food.

When the explorers sent an early package of specimens to President Jefferson in April 1805, the samples included four live magpies. This seems a passive-aggressive gesture on Lewis' part. Those birds would have been a real handful back at the president's residence in D.C.

A relative of jays and crows, the magpie is intelligent and social. On our porch in Summit Park year after year, my wife and I saw generational training sessions, led by older magpies teaching younger ones how to manage the intricacies of various birdfeeders.

Magpies work in pairs. One suspects that they invented the pick-pocket methodology. One to distract, one to steal.

What do they have to do with pies? Nothing . . . apparently "pie" was Old English for bird. But don't leave your pies to cool on the porch. The magpies will steal them.

A member of the Thrush family, mountain bluebirds (Sialia currucoides) used to proliferate in the Wasatch Back. Back then, mines had a voracious appetite for wood to be used for fuel, building material, and underground scaffolding. This led to the clearcutting of hills for miles around. Look at old photos of our big mines, and you'll see hillsides chopped down to a nubble.

With a constraint on their preferred arboreal habitat, the mountain bluebirds declined in population. Luckily, that trend has reversed in recent decades as hillsides revegetated. Today, most experts categorize these sky-blue flyers as a species of low conservation concern.

They live six to ten years and feed on beetles, grasshoppers, and caterpillars. They consume about 12 percent of their body weight daily. Wouldn't that be nice! Like the cadre of Park City kiter/surfer residents who descend on Baja to escape the snow, mountain bluebirds breed here in the milder months and head south to Mexico for the winter.

A local and passionate advocate for mountain bluebirds is Letitia Lussier. She has been instrumental in Utah Mountain Bluebird Trails, a local conservation project that she started in 1995 to help declining native mountain bluebird populations.

"During the mining days, we lost a lot of habitat for 'cavity nesters' like bluebirds and tree swallows. The project is an attempt to help these birds come back in healthy numbers."

Lussier has installed—and trained volunteers to monitor—some seventy nesting boxes located around the county.

She is also one of the original ski instructors at Deer Valley, starting her role in 1981. Lussier has the longest tenure among the current instructor crew.

Mountain bluebirds are regarded as a sign of joy and hope. Keep your binoculars at the ready. We think the efforts to bring them back are working!

BEAVER BELIEVERS

This writer's dad always said, "Buy land on water." When my wife and I bought a townhouse in Kimball Junction in 2018, we thought we were pretty smart just to buy land on a trail system. Little did we know that the trickle of water running just beyond the fence in Swaner Preserve would turn into a duck pond five years later. That landscape transformation was directly due to the efforts of a beaver family that took up residence near the Swaner EcoCenter in 2020.

The first generation of beavers (Castor canadensis) began their efforts near the EcoCenter, damming the stream into a nice-sized pond (about two tennis courts' worth of area). Immediately muskrats, ducks, and other avian life took up residence. Kits (baby beavers) followed soon after and the entire family started upstream along the Millennium Trail, engineering sticks and mud to adjust the sporadic stream into a series of small ponds that attract more muskrats, ducks, sandhill cranes, kingfishers, and other species.

We were deeply dismayed when the five beavers in the vicinity succumbed to Tularemia in early 2024. This is a nasty virus that usually strikes jack rabbits and deer, but it decimated the local beaver clan, and more in neighboring counties. We can only hope that other beavers move upstream from East Creek to reclaim the territory, or that state-led beaver relocation efforts bring a viable population back to the area.

We're a little concerned that the sump pump in our crawlspace has been working overtime ever since our duck pond appeared, but the efflorescence in the ecosystem that the beavers created is well worth it. We're Beaver Believers!

We're also fans of the muskrats (Ondatra zibethicus). While they don't have the engineering skills of the beaver, they are fun to watch.

Marmots, Potguts, and Ermine

When you're hiking up above 8,000 feet, you're in prime habitat of the yellow-bellied marmot (Marmota flaviventris). You'll know it when you hear a piercing, high-decibel shriek. That's the "whistle pig" telling you that you're not welcome around these parts.

Weighing as much as eleven pounds with a length up to twenty-seven inches, the marmot is the largest and loudest member of the squirrel family. They are cousins to the groundhog. The marmot's coat is a beautiful dark brown, with the aforementioned lighter-colored fur on the belly. They love rocky hillsides and even hang out in the old stonework of the Silver King Coalition Mill below Park City's Bonanza and Payday lifts.

Living in burrows, they eat plants, insects, and the occasional bird's egg, and typically hibernate in the fall and winter.

A few are known to live at lower elevations, closer to town, and they apparently have a yen for finance. There's been a brace of marmots hanging out for years near the bike path that runs by the KeyBank branch in the Snow Creek center. Another bunch frequents the rock wall by Zions Bank on Kearns Boulevard. You can have a stare-down as you use the drive-through.

Marmots have mixed popularity. Some people love them and find their screeches endearing. Others—especially those who backpack in the Uintas—think them an annoying pest due to their habit of chewing through backpack material to get to crunchy granola bars. The lesson? When you're camping, bears aren't the only species that call for bear-proofing measures.

On its birth certificate, the potgut's formal name is the Uinta ground squirrel (Urocitellus armatus). It's a rodent about a foot in length and eight ounces in weight. When it's scrunched up and hiding in the grass, it looks roly-poly, hence its informal name. When it stands up tall by its burrow entrance, it does a decent meerkat imitation, looking quite slim.

Potguts hibernate in the fall and winter and appear above ground from April to August. They are herbivores for the most part, eating grass, seeds, and leaves, but they'll gulp down an earthworm or two.

They emit a variety of chirps and other vocalizations, some for territorial and mating purposes, and some to warn of raptors overhead. They live in burrows, usually in meadows, or perhaps in your own backyard.

Their best party trick involves bikers. While you are wheeling away down some paved path, the potguts seem compelled to wait until you are close. Then they dash across the path right in front of you. At the very least, this leads to your heartbeat elevating precipitously. At worst, it leads to an ex-potgut and . . . Bingo! . . . You're wheels-up in a ditch.

The city and county recently put in place laws that limit bikes and e-bikes to fifteen miles per hour on major bike paths such as the Rail Trail, Millennium Trail, and Poison Creek Trail (but not on singletrack routes). This writer has lived by the supposedly regulated five-mile-per-hour paved path through Newpark for a number of years. It takes true optimism to think that people will actually obey the countywide fifteen-mile-per-hour speed limit. Perhaps the best way to encourage compliance is to encourage infestations of potguts. Mind your speed when you're in their territory!

Park City appreciates a slim build, and the ermine fits the bill. Also known as a stoat, the ermine (Mustela erminea) is a member of the weasel family. In the winter, its fur turns completely white, except at the tip of their tails. When they scamper across the snow, at first you might think you're seeing a bouncing leaf or piece of bark blown by the wind.

Ermines run about a foot in body length, with a three-to-five-inch tail. They weigh about nine ounces. Despite the similarities in these measurements to those of the potgut, ermine appear far more lithe. It's probably due to their carnivorous Keto-like diet and, of course, their elegant fur, which British royalty favors for their ceremonial gowns.

Several times over the years, I've seen ermine underneath the Carpenter chairlift and on the Webster ski run. Once I spied one carrying an ill-fated mouse in its mouth.

Knowing that some people have ferrets as pets, it's reasonable to ask if ermine can be domesticated. The answer is no, and furthermore, ferrets make terrible pets.

WILDLIFE BRIDGES AND UNDERPASSES

UDOT installed the nation's first wildlife crossing in 1975, per the Wildlife Crossing Initiative. The bridge spans I-15 near the town of Beaver. Nowadays, Utah boasts more than fifty wildlife crossing structures (bridges and tunnels).

One of our favorites is the bridge over I-80 at the very top of Parley's Summit. Built in 2018 for $5 million, it is in constant use, as one can see from delightful videos regularly posted by the State's Department of Natural Resources. (There are a lot more mountain lions in the neighborhood than this former Summit Park resident ever knew about!) The location of the bridge is smack dab in the middle of a moose migration route, so it serves very well.

Does $5 million pencil out? A USU review states that every year in the U.S., wildlife vehicle collisions (WVCs) kill more than 200 people and injure 26,000, at a cost of more than $8 billion. The "net social improvement" of a wildlife crossing structure is estimated to be more than $15 million over its service life, with the benefit outweighing the cost by more than double. Reduction of incidents ranges up to seventy-seven percent.

The study describes I-80 as an "epicenter" of WVCs and indicates that, between 2010 and 2021, the estimated cost of a collision was:

- Mule deer = $10,862
- Elk = $24,036
- Moose = $39,851

Prior to the bridge's construction, I-80 was experiencing 100 WVCs a year in 2016 and 2017, so the cost of the Parley's structure sounds good to us. Since it was built, I-80 WVCs have plummeted.

If you have problems with the USU analysis, take it up with the scientists. They state that the study uses a difference-in-differences estimation with count data in the negative binomial distribution context to quantify the causal effect of wildlife structures on WVC reductions. So there; you've been warned.

There are wildlife crossing structures elsewhere in the county, namely the underpasses at I-80 near Silver Creek and on U.S. Route 40 south of Home Depot. There is an underpass at Kimball Junction that makes it easy for the elk and raccoon to get to their Orangetheory fitness classes, but it's not officially designated a crossing.

Concerned citizens are advocating for more crossings, especially along Route 224. If there is an underlying theme in this entire document, it's to slow your roll. Dawn, dusk . . . really all the time. You don't have to push the pedal to the metal. Give our wildlife a fighting chance.

ART, MUSIC, FILM, MUSEUMS, AND THINGS YOU HAVE TO SEE TO BELIEVE

*Between snow sports, summer sports, and working for a living,
we still manage to enjoy the cultural side of things
around here to an admirable degree.*

PUBLIC ART AND ART BY THE PUBLIC

The phrase "public art" is a loaded one. What passes for culture out in the open sometimes lands on the scale between "Meh" and "WTF?" Summit County is no different than other locales when it comes to hits and misses.

Those silvery outlines of moose and elk on Route 224? They are like giant cookie cutters or holiday ornaments. Built with good intentions, they are supposed to make you think, "Ah, wildlife ahead . . . I should slow down." Subtle.

The glade of 150-or-so shiny tubes of metal out near the Quinn's Junction dog park? Is it an aspen grove? Slot canyon? Rabid porcupine? No idea, but it grows on you.

The metal "Making Tracks" slices of mystery south of Meadows Drive on Route 224? Unfathomable.

In Newpark, there's a perfectly wholesome sculpture of two kids climbing an eight-foot-tall slab of sandstone. A sign at the base says, "Thank you for not climbing." Mixed messages.

The Olympic Flame-y thing on Kearns Avenue and Bonanza Drive? Tries a little too hard.

Franz the bear on Main Street? Sit down next to him and rub his belly. It's good luck.

The painted Rocky Mountain Power utility boxes around town? Pretty good stuff.

Artwork in various tunnels and underpasses? Not bad, and the shade is enjoyable on warm days. One mural displays a female miner in a yellow slicker . . . very inclusive, but not all that accurate historically. Women didn't break into the underground ranks until the 1970s.

Banksy has several works of art in Park City, most notably the camera man and flower at 402 Main Street. Come to your own judgment.

The County recently installed two sculptural works at the Pinebrook/Jeremy Ranch exit off I-80. The roundabouts here are known as the Ben Hur Chariot Race facsimile, so perhaps a gladiator theme would have sufficed. As it is, there are impressively large moose and sandhill crane statues in the two roundabout center islands.

The 2002 Winter Olympic towers—one in Kimball Junction and the other at the Olympic Welcome Plaza near Route 224 and Kearns Boulevard—are pretty cool exceptions to public art mediocrity/obscurity. We can still enjoy the great branding those Games brought, even though the freestyle skier isn't wearing a helmet. The 2034 Olympic Games branding? Don't get me started.

Then there are the unsanctioned or privately funded art exhibits, such as the shoe trees along Poison Creek and Deer Valley Drive near the Marriott Summit Watch hotel. Currently seven willow trees are shackled with a display of dangling footwear. There are several different stories about the origin and meaning of this display. No doubt alcohol was involved. It was probably done in the spirit of pure and admirable mischief, but stopping at one tree would have been enough. No doubt a lot of the footwear would have had a better life at Goodwill or the Christian Center thrift store.

Up on the Last Chance run, Deer Valley skiers have a chance to experience artwork staged by homeowners adjacent to the trail. There are the bronze elk and the feisty wooden raccoons. Then you come upon the

Bear House, with its gang of cartoon-like ursine characters. The Bear House is proof that having a lot of money and having good taste are not necessarily related, but the exhibit will make you laugh. Kids love it. Rounding out the run are the red cedar totem pole and the metal moose.

The Whale: We know it's down in Salt Lake City, but if you have a chance, drive by 900 South and 1100 East to see the leviathan breach the roundabout at this intersection. More ambitious visitors can run 630 laps around the intersection to complete a 26.2 mile "whaleathon." All hail the Whale!

The presence of the Whale in landlocked Utah is as big a mystery as why the University of Utah has a department of Naval Studies.

The backstory: During World War II, the U.S. Navy managed a significant amount of radio traffic in the Pacific Theater via facilities near the University of Utah campus. Utah was relatively safe from the risk of Japanese bombing versus West Coast cities.

Galleries

There are around twenty art galleries in Park City, a good number of which are located on Main Street. Most of these businesses tolerate one of our town's favorite activities, the Friday night looky-loo gallery stroll. These are perfect excursions when you have out-of-town visitors (or you're from out of town yourself). The outings involve a tour of the showrooms, with absolutely no intention of buying anything. It's a great way to experience Main Street and raise your aesthetic sophistication at the same time, or demonstrate your sophistication to your out-of-town visitors.

With its wonderful moose and grizzly bear portraits, the Mangelsen photo gallery on Main Street is always a treat. The Mountain Trails Gallery at the top of Main Street has very pleasing bronzes and a cool old bank vault from our mining heyday. Don't miss the Kimball Art Center. It has a gallery filled with different exhibits on rotation, and it is one of Summit County's long-time non-profits. It's off Kearns Boulevard with plenty of parking, but moving in the future to Kimball Junction.

Also in the Kearns Boulevard area is the Create PC local artists cooperative. Supported by the Arts Council, the two-story facility rents space for artists to create, display, and sell paintings, photography, ceramics and more. If you're looking for artwork depicting local scenes, this is the place. It is open to the public Wednesday through Sunday, from 12:00 to 6:00 p.m.

If you find yourself with the disposable income to purchase a painting, sculpture, or photograph from one of these galleries, have at it. They add a cultural frisson to our scene, and it's nice to give them the business versus some fancy pants place in New York or Los Angeles.

THE MUSIC SCENE, OR RAGE AGAINST THE CPAP MACHINE

Sitting outdoors with a bottle of something chilled while listening to cool tunes is a why-we-live-here moment. Park City's music scene is a mix of plucky local acts and national performers who range from big names to acts that are past their freshness date.

The plucky local acts can be found at bars, at events like the Park Silly Market, and at outdoor venues such as the Pendry, Newpark Plaza, or Billy Blanco's. Most of these events are free of charge. They add a vibrant beat to our lives. A good resource on this scene is *mountaintownmusic.org*, another great area non-profit worthy of your support. This organization stages more than 200 free outdoor concerts during the summer at various locations.

You can also track upcoming concerts at the Park City Performing Arts website: *parkcityinstitute.org*.

For Fourth of July fun, check out *forumfest.com/schedule-of-events/*.

In August, the Park City Song Summit is a go-to event: *parkcitysong-summit.com/pages/lineup*.

A good resource for the name acts coming year-round to Deer Valley, the Egyptian Theatre, and elsewhere can be found here: *stayparkcity.com/how-to-pc/music/*.

The concerts range from rock and pop to blues to classical. A lot of the popular acts arose when "doobie" was the operative phrase versus today's "medicinal" terminology. A sub-set of these golden oldie acts can still hold a tune, especially if the road crew provides O_2 for the performers between sets. Be warned though regarding the "wrinkled rockers" who pass through on tours. If whatever iteration of the Beach Boys comes to town, they might want to change the lyrics of "Kokomo" to "Lumbago, Montego. Baby, why don't we go . . ."

CELEBRITIES, SUNDANCE, AND OTHER FESTIVALS

We get a lot of celebrities passing through Park City. The Sundance Film Festival has been one vector, bringing all the PIBs (People in Black) to town. Skiing is another, and our well-heeled political donor base is yet another.

Don't worry. If you ignore the celebrities long enough, they will go away and stop disrupting traffic or restaurant reservations. If you see one, go on with your day. Avoid eye contact. Do not under any circumstances ask for a selfie or an autograph. Neither bother them nor encourage them.

To their credit, most celebrities who come here want to keep a low profile and enjoy our town as all of us do. They go incognito which translates to lots of winter layers, goggles, and buffs. The exception may be the Kardashians, who apparently love to parade about the Montage pool area. To our credit, when Park City residents spot a celebrity, we usually nod, or smile, or ignore them so they can enjoy their day.

Our friend Jennifer Marie had a "celebrities are just like us" moment, when she encountered a *Sex in the City* star in the Stein Eriksen restroom going toe-to-toe with their four-year-old. The discussion involved the need for proper hand washing. Parenting 101.

Jennifer Marie also breezed past a Charlie's Angels movie star in the Post Office on Main Street. Thinking the woman looked familiar, she said, "Hello, how are you?" and moved along. Only later did Jennifer Marie realize the individual in question was a familiar face from the silver screen, not from day-to-day life (as attractive as Parkites may be).

In this writer's role as a Deer Valley hiking guide, I've led internet influencers around our beautiful trails. This is nerve wracking. After iPhone videoing a lovely sylvan scene, the influencers spend the next half mile of the hike editing their work, with their eyes on their phones, not on the trail. Be assured, my first aid kit was at the ready.

Our celebrity count will no doubt drop now that the Sundance Film Festival has left for Boulder, Colorado as of January 2026. Whether the loss of Sundance will decrease the number of celebrity skiers we encounter is a different question. Nonetheless, we're sad to see it go, and we wish Boulder, Colorado good luck when their run begins in January 2027. The organizers there will have their work cut out for them replicating Park City's transit system and volunteer network. As Tom Clyde, Park Record columnist, points out, the sequel is seldom as good as the original.

For the rest of us, Park City is awash with festivals. Savor the Summit, Jan's Winter Welcome, the National Ability Center's Barn Party, the Kimball Arts Festival, the Wine Festival, the Park City Silly Market through the summer . . . the list goes on. There's even an Anti-Gala. Suffice it to say our community has chronic bouts of festival and event fatigue.

If your net worth allows, you can attend all these high-end experiences and, in several cases, drop $250 or more a seat. The less expensive events, like the Arts Festival and Silly Market, are a great way to visit Main Street with 10,000 of your closest friends. (Did we mention there's this great free bus system here?)

Beside the thousands of dollars these festivals raise for worthy non-profits, the events fulfill other purposes, such as providing opportunities to show off fancy clothes, jewelry, and newly enhanced body parts like . . . err . . . Botoxed lips.

An equally rewarding though less expensive way to experience Park City's event schedule is to volunteer. Helping to pull off these events can be fun and fulfilling and a great way to make new friends in the community. Otherwise, a number of these shindigs call for sheltering in place.

Must-See Museums

The Park City Museum: Situated on Main Street, this place punches above its weight. For its size (about 6,500 square feet of exhibit space), it delivers more interactive fun and interest in three floors than museums twice its size. It specializes in mining and skiing history, and has a gallery to host temporary exhibits several times a year. Some best practices:

- Push every button you see on the displays.
- Take a family photo in the mine elevator "cage" in the basement.
- Sit in the Skier Subway and watch the video. This may be the worst ski lift ever.
- Go ahead. Push the dynamite plunger. We dare you.
- Join the crowd and buy a bag of colorful polished rocks in the gift shop. It's the biggest selling item in the entire array of cool gifts.

Open 10:00 a.m. to 5:00 p.m. daily, the museum hosts a tour of historic homes in June and a tour of Glenwood Cemetery with reenactors playing graveyard residents in the fall. It also offers a series of free history lectures throughout the year. All are engaging events. During the summer, the museum conducts walking tours of Main Street at ten dollars a pop (or twenty-two dollars for a walking tour/museum ticket combo). It also hosts history hikes in the area for its members. Museum membership

(2024) is a modest fifty-five dollars a year for individuals and one hundred dollars for families.

Utah Olympic Park: Alf Engen was a pioneer in bringing skiing to Utah in the 1930s, and for a time, he held the world record for the longest ski jump, set at Ecker Hill in the Pinebrook neighborhood. When the 2002 Olympics hit town, and a museum was opened at the Olympic Park, it was the natural choice to name it after Alf.

Open 9:00 a.m. to 6:00 p.m. daily, the museum is free and covers Utah ski history and many aspects of the 2002 Winter Olympics. The interactive displays are top-notch. If you visit during the summer, you may be able to watch the "Flying Aces" perform astonishing aerial twists and turns into the training pool. It's like a thin-air rock concert. The museum is already gearing up for the 2034 Winter Olympic Games, recently awarded to Utah.

For a modest fee you can tour the bobsled, luge, and skeleton runs and other facilities. Hanging your toes over the top of the 120-meter ski jump is an experience not to be missed. Summer visitors can purchase rides on the outdoor zip lines, ropes courses, and alpine coaster.

The Swaner EcoCenter: This is a delight if you are at all interested in matters ecological or if you need to entertain some little ones for the morning or afternoon. Take your guests up to the viewing tower to look for elk, cranes, eagles, and hawks out on the preserve. Don't miss whatever interesting exhibit is on display on the ground floor. The small gift shop is a great source for nature-oriented gifts. The Center is usually open Wednesdays to Sundays from 10:00 a.m. to 4:00 p.m.

The Summit County Historical Museum: Located in the basement of the County Courthouse in Coalville, this museum is free and open Monday through Friday, 8:00 a.m. to 5:00 p.m. It specializes in "butter-churn" exhibits, meaning lots of domestic accoutrements like old sewing machines, stoves, and other artifacts. While there's no need to take digitalis to calm your heart before entering, the collection has its quaint charms.

Echo Church: Back in 1869, when the Transcontinental Railroad was completed at Promontory Point north of the Great Salt Lake, the small town of Echo was an important way station on the line. Today, the village is quiet, almost deserted. According to the Summit County website: "Built in 1876 in a Late Gothic Revival style by a carpenter named John Shill,[Echo Church's] function was originally a church for the Protestants that were attempting to establish themselves in Utah. The building was used as a church on the weekends and as a school for the local children of the area."

The church/museum has interesting rotating exhibits and is generally open on Saturdays from 11:00 a.m. to 4:00 p.m. from late May to Labor Day weekend. It's a good place for weddings too. Admission is free, donations suggested. It's worth checking their Facebook page to verify before beelining its way.

You can learn interesting facts, such as how town owner Brigham Young, Jr. designed "Echo City" in 1868 with twelve avenues named after his wives and the cross streets for Union Pacific dignitaries. The man knew how to curry favor in the personal and professional arenas.

If the church is closed, you can still make a good day of it by driving I-80 up Echo Canyon with its beautiful red rock cliffs. Early Latter-day Saint William Clayton gave the following description of Echo Canyon in his diary: "There was a very singular echo in this ravine. The rattling of the wagons resembled carpenters hammering at boards inside the high rock. The report of a rifle echoed from rock to rock for some time. The lowing of cattle and the braying of mules seemed to be answered beyond the mountains. Music, especially brass instruments, had a very pleasing effect. The echo imitated every note. The high rocks on the north and high mountains on the south with a narrow ravine for a road formed scenery at once more romantic and more interesting than any I had ever witnessed."

Heber City has three museums, namely the Daughters of the Utah Pioneers and the Heritage Ranch Museum, which capture ranch and farm life more than a hundred years ago, and the Commemorative Air Force Museum at the Heber Airport, which highlights aviation history.

Natural History Museum of Utah (NHMU): Okay, yeah, you caught us promoting another Salt Lake City cultural attraction, but holy moly, the wall of ancient Ceratopsians in this museum is mind-blowing. Let's admit it, folks, being a half-hour drive from Salt Lake City is one of the positive aspects of living in Summit County. We won't apologize for that!

NHMU is open from 10:00 a.m. to 5:00 p.m. most days, but on Wednesdays it is open until 9:00 p.m.

THE FILM SERIES

Using a $40,000+ loan for equipment from the Park City Council in 1995, a project of the Park City Arts Council grew into what is now the Park City Film Series. Mayor Brad Olch and the City Council were initially reticent to fund the loan, and payback terms were bandied back and forth, but ultimately the forces of light prevailed. We all are the beneficiaries.

At the time, Arts Council president Joanna Charnes said that films are artistic, cultural, and educationally enriching, and can enhance Park City's "positive cultural and lifestyle image," bringing people of the community together.

Three decades later, Park City Film is a consistently elevating experience for Park City and Summit County residents, and with the help of volunteers, it meets its mission of creating community through film. The non-profit brings thought-provoking, independent works that are not generally available through commercial outlets, and it hosts discussions on topics raised by these films. A good number of these films debuted at the Sundance Film Festival. This is not Hollywood schlock.

Typically airing Friday, Saturday, and Sunday nights at the Jim Santy Auditorium at the Park City Library, the films are a screaming deal, with tickets currently costing less than ten bucks. The popcorn is great, and there are cool door prizes! The Park City Film Series recently expanded its lease to accommodate more screenings year-round.

Park City Film offers Assisted Listening devices for films screened in the Santy and transmits Closed Captions and Audio Descriptions for films when available. American Sign Language interpretation for post-film discussions is available upon request with a one-week lead time. The auditorium is wheelchair accessible with six spots for wheelchairs and twenty-two accessible seats. Bathrooms are also ADA accessible.

Things You Have to See to Believe

In Park City and Park City adjacent, there are some activities and events that defy all expectations and must be witnessed in person to grasp just how weird and amazing they are.

County Fair and Rodeos: Those of us who live in Park City and the Snyderville Basin often forget that ranching and farming are important pursuits in our county. A good cure for this blinkered vision is to attend the Summit County Fair, which takes place in August in Coalville.

There's an eight-day schedule of archery, horse riding, concerts, exhibits, baking contests, demolition derby, food booths, livestock judging, and more. There's an exciting Professional Rodeo Cowboys Association (PCRA) rodeo, as well as a heartwarming and hilarious Little Buckeroos event that features mutton busting and calf riding. You can find more information at *summitcountyfair.org*

If you've never seen mutton busting, prepare to have your world view rocked. It's hard to know for whom or what to root . . . the sheep or the six-year-old! There are no set rules and, thank goodness, no national organization, and the kids generally wear helmets.

In concert with the County Fair, Kamas holds Fiesta Days & Rodeo. Around the Fourth of July, Oakley holds a fair and rodeo as well. All of these events are a good excuse to don some denim, smell the hay, and eat a corn dog.

Skijoring: Roughly translated from the Norwegian, skijoring means "ski driving." At the annual February event in Heber, a horse and rider pull a skier or snowboarder through a weaving course of jumps and gates. There's something to do with grabbing a ring. Points are deducted for missing the ring and other shortfalls that are mysterious to all except the event judges. It's very confusing, there are some good wipeouts, and most runs are over in twenty seconds or less. Needless to say, it's a sport that requires the on-site presence of Emergency Medical Technicians and large animal veterinarians.

The event is a great excuse to dress in warm, cowpoke finery, so on and off the course, the people watching is at the highest level.

World Cup Moguls and Aerials: Typically in February, Deer Valley Resort hosts the World Cup Moguls and Aerials. The Champion run at Snow Park is known as the longest and steepest mogul run on the international circuit, and the crew of volunteers that prepares the course does a stand-out job. The racers in single and dual formats blast down a course of hand-carved moguls, perform two flips, and race to the finish line in knee-ligament defying turns.

The White Owl run is the site of the aerials jumps, which launch the athletes to impossible heights as they twist and turn in mid-air. A gymnast background is a plus in this sport.

Television does not do these sports justice. The skill and daring of these competitors are best seen in person to be fully understood and appreciated. The toll these competitions take on the participants is less appreciated. Ashley Caldwell, Park City local and aerials gold medalist at the Beijing Olympics, told me, "At the start of the season, my height is five-foot, seven inches. At the end, I'm five-foot, six."

The spectator area is close to the runs and has a rock-concert vibe. Most of the finals are at night, so dress in plenty of layers, and bring a square of cardboard or carpet to stand on, to keep your feet warm. Since you are watching the world's top competitors, it's our own private Olympics year in, year out. *Skol!*

THE FUTURE IS HERE

Between the transition from a mining economy to a recreation-based one, Park City suffered some "ghost town" years.
Can we avert future downturns? By working together, yes!

THE ONCE AND FUTURE OLYMPICS

Utahns are justly proud of the roles played by the State, Park City, and Summit County in the 2002 Winter Olympic Games. We parlayed our collective experience in hosting large events like the Sundance Film Festival and World Cup contests into a smoothly run "welcome to the world." Our spirit of volunteerism was on ample display, and at the last moment, the weather cooperated and brought snow.

Admittedly, I was a little hesitant leading into the 2002 Games. We caught one ski jumping event before taking a plane to the Hawaiian Islands. My wife and I had expected traffic snarls back in Utah, but each day we were away, the news from home was positive and the Games' logistics appeared to be running smoothly.

We returned for the last week and attended bobsled, biathlon, women's giant slalom and another jumping event.

Some observations:

First, the Salt Lake organizing committee borrowed municipal buses from all over the country, including from Denver, Phoenix, Los Angeles, San Francisco, and more. I was worried when I boarded San Francisco's 45 Stockton bus during that first event at the Olympic Park. I had ridden that line often when I lived and worked in the Bay Area. The bus creaked and sputtered its way up the long climb to the venue, but despite my qualms, it made it to the top. When I returned two weeks later, there were nothing but Denver buses at the site.

"Where are the San Francisco buses?" I asked a volunteer.

"Oh, they are down in the valley. They couldn't take the climb," he remarked.

Note to the 2034 organizing committee: Start cozying up to Denver now.

Second, several years after the Games, my wife purchased a spot in a skeleton clinic for my birthday. Skeleton is the Olympic sport that involves coasting down the bobsled track headfirst on a tea tray, as opposed to luge, which is feet first on a tea tray. The clinic cost $150 for three runs (starting from Turn Six). I topped out at sixty miles per hour, which was a life experience. Don't try to slow down by dragging your toes; you'll ruin a good pair of boots.

The Olympic Park no longer offers skeleton clinics for the general public. They do still offer bobsled rides, steered by professional drivers.

Nonetheless, I can advise you on how to save $150. Just go to the paint department at Home Depot, and stick your head in the paint-shaking machine for a minute. It will closely replicate the experience of careening down the icy track on a skeleton tea tray.

Be aware that skeleton athletes think luge athletes are crazy, who think bobsled athletes are crazy, who think Skeleton athletes are crazy. It all works out, but the inside word is that bobsledding carries the highest risk of decapitation.

Third, the 2002 Games were held in the shadow of 9/11. The airspace around Park City's venues was locked down tight. There were surface-to-air missile installations tucked around our hillsides, ready for any alert. Friends who went off backcountry skiing returned with tales of being politely but firmly told to move along by winter-camo'd soldiers appearing out of nowhere carrying automatic weapons. Some friends were even accosted by rocket-armed helicopters rising up the canyon and hovering nearby. Others recall a metal detector erected on Deer Valley Resort's Little Stick run.

I rode up a chairlift with a guy who claimed he spent the Olympics in a bunker in Alexandria, Virginia, watching the airspace for hostile anomalies. The 2034 Olympics will be that much more interesting from a security standpoint, what with the number of drone taxis that will be in the airspace by then.

Lastly, U.S. Ski and Snowboard, the governing body for Olympic skiing and snowboarding, operates the 85,000-square-foot Center of Excellence out near U.S. Route 40 and State Route 248. This is a magnificent multi-million-dollar gymnasium combined with a biomedical lab. The young athletes are tested and screened almost daily on blood chemistry, oxygen intake and recovery time, all to gain a hundredth of a second advantage over the Austrians. We believe that athletes at the Center of Excellence do not drink the local water, for fear of potential lead contamination in the water. A tour of Park City's Water Division facilities indicates that our culinary water is well within EPA standards, thanks to some amazing engineering at the 3Kings Water Treatment Plant, but you can understand that the Ski Team might still have some concerns, or is operating on decades-old assumptions.

In July 2024, Utah was awarded the 2034 Winter Games. We have every hope and reasonable expectation that they will run as smoothly. Dust off your volunteer jacket and get those pin collections out of storage.

SALT FLAT CITY

In the early days, Park City residents spoke of "going down to Zion" when they traveled to Salt Lake City. As has been mentioned or implied elsewhere, Park City and Summit County remain intimately tied to the Salt Lake Valley. It's where we all go for cultural amenities like the symphony and ballet or professional basketball, soccer, and hockey games. We obtain specialized medical care at the centers run by the University of Utah and Intermountain Healthcare. There are Costco, Target, and Trader Joe's stores down there. If you're a Republican, you can even go there to petition the government for redress of grievances.

In turn, Salt Lake Valley residents head up the hill to escape the summer heat, hike and bike Bonanza Flat, and stroll our streets during events searching for the Java Cow shop.

If there are future editions of this publication, we may need to change "Salt Lake" to "Salt Flat" because of climate change and water use policy. The intermountain West is in the midst of a mega-drought, and we're losing the Great Salt Lake. It's a fraction of its former size, due in part to lower precipitation, and the fact that the rivers that feed the lake are tapped for other uses. When it's completely gone, what shall we call the capital city?

About 80 percent of water usage in Utah goes to agriculture, and a large portion of that goes to alfalfa farming. In turn, our ag businesses export a lot of alfalfa out of state. So in effect, we're sending water, which could restore the Great Salt Lake, to China—or worse, to Colorado.

As stretches of lake shoreline are exposed and dry out, toxic dust is carried east. There are not a lot of comprehensive studies yet, but presumably some of that pollution makes its way to Summit County.

There are encouraging efforts to mitigate the crisis, and every once in a while, the State Legislature can surprise citizens in a good way. In 2023, a number of bills passed to protect streamflow to the lake and to compensate farmers for water rights. Funding for landscape conversion, monitoring, and municipal water planning were beefed up. And we now have a position called the Great Salt Lake Commissioner to coordinate a state-level plan to save the lake.

More recently:

- In the 2025 session, legislation allows water districts to use tiered pricing to encourage conservation.
- Utah State University and the University of Utah are collaborating on a Great Salt Lake Strike Team to provide data and recommendations to policymakers.
- The State's forestry division removed 15,000 acres of invasive, water-hogging phragmites, which are large, perennial reed grasses.
- The Great Salt Lake Commissioner released a strategic plan in January 2024, listing major steps and milestones, and followed up with a "2034 Plan for a Healthy Great Salt Lake," which is an indication that the spotlight of the 2034 Winter Olympics may spur us to further action.
- A number of water districts and companies have released significant amounts of water into the lake, or have agreed to forego using as much water as in the past.

- In April 2026, the Larry H. and Gail Miller Family Foundation, Maverik (the gas station/convenience store business), and the J. Willard and Alice S. Marriott Foundation committed $10 million each to the Great Salt Lake Rising initiative (*https://gslrising.org/*).

All of these efforts are an uphill grind and subject to legislative and citizen fatigue. Residents of Summit County must contribute their ideas and actions now and in the future. The problem of the Great Salt Lake is a problem for all of us, not just those who live in the valley.

You can keep tabs on Strike Team progress here: *gardner.utah.edu/great-salt-lake-strike-team/*

Things to Change

With apologies to Gil Scott-Heron, the revolution may or may not be televised. In the meantime, there may be opportunities to fix a few minor, nagging issues at the local level. Here are a few suggestions.

T-shirt companies in town will not be able to sell shirts with exaggerated depictions of our mountains. Our mountains are beautiful and impressive in their own right, but Wasatch Back ridgelines are understated and gentle compared to the steeper prominences of the Wasatch Front and Uintas. If the peak on a "Park City" tee looks like Denali, the Matterhorn, or K2, it's false advertising.

And no grizzly bear images either, please. "Old Ephraim," one of Utah's last Ursus arctos horribilis, was trapped and killed in Logan Canyon in 1923.

A dog owner found leaving a bag of crap on the side of a trail for someone else to deal with will have to walk or bike the entire length of the Mid-Mountain Trail dressed in a tutu, a la the Poop Fairy. Actually, a good portion of our population likes to do just that while recreating anyway, especially around Tour Des Suds time. Perhaps walking the trail while sporting a garland of used poop bags might be a better deterrent.

A few April Fools' Days ago, Mountain Trails Foundation made a brilliant social media post, about receiving a grant for purposes of DNA testing on the canine leave-behinds in order to track them back to the dog owners. Technology continues to advance; it might be time to make that a reality!

Anyone promoting their vacation rental or property for sale with the phrase "Ski-In Ski-Out" will be required to post a certification video showing the exact routes to and from the property and the slopes. The video should consist of a single, long, tracking cut, like the Copacabana Restaurant scene in *Goodfellas*. No cutaways. Trust but verify.

Moose are susceptible to infestation by wood ticks. A single moose can have thousands of the pests feeding on blood, causing higher rates of mortality in yearlings and reduced reproduction by females. Anyone caught letting their dogs pester moose will have to join a DHHS "tick drag." Anyone who collides with and kills a moose while travelling above the speed limit on Route 224 will have to dress it out and live solely off moose meat for the next month.

The phrase "bumping chairs" describes how lift operators hold back an approaching chairlift to give the guest a more gentle seating. If you are caught berating a chairlift operator, you'll be required to bump chairs for the next hour.

Of course, if you are caught berating any Deer Valley employee in any department, may God have mercy on your soul. If the employee is not a J-1, chances are that he or she is a former C-level executive, Delta pilot, or military officer (or all of the above). There's enough retired executive talent in Deer Valley's part-time workforce to come off the bench and run a dozen Fortune 500 companies. They know how to deal with entitled lightweights.

Hotels and rentals in Summit County will be required to post exact drive times to and from the Salt Lake City International Airport. None of this "Oh, and we're a half-hour drive to a major airport" when in reality your location is a forty-nine-minute drive to SLC.

The city will have to cease using "Empire Creek" as the name of the stream that flows along Deer Valley Drive and City Park. It was known as "Poison Creek" in the mining days. We had a problem with heavy metals and effluent back in the day. And there are occasional effloresces of red algae in the waters flowing by Marriott Summit Watch today. Acknowledging our past will help us deal with the future.

Why is there a store called Kemo Sabe on Main Street, which after all, occupies ancestral lands of the Utes? What does that say about ourselves? If it's any consolation, they are taking the rest of the Intermountain West down with us, what with shops in Aspen, Vail, Jackson, Round Top, and Whitefish.

The empty flashing-light cop cars sitting at various intersections serve no purpose that the citizenry can determine. Cops will have to be sitting in the cars and perhaps, if it's not a bother, actually enforce traffic laws at these busy intersections.

Furthermore, from 3:00 to 6:00 p.m., you should be able to turn right/north from both lanes on Deer Valley Drive when you get to the junction with Park Avenue (the Cole Sports/Jans intersection).

Ski resorts like Vail will not be able to hold holiday fireworks celebrations unless they are paying their staff living wages. In late 2024, Park City ski patrollers went on strike, asking for, among other benefits, base pay to rise from twenty-one dollars to twenty-three dollars an hour. Ralph, a friend who was a patroller for decades, points out that the cost of a single burst of fireworks on New Year's Eve would probably take care of a patroller's annual pay differential. "Boom! That's one patroller. Boom! That's another patroller. Vail can afford a two-dollar raise."

Let's talk about real problems. Wordle is going to run out of five-letter words in less than ten years. Wordle will have to recognize technical terminology, especially from mining. The words, "winze" and "stope" and other ephemera will be added to the master list.

THINGS WE LOVE
(AND SOME WE FEAR)

Loves:

- Flammulated owls: They eat bark beetles
- Open space
- Bike paths
- Red Bicycle bread: Buy two (one to nibble in the car)
- High Valley Transit and the Park City free bus systems: 1.5 million riders can't be wrong
- Rasta Pasta at 11 Hauz
- Deer Valley expert mountain host tours, especially on powder days
- Caesar salad at 7880: But don't tell anybody about 7880 . . . it's a secret
- Summit Bikeshare: New stations added each year
- The hike to the Notch in the Uintas: You might see mountain goats. And the hikes around Christmas Meadows, where you might see moose.

- Samak Store beef jerky and smoked salmon and trout
- Woodland Biscuit Company's breakfast and brunch
- The rock chairs on top of Summit Park
- Any story about Mother Urban, Park City's famous madam
- Silver Fork Lodge in Big Cottonwood Canyon
- Olympic collector pins with Bagley cartoon designs . . . we can't wait for the 2034 versions

Fears:
- Thirteen-year-olds on e-bikes
- Paid parking at the resorts
- Early-season skiing on the "white ribbons of death"
- Unchecked growth and traffic on Routes 224 and 248
- The State Legislature
- Property tax notices from the county assessor

CHALLENGES

The biggest unknown our community faces regarding our economy and quality of life is the long-term impact of climate change. Ski seasons will shorten. We will lose the first and last week or two of what we now think of as normal seasons, and the elevations at which snowfall is significant will rise. Ski resorts will see fewer guests in the early season and will have to adjust to lower revenue from curtailed Christmas Week sales. Lifts at lower altitudes will spend more of their lifetimes as commuter routes from parking lots to higher parts of the mountain where the actual skiing will take place. An extended mountain bike season in May and October may provide a modest offset.

Long term, who knows? Skiing may only be a viable activity above 8,000 feet in elevation. The configuration of our current resorts may change radically in coming decades. We got a preview in the historically low-snow 2025–2026 season.

Climate change also affects the amount of water we'll be able to access for future development. As cowboy musician Dave Stamey sings: "And where the water's coming from, ain't nobody knows."

The biggest changes to Summit County over the next few years are going to be the changes happening in Wasatch County. The hills around Jordanelle Reservoir are already starting to fill with houses and townhomes. The expansion of Deer Valley will propel this lakeside development at an even faster pace. The crush of people coming to this area will strain all the infrastructure, and impacts will spill over into Summit County.

A sub-set of this growth will happen in the town of Hideout, which is expanding due to some shady dealings in the State Legislature: a state law, valid for only four months, allowed Hideout to annex land in a different county. The case went to the Utah State Supreme Court, which unfortunately, but perhaps not shockingly, allowed this very hostile take-over to happen.

A strength of Park City is historic Main Street and the sense of place it gives to visitors and residents alike. Businesses, residents, and the city government don't seem likely to do much to change that community positive. The discussion has shifted to other parts of town, and there are opportunities to bring more character and quality-of-life amenities to Bonanza Park and Quinn's Junction.

The County has a similar opportunity at Kimball Junction. Decades ago, the County Council was accused of trashing the neighborhood in its drive to secure retail businesses generating sales tax revenue. Thankfully, the Newpark development brought walkability and a variety of retail and housing options, so perceptions of Kimball Junction have improved. With the advent of Dakota Pacific development and UDOT upgrades, further progress (or peril) is possible.

If you have attended aviation industry trade shows over the last decade, you'll know that air taxis (either piloted or drones) have been the next big thing. "Wait until next year" seems to be the rallying cry. Technologic and regulatory hurdles are finally starting to fall, and the next big thing might actually take place in the near future. This could have positive impacts on our vehicle traffic, but could vastly complicate other aspects of life, such as noise pollution, aviation safety, wildfires, privacy, and more.

Park City's ski slopes are directly tied to those in Big and Little Cottonwood Canyons. These days, when a snowstorm closes the Cottonwood Canyons for plowing and avalanche mitigation, half of Salt Lake City heads our way to ski the pow. If the Wasatch Front can solve its traffic problems in those canyons, it will have a direct and positive impact on our quality of life. It's easy for us to say, "Oh, that's their problem." If we don't weigh in on public comment opportunities, then shame on us. We won't be in a position to complain on those big-dump days.

On the positive side, Summit County remains committed to preserving open space. The efforts of the County, Basin Recreation, Park City, non-profits, and our generous residents have defined our community and quality of life in immeasurable ways. A recent and massive acquisition of the 910 Ranch (8,588 acres in all) near Jeremy Ranch continues this trend and will have generational benefits. However, it will be a complex puzzle to solve. The easement is held by the State's Department of Natural Resources, and they will have to navigate political pressures from other state entities such as UDOT and the Legislature.

One of the trickiest problems for any resort community to solve is affordable housing. A 2021 study for Park City showed that out of 10,440 housing units, 32.6 percent were owner-occupied and 11.2 percent renter-occupied. The rest were mostly second/vacation homes. In 2025, Summit County estimated that 38 percent of housing stock is "empty," meaning neither owners nor long-term renters live in them.

A 2022 study by the Kem C. Gardner Institute showed 21.5 percent of Summit County housing stock is in the short-term rental category. And the category is on the rise. According to a 2024 follow-up study, Summit County leads the state with approximately 23 percent of all housing listed as short-term rentals, and at 41 percent, Park City proper has the most short-term rentals of any city in the state. "I live in Park City" is a phrase growing in rarity.

Wasatch County does not have a large pool of unoccupied units, but as one of the fastest-growing in the state, it faces high demand, high housing and rental prices, and a gap in supply.

Like the mining companies of old, Park City Mountain and Deer Valley Resort have taken steps to source or develop staff housing. This is a trend that will most likely continue as home prices continue to rise in Summit County. Maybe the ski companies could start offering no-cost housing loans to staff, like the Hecla mining company did decades ago.

There's some hope that the private and federal investment brought by the 2034 Olympics can be harnessed to improve our housing stock. Otherwise, we'll slide further down the path to being a "hollowed-out" town with predominately second homeowners and VRBO investors.

The long-term solution will rest on zoning changes and infrastructure investments that allow for more concentrated multi-family housing options with well-functioning public transportation. Whether or not our voters will have an appetite for all that remains to be seen.

END BITS

Congratulations, you made it!
Just a few items in conclusion, unless you want to
comb through the thirty pages of reference material.

Afterword

Nobody reads afterwords. Go out and have some fun. Take a hike. Ride a bike. Find a powder stash. Donate to or volunteer at a non-profit. Toast our community with a glass of Old Town Cellars Townie Rosé. We are blessed to live here.

Author's Biography

Michael O'Malley has skied in Park City since 1980 and lived here since 1997. He now spends part of his time in Olympia, Washington, where you don't have to shovel rain. A graduate of Pomona College, where he met his wife Lauren, he's held marketing positions in a variety of industries over his career, the most recent stint with the Economic Development Corporation of Utah. Other pursuits include four decades as a whitewater river guide, three decades as a lacrosse referee, and two decades as a mountain host and hiking guide at Deer Valley Resort. He leads Fox School of Wine's "Mines & Wines" tours, and volunteers at the Park City Museum, regularly contributing to the "Way We Were" history article series.

REFERENCES

Fundamentals

Space

Wikipedia. "Rhode Island." Last Modified May 22, 2025 at 22:35. https://en.wikipedia.org/wiki/Rhode_Island.

Wikipedia. "Summit County, Utah." Last Modified May 17, 2025 at 22:21. https://en.wikipedia.org/wiki/Summit_County, Utah.

Wikipedia. "Wasatch County, Utah." Last Modified April 10, 2026 at 14:47. https://en.wikipedia.org/wiki/Wasatch_County,_Utah

Time and Geology

Boutwell, J. M. and L. H. "Geology and ore deposits of the Park City district, Utah." U.S. Geological Survey, 1912. https://doi.org/10.3133/pp77.

State of Utah, Department of Natural Resources. *Geologic Resources of Summit County, Utah*. PDF file. 1990. https://ugspub.nr.utah.gov/publications/public_information/pi-7.pdf.

Weller, Kristine. "Summit County home to significant portion of Californians moving to Utah." *KPCW*, August 16, 2024. https://www.kpcw.org/park-city/2024-08-15/summit-county-and-surrounding-counties-saw-significant-portion-of-california-migrants-in-2022.

Park City Proper

Wikipedia. "Park City, Utah." Last modified June 8, at 01:22, https://en.wikipedia.org/wiki/Park_City,_Utah.

The People

Kamas Valley History Group. Accessed June 20, 2025. https://kamasvalleyhistory.org/.

Kem C. Gardner Policy Institute. "Travel & Tourism County Profile. In Summit County." 2023. https://assets.simpleviewinc.com/simpleview/image/upload/v1/clients/parkcity/County_Profiles_2022_Nov2023_e6b63aea-705c-4aee-a629-23780007680d.pdf.

"Mile Post 2023." Park Record, August 14, 2024. https://www.parkrecord.com/2023/10/04/mile-post-2023/

Ski Utah. "Ski Utah Resort Histories | Park City Mountain." https://www.skiutah.com/blog/authors/lexi/ski-utah-resort-histories-park-city/.

Summit County. "I Love History." https://ilovehistory.utah.gov/summit-county/

Summit County, UT - Official Website. "Historical Overview | Summit County, Utah History & Heritage" https://www.summitcounty.org/796/Historical-Overview#.

United States Census Bureau QuickFacts. "Summit County, Utah. Census Bureau QuickFacts." https://www.census.gov/quickfacts/fact/table/summitcountyutah/POP010210.

USAFacts. "Summit County, UT population by year, race, & more." 2025. https://usafacts.org/data/topics/people-society/population-and-demographics/our-changing-population/state/utah/county/summit-county/.

Yanasak-Leszczynski, Josephine. "The earlier people of Summit County." 2015. https://parkcityhistory.org/wp-content/uploads/2015/04/www20150422-American-Indians-in-Summit-County-Yanask-Leszczynski.pdf.

Park City Past – Mining

Silver Camp Versus Lead Camp

Droste, Keith A. "Park City Mining Dist Total Production seven operations no $." Spreadsheet. Author's personal files, 2011.

O'Malley, Michael. "Conversations with Lynn Cier." Author's personal files, 2024.

Not So Much as a Hatful of Ore – A Lynching on Main Street

Alexander, Thomas G. *Utah, the Right Place: The Official Centennial History.* Salt Lake City/Gibbs Smith, 1996.

"An Old-Timer Visits." *Park Record,* September 19, 1920. https://newspapers.lib.utah.edu/ark:/87278/s6jd604p/7964563.

Berg, Manfred. *Popular Justice: A History of Lynching in America.* Rowman & Littlefield Publishing Group, 2011.

Colorado Encyclopedia. "Lynching in Colorado." https://coloradoencyclopedia.org/article/lynching-colorado#:~:text=Between%201859%20and%201919%2C%20Coloradans,towns%20across%20the%20Colorado%20Territory.

Compton, Hal. "The Lynching of 'Black Jack' Murphy." *Park Record,* March 23, 2006. https://newspapers.lib.utah.edu/ark:/87278/s60614cj/22577821.

"Dad's Column." *Park Record,* April 17, 1931. https://newspapers.lib.utah.edu/ark:/87278/s62v3jh7/7999008.

Gerlach, Larry, R. "Ogden's 'Horrible tragedy': The Lynching of George Segal." *Utah Historical Quarterly* 49, no. 2 (1981). https://issuu.com/utah10/docs/uhq_volume49_1981_number2/s/133666.

Knowlton, Christopher. Cattle Kingdom: The Hidden History of the Cowboy West. Damon Dolan/Houghton Mifflin Harcourt, 2017.

NAACP. "History of lynching in America." 2022. https://naacp.org/find-resources/history-explained/history-lynching-america.

Rueda, Jacob. "Historian reflects on Utah's history with lynching and prejudice." *KSL NewsRadio,* December 30, 2022. https://kslnewsradio.com/1966468/utah-historian-reflects-on-the-states-history-with-lynching-and-prejudice/.

Tanner, Courtney. "Two Black men were once lynched in SLC. Here's what we know about their stories." *The Salt Lake Tribune,* June 12, 2022. https://www.sltrib.com/news/2022/06/12/two-black-men-were-once/.

"The Lynching of 'Black Jack' Murphy." *Park Record,* February 3, 1977. https://newspapers.lib.utah.edu/ark:/87278/s6t44wtc/8204108.

User, S. n.d. "Lynchings: By State and Race,1882-1968 *. Famous Trials." https://famous-trials.com/sheriffshipp/1083-lynchingsstate

Dynamite at the Daly West Mine

Hamburger, Jay. "Confirmed: Opening is a mine shaft." *Park Record,* June 25, 2011. https://newspapers.lib.utah.edu/ark:/87278/s6t47gn9/22607833.

Hamburger, Jay. "Mining-era explosives unearthed in Empire Pass." *Park Record,* October 8, 2008. https://newspapers.lib.utah.edu/ark:/87278/s6wx1650/22595124.

McLaws, Chris. "Park City's First Hospital." *Park Record,* June 21, 2016. https://www.parkrecord.com/entertainment/park-citys-first-hospital/

Miller, J.B. "Penned Like Rats in a Trap." *Salt Lake Telegram,* July 16, 1902. https://www.newspapers.com/article/salt-lake-telegram-1902-jul-16-utahs-dal/14422249/.

"Mine shaft collapses at American Flag." *Park Record,* May 25, 2011. https://www.parkrecord.com/2011/05/25/mine-shaft-collapses-at-american-flag/.

The Luck of the Irish is Not Evenly Dispersed

"A Horrible Death." *Park Record,* November 18, 1899. https://newspapers.lib.utah.edu/ark:/87278/s6gq80zp/8328859.

Cater, Ben. "Grassroots healing: The Park City Miners' Hospital." *Utah Historical Quarterly* 78, no. 4 (2010). https://issuu.com/utah10/docs/uhq_volume78_2010_number4/s/10369006.

Dwyer, Robert J. "The Irish in the building of the Intermountain West." *Utah Historical Quarterly* 25 (1957). https://issuu.com/utah10/docs/volume_25_1957/s/96070.

"How Irish Is Utah? Here's a Map Showing the Claimed Irish Ancestry of Each Utah County." Reddit, 2016. https://www.reddit.com/r/SaltLakeCity/comments/b16xkq/how_irish_is_utah_heres_a_map_showing_the_claimed/.

Import, P.R. "Park City's Leprechaun trail: raising a pint to the 'Emerald Island' since 1880." *Park Record,* March 17, 2007. https://www.parkrecord.com/news/park-citys-leprechaun-trail-raising-a-pint-to-the-emerald-island-since-1880/

"Michael H McCarthy" Find a Grave, January 11, 1870. https://www.findagrave.com/memorial/30421678/michael-h-mccarthy.

"Mine Disasters in the United States." United States Mine Rescue Association. https://usminedisasters.miningquiz.com/saxsewell/daly_west_news_only.htm.

The Silent Sentinel. "1906: The Ties That Bind." *Echoes of the Past: Building 55*, August 26, 2014. https://thesilentsentinel55.weebly.com/project-blog/archives/08-2014.

United States Census Bureau. "1910 Census: Abstract of the Thirteenth Census of the United States." Effective January 1913. https://www.census.gov/library/publications/1913/dec/abstract.html.

"Utah and Ireland have long-standing bond beyond St. Patrick's Day." *FOX 13 News Utah (KSTU)*, March 17, 2021. https://www.fox13now.com/news/local-news/utah-and-ireland-have-longstanding-bond-beyond-st-patricks-day.

Utah, H. S. O. "Irish Heritage in Utah." *Hibernian Society UT*, January 27, 2021. https://www.irishinutah.com/post/irish-heritage-in-utah.

Westwood, Brad. "Irish, Cornish, Welsh and Jewish immigrants and Salt Lake City's West Side." *Utah Department Of Cultural & Community Engagement*, 2023. https://heritageandarts.utah.gov/the-roots-of-post-civil-war-immigration-and-salt-lake-citys-west-side/.

Whitley, Colleen. *From the Ground Up: A History of Mining in Utah*. University Press of Colorado, 2006. https://doi.org/10.2307/j.ctt4cgn2r.

Williams, Carter. "Looking back at Irish history in Utah." *KSL.com*, March 17, 2017. https://www.ksl.com/article/43517003/looking-back-at-irish-history-in-utah.

ZIPAtlas. "Percentage of Irish population in Utah by city in 2025." Last modified 2025. http://zipatlas.com/us/ut/city-comparison/percentage-irish-population.htm.

Core Samples of Woe in Park City's Cemeteries

Ahmad, Farida. B., & Robert. N. Anderson. "The leading causes of death in the US for 2020." JAMA, 325(18), 1829-1830 (2021). https://doi.org/10.1001/jama.2021.5469.

Bloom, Anna. "Kimball finds more than 1,000 burials unrecorded." *Park Record*, November 16, 2005. https://www.parkrecord.com/news/kimball-finds-more-than-1000-burials-unrecorded/.

Nangle, B. E., Neerings, K., Duncan, J. D., Muirbrook, M. *Utah's Vital Statistics 100 year Anniversary 1905 to 2005*. Utah Department of Health, Center for Health Data, & Office of Vital Records, 2005. https://ibis.utah.gov/ibisph-view/pdf/opha/publication/OVRS_100YearReport.pdf.

O'Malley, Michael. "Spreadsheet adapted from Glenwood Cemetery 'Book of the Dead.'" Author's personal files, 2022.

"Stats of the State of Utah." National Center for Health Statistics. Last modified April 9, 2018. https://www.cdc.gov/nchs/pressroom/states/utah/utah.htm.

The Deadly (and Miraculous) Quincy Avalanche

"The Deadly Avalanche." *Park Record*, January 31, 1903. https://newspapers.lib.utah.edu/ark:/87278/s6nk4h8k/8338455.

Invisible Death in the Daly West

"Dead-Air Pocket in Mine Kills Three in Park City." *Deseret News,* April 24, 1942. https://newspapers.lib.utah.edu/ark:/87278/s67q3x98/25602222.

"Park City Property to be under New Management." *Park Record,* April 9, 1942. https://newspapers.lib.utah.edu/ark:/87278/s6155kn0/8113244.

"Pertaining to the Mine Accident of April 23rd." *Park Record,* May 7, 1942. https://newspapers.lib.utah.edu/ark:/87278/s6h42v2j/8113542.

"The Most Dangerous Gases In Mining" Chart Industries, Inc, November 9, 2023. https://www.chartindustries.com/Articles/The-Most-Dangerous-Gases-In-Mining.

"Three Well Known Miners Die from Poison Gas." *Park Record,* April 30, 1942. https://newspapers.lib.utah.edu/ark:/87278/s6mw3kqn/8113465.

The Fatal Flagstaff Fall

Brown, Hollie. "Abandoned Mine Reclamation Project Completed in Eureka." *Utah Division of Natural Resources,* July 11, 2023. https://drilldown.ogm.utah.gov/2023/07/11/.

"Flagstaff Mine Claims Life of Salt Lake Boy." *Summit County Bee and Park Record,* August 22, 1963. https://newspapers.lib.utah.edu/ark:/87278/s69w1j42/8108232.

UPI. "Boy Dies in Fall Down Mine Shaft." *Provo Daily Herald,* August 19, 1963. https://newspapers.lib.utah.edu/ark:/87278/s6hx5txd/23816119.

Deer Crest Views: The East Ontario and Boiler Point

Historic Aerials. Accessed June 20, 2025. https://www.historicaerials.com/.

Knudson, Max B. "DEER CREST: A NEW NAME, a NEW VISION." *Deseret News,* September 8, 1996. https://www.deseret.com/1996/9/8/19264181/deer-crest-a-new-name-a-new-vision/.

Nicholas, David. "A Smattering of Gold." Park City Museum, September 28, 2021. https://parkcityhistory.org/a-smattering-of-gold/.

O'Malley, Michael. "Email correspondence with Don Taylor." *Author's personal files,* March 2024.

O'Malley, Michael. "Email correspondence with McKay Edwards." *Author's personal files,* January, 2024.

"Park City Cons. Pays off Debts." *Park Record,* May 15, 1941. https://newspapers.lib.utah.edu/ark:/87278/s6tx4htr/8035190.

Geology and Labor in the Park City Consolidated

Wiles, Gloyd M. *Information Circular.* Department of the Interior – United States Bureau of Mines, April 1936.

The Metallic History Signs

Elliott, Sally. "The Way We Were." Park City Museum, March 5, 2014. https://parkcityhistory.org/wp-content/uploads/2014/03/The-Unfortunate-Fate-of-the-Kearns-Keith-Mill.pdf.

McQuay, Jana. "Park City Resort dubs new base lodge 'Legacy.'" *Deseret News,* January 19, 2024. https://www.deseret.com/1999/7/25/19457374/park-city-resort-dubs-new-base-lodge-legacy/.

The Silver Mine Adventure

Gackle, Dalton. "Whatever Happened to the Silver Mine Adventure?" Park City Museum, October 29, 2020. https://parkcityhistory.org/whatever-happened-to-the-silver-mine-adventure/.

Knudson, Max B. "SILVER LINING: PARK CITY FIRM TURNS UNPROFITABLE MINE INTO TOURIST ATTRACTION." *Deseret News,* June 9, 1996. https://www.deseret.com/1996/6/9/19247477/silver-lining-park-city-firm-turns-unprofitable-mine-into-tourist-attraction/.

O'Malley, Michael. "Conversations – source name withheld by request." *Author's personal files.* August 2025.

Park City Past – Other Pursuits

The Pony Express was Here . . . for About Six Weeks

Barlow, Jacob. Kimball Stage stop. JacobBarlow.com, April 5, 2023. https://jacobbarlow.com/2023/05/04/kimball-stage-stop/.

Iwasaki, Scott. "Park City Museum jumps on the Pony Express." *Park Record,* May 12, 2024. https://www.parkrecord.com/2011/03/25/park-city-museum-jumps-on-the-pony-express/.

Van Eyck, Zack. "Pony Express sites to be recognized." *Deseret News,* January 17, 2024. https://www.deseret.com/2002/7/20/19667238/pony-express-sites-to-be-recognized/.

Butch Cassidy in Park City?

McLaws, Chris. "Did Butch Cassidy rob the Oak Saloon?" Park City Museum, September 21, 2020. https://parkcityhistory.org/did-butch-cassidy-rob-the-oak-saloon/.

"News Summary." *Coalville Times,* May 20, 1898. https://newspapers.lib.utah.edu/ark:/87278/s6np2z30/657189.

The Jordanelle Japanese Internment Farm

Nichols, Jeffrey D. "The Japanese Agricultural Colony at Keetley, Wasatch County." *History Blazer,* 1995. https://historytogo.utah.gov/japanese-agricultural-colony/.

Taylor, Sandra C. "Japanese Americans and Keetley Farms: Utah's Relocation Colony." *Utah Historical Quarterly* 54, no. 4 (1986). https://issuu.com/utah10/docs/uhq_volume54_1986_number4/26.

Copper Bottomed Conscience: The Michigan Bunch and Main Street

"A Card." *Salt Lake Tribune,* June 28, 1877. https://newspapers.lib.utah.edu/ark:/87278/s62v3r1f/12997225.

"A Correction." *Park Record,* December 1, 1883. https://newspapers.lib.utah.edu/ark:/87278/s6w96c9j/8286793.

Brumley, S. and Michael O'Malley "Edward P. Ferry: Park City's First Capitalist.ppt." *Author's personal files,* December 2024.

"In Favor of Nims." *Deseret News,* June 6, 1888. https://newspapers.lib.utah.edu/ark:/87278/s6bv8b7j/2669947.

"Park City Aroused." *Salt Lake Tribune,* November 25, 1886. https://newspapers.lib.utah.edu/ark:/87278/s6x07gw0/12989469.

"Preliminary Examination." *Salt Lake Tribune,* June 29, 1877. https://newspapers.lib.utah.edu/ark:/87278/s6z337mb/12997265.

"Red Hot!." *Salt Lake Tribune,* June 27, 1877. https://newspapers.lib.utah.edu/ark:/87278/s6b86j1q/12997107.

"The Marsac Title." *Park Record,* October 1, 1881. https://newspapers.lib.utah.edu/ark:/87278/s6hh7n53/8291458.

"The Masrac Title." *Park Record,* September 24, 1881. https://newspapers.lib.utah.edu/ark:/87278/s6xs6xkw/8290787.

Thompson, George A. and Fraser Buck. *Treasure Mountain Home: Park City Revisited.* Dream Garden Press, 1983.

Whitley, Colleen, ed. *From the Ground Up: A History of Mining in Utah.* University Press of Colorado. 2006. https://doi.org/10.2307/j.ctt4cgn2r.

Wikipedia. "Thomas W. Ferry." Last modified April 14, 2025. https://en.wikipedia.org/wiki/Thomas_W._Ferry.

Wright, Dean F. "A History of Park City, 1869 to 1898." Master's Dissertation, University of Utah, 1971.

The Big White Barn

Park City Utah. "McPolin Farm" https://www.parkcity.org/departments/mcpolin-farm.

Summit Land Conservancy. https://www.wesaveland.org/.

Sawmills and Stills: Thaynes Canyon Through the Years

"Alleged Bootleggers Tracked to Lair." *Park Record,* July 15, 1921. https://newspapers.lib.utah.edu/ark:/87278/s64180fz/7967791.

Elliott, Sally. "North Park still central to Park City's story." *Park City Museum*, December 13, 2019. https://parkcityhistory.org/north-park-still-central-to-park-citys-story/.

"It Was Not Bob Hanley." *Park Record*, September 5, 1924. https://newspapers.lib.utah.edu/ark:/87278/s6d2311x/7974356.

"Park Float." *Park Record*, September 5, 1924. https://newspapers.lib.utah.edu/ark:/87278/s6d2311x/7974399.

WikiTree FREE Family Tree. "John Johnson Thayne (1825-1910)" Last modified April 14, 2020. https://www.wikitree.com/wiki/Thayne-56.

Entrepreneurism and the White Mule

"Alleged Bootlegger Sticks Gun a Gun in Officer's Belly." *Park Record*, August 26, 1921. https://newspapers.lib.utah.edu/ark:/87278/s66t1q15/7968435.

"Another Still Found." *Park Record*, September 11, 1925. https://newspapers.lib.utah.edu/ark:/87278/s6jd6054/7978244.

"Another Still Seized." *Park Record*, January 18, 1929. https://newspapers.lib.utah.edu/ark:/87278/s6p85f7w/7990964.

"Another Woman Arrested for Bootlegging." *Park Record*, July 14, 1922. https://newspapers.lib.utah.edu/ark:/87278/s6d51q8m/7971956.

"'Booze' Kills Parkites." *Park Record*, January 2, 1925. https://newspapers.lib.utah.edu/ark:/87278/s62j7f5x/7975642.

"Carlson and Siddoway Guilty of 'Moonshining'." *Park Record*, August 21, 1925. https://newspapers.lib.utah.edu/ark:/87278/s6xp8789/7978034.

"Hamlin Arrested for 'Bootlegging'." *Park Record*, September 3, 1920. https://newspapers.lib.utah.edu/ark:/87278/s6st8s5q/7964410.

"It Was Not Bob Hanley." *Park Record*, September 5, 1924. https://newspapers.lib.utah.edu/ark:/87278/s6d2311x/7974356.

"Park Float." *Park Record*, January 9, 1925. https://newspapers.lib.utah.edu/ark:/87278/s6t44wgw/7975864.

"Park Float." *Park Record*, May 4, 1923. https://newspapers.lib.utah.edu/ark:/87278/s64t7mws/8073934.

"Police Court." *Park Record*, November 12, 1926. https://newspapers.lib.utah.edu/ark:/87278/s6j39vxc/7982744.

"Police Officers Doing Good Work." *Park Record*, November 26, 1920. https://newspapers.lib.utah.edu/ark:/87278/s6446ps0/7965277.

"Still Confiscated." *Park Record*, August 29, 1924. https://newspapers.lib.utah.edu/ark:/87278/s6ht3rpn/7974264.

The Empire Canyon Landslides

"Landslide, Flooded Canal Threaten Park." *Park Record*, June 1, 1967. https://newspapers.lib.utah.edu/ark:/87278/s6z90g03/8128744.

Ruddell, Mahala. "A Landslide Brought It Down." *Park Record,* July 20, 2016. https://newspapers.lib.utah.edu/ark:/87278/s6fz1pnc/23671387.

Three Historic Aerial Crashes

Leatham, Steve. Perfect courage | Park City Museum. Park City Museum, December 12, 2019. https://parkcityhistory.org/perfect-courage/.

Leatham, Steve and David Nicholas. "A Hell of a roar." Park City Museum, January 31, 2020. https://parkcityhistory.org/a-hell-of-a-roar/.

O'Malley, Michael. "Oral history folder in Park City Staff – Interview with Jack Leavitt." Park City Museum research library files, December 2022.

Warren, Larry. *Park City: Mountain of Treasure.* Mountain Sports Press, 2003.

Polygamy

Fisher, D. "Reynolds v. United States (1879)." The Free Speech Center, December 23, 2024. https://firstamendment.mtsu.edu/article/reynolds-v-united-states/.

"John Singer's Long Struggle with the Law Recounted." *Park Record,* January 25, 1979. https://newspapers.lib.utah.edu/ark:/87278/s6tt5tnk/8213155.

"Law Officer's Shot Ends John Singer's Life." *Park Record,* January 25, 1979. https://newspapers.lib.utah.edu/ark:/87278/s6tt5tnk/8213136.

"Singer Case Closed?." *Park Record,* May 3, 1979. https://newspapers.lib.utah.edu/ark:/87278/s60s0s39/8201524.

"Supreme Court won't hear Singer Appeal." *Park Record,* March 7, 1985. https://newspapers.lib.utah.edu/ark:/87278/s6b8997n/8259634.

"The Manifesto And The End Of Plural Marriage." *The Church of Jesus Christ of Latter-day Saints,* January 1, 2016. https://www.churchofjesuschrist.org/study/manual/gospel-topics-essays/the-manifesto-and-the-end-of-plural-marriage?lang=eng.

"Why?." *Park Record,* January 25, 1979. https://newspapers.lib.utah.edu/ark:/87278/s6tt5tnk/8213126.

Park City Present

Best Places to Get Business Done: Morning Edition

Atticus Coffee & Teahouse. Accessed June 20, 2025. https://www.atticustea.com/#.

Barnes & Noble. "The Book Store." Accessed June 20, 2025. https://www.barnesandnoble.com/b/books/_/N-29Z8q8.

Cupla Coffee. "Park City." Accessed June 20, 2025. https://cuplacoffee.com/locations/park-city-coffee-shop/.

Daily Rise Coffee. "Daily Rise Coffee Park City." Accessed June 20, 2025. https://dailyrisecoffee.com/pages/daily-rise-coffee-park-city.

Deer Valley. "Deer Valley Café." Accessed June 20, 2025. https://www.deervalley.com/things-to-do/restaurants/deer-valley-cafe.

Five5eeds. Accessed June 20, 2025. https://www.five5eeds.com/.

Hill's Kitchen. "Our Story." Accessed June 20, 2025. https://hills-kitchen.com/our-story/.

Hugo Coffee Park City Visitors Center. Accessed June 20, 2025. https://hugocoffeepcvisitorcenter.com/.

Lucky Ones Coffee. "About." Accessed June 20, 2025. https://www.luckyonescoffee.com/about.

Montage Deer Valley. "Buzz Cafe." Accessed June 20, 2025. https://www.montage.com/deervalley/dining/buzz/.

Park City Bread and Bagels. "Menu." Accessed June 20, 2025. https://pcbagelsutah.com/menu-1.

Park City Gardens. "Garden Cafe." Accessed June 20, 2025. https://www.parkcitynursery.com/garden-cafe.html.

Silver Star Café. "About Us." Accessed June 20, 2025. https://www.thesilverstarcafe.com/about-us.

Stein Eriksen Lodge. "First Tracks Kaffe." Accessed June 20, 2025. https://www.steinlodge.com/dining/first-tracks-kaffe.

Urban Sailor Coffee. "Home." Accessed April 15, 2026 https://urbansailorcoffee.com/

Please and Thank You: The J-1 Picture

Department of State. "Facts and Figures." Accessed June 20, 2025. https://j1visa.state.gov/basics/facts-and-figures/.

Higgins, Sean. "Seasonal resort employees are leaving. That means changes for PCMR and Deer Valley." *KPCW*, March 15, 2022. https://www.kpcw.org/park-city/2022-03-15/seasonal-resort-employees-are-leaving-that-means-changes-for-pcmr-and-deer-valley.

A Refuge from Billboards

"County Reaffirms Billboard Stance." *Park Record,* November 10, 1977. https://newspapers.lib.utah.edu/ark:/87278/s6p281wh/8214581.

O'Malley, Michael. "Cities of Kamas and Park City GRAMA requests." *Author's personal files*, 2024.

Supermarkets and Farmers Markets

Anaya's Market: Situated in Silver Creek, this is the place for Latin American foods and flavors. Good values in the bakery, meat department, and spice rack.

Copper Moose Farm. "Home." Accessed June 20, 2025. https://coppermoosefarm.com/.

Good Earth Markets. "Home." Accessed July 11, 2025. https://goodearthmarkets.com/

Iwasaki, Scott. "Park City Farmers Market relocates to First Time chair lift lot." Park Record, May 7, 2024. https://www.parkrecord.com/2024/05/07/park-city-farmers-market-relocates-to-first-time-chair-lift-lot/.

Tagge's Famous Fruit & Veggie Farms. Accessed June 20, 2025. https://www.taggesfruit.com/.

Co-working Spaces

Assemble Park City. "Home." Accessed June 20, 2025. https://assembleparkcity.com/.

Elevated. "Home." Accessed June 20, 2025. https://elevated1775.com/.

Kiln. Accessed June 20, 2025. https://kiln.com/.

Wright, J'Nel. "Mile Post: Rise of the remote worker." *Park Record*, September 25, 2021. https://www.parkrecord.com/2021/09/25/mile-post-rise-of-the-remote-worker/.

Garbage and Recycling

Momentum Recycling. "Park City Residential Glass Recycling Service." Momentum Recycling, January 7, 2025. https://utah.momentumrecycling.com/parkcity/#av_section_2.

O'Malley, Michael. "Notes from landfill tour sponsored by Recycle Utah." *Author's personal files*, September, 2024.

Recycle Utah. Accessed June 20, 2025. https://recycleutah.org/.

Republic Services. "Summit County, UT." Accessed June 20, 2025. https://www.republicservices.com/municipality/summit-county-ut.

Summit County Utah. "Summit County Landfills | Three Mile & Henefer Landfill Services." https://www.summitcounty.org/778/Summit-County-Landfills.

Thrift Stores and Other Bargain Hunting

Christian Center of Park City. "Park City Thrift Store." Accessed June 20, 2025. https://ccofpc.org/thrift-park-city/.

Christian Center of Park City. "Summit Exchange." Accessed June 20, 2025. https://ccofpc.org/summit-exchange/.

PC SKI SWAP. Accessed June 20, 2025. https://www.parkcityskiswap.com/.

Recycle Utah. Accessed June 20, 2025. https://recycleutah.org/.

ReStore Park City. "Park City Restore - Thrift Store & Boutique." Accessed June 20, 2025. https://parkcityrestore.com/.

Right at Home Designs. "Home." Accessed June 20, 2025. https://rightathomedesigns.com/.

St. Mary's Park City. "St. Lawrence Thrift Store." Accessed June 20, 2025. https://www.stmarysparkcity.com/st-lawrence-thrift-store.

9/11 and the Ecker Hill Flag

O'Malley, Michael. "Author's conversations with Scott Zuckerman of Kamas, Jim Ayers – formerly of Pinebrook and now in Alabama, and Mat Young of Pinebrook." *Author's personal files*, August, 2024.

Ski Town Life and Day-to-Day Stuff
How to Get Your Pass Pulled at the Ski Resorts
Summit County Utah. "Summit County Code." Accessed June 20, 2025. https://www.summitcountyutah.gov/2583/Summit-County-Code.

Non-profits
Internal Revenue Service. "Exempt Organizations Business Master File Extract (EO BMF)." Accessed June 20, 2025. https://www.irs.gov/charities-non-profits/exempt-organizations-business-master-file-extract-eo-bmf.
Park City Community Foundation. Accessed June 20, 2025. https://parkcitycf.org/.

Libraries (And The Miners Hospital Ghost)
Clyde, Tom. "Way We Were: The Tina Touch." *Park Record,* June 18, 2024. https://www.parkrecord.com/2024/06/18/way-we-were-the-tina-touch/.
McLaws, Chris. "Park City's first Hospital." *Park City Museum*, April 23, 2020. https://parkcityhistory.org/park-citys-first-hospital/.
Park City Library. Accessed June 20, 2025. https://parkcitylibrary.org/.
Salt Lake City Public Library. "Home." Accessed June 20, 2025. https://resources.slcpl.org/.
Summit County Library. "Homepage." Accessed June 20, 2025. https://www.thesummitcountylibrary.org/.

Really, Gas Fire Circles?
Kaplan, Sarah. "Covid-19 sparked a run on outdoor heaters and fire pits. Which is better for the planet?" *The Washington Post,* December 11, 2020. https://www.washingtonpost.com/climate-solutions/2020/12/11/climate-curious-heaters/.
Park Record Staff. "Spring Home 2024." *Park Record,* August 14, 2024. https://www.parkrecord.com/2024/03/15/spring-home-2024/.

Clam Chowder
Boston Harbor Marina. "Home." Accessed June 20, 2025. https://www.bostonharbormarina.com/.
Cove Olympia. "Home." Accessed June 20, 2025. https://www.coveolympia.com/.
Deer Valley. "The Sticky Wicket." Accessed June 20, 2025. https://www.deervalley.com/things-to-do/restaurants/the-sticky-wicket.
Facebook. "Ken's Place Seafood Restaurant." Accessed June 20, 2025. https://www.facebook.com/KensPlace1927/.
Gilbert's Chowder House. Accessed June 20, 2025. https://www.gilbertschowderhouse.com/.
Harmons Grocery. Accessed June 20, 2025. https://www.harmonsgrocery.com/.
The Bake Shop. Accessed June 20, 2025. https://www.thebakeshopparkcity.com/.

High-Altitude Baking

High Altitude Bakes. "High Altitude Baking." Accessed June 20, 2025. https://highaltitudebakes.com/high-altitude-baking/.

King Arthur Baking. "High-Altitude Baking." Accessed June 20, 2025. https://www.kingarthurbaking.com/learn/resources/high-altitude-baking.

The Bake Shop. Accessed June 20, 2025. https://www.thebakeshopparkcity.com/.

Avalanche Routes

Deer Valley Resort. "Have a Blast with Avalanche Mitigation at Deer Valley Resort." 2014. Video, 3 mins., 52 secs. https://www.youtube.com/watch?v=Q2RkwId31t8.

Wikipedia. "Pentaerythritol tetranitrate." Last modified June 9, 2025. https://en.wikipedia.org/wiki/Pentaerythritol_tetranitrate.

The Xbox Injury and KDS

O'Malley, Michael. "On-slope experience." *Author's personal files*, December 2017.

Snow Park Observations

Good Reads. "A quote from Tribe." Accessed June 20, 2025. https://www.goodreads.com/quotes/7717738-when-you-throw-trash-on-the-ground-you-apparently-don-t.

Hampshire, David. "Otto Carpenter: The Man Behind Snow Park." Park City Museum, April 3, 2024. https://parkcityhistory.org/otto-carpenter-the-man-behind-snow-park/.

Divine Guidance: Snowboards at Deer Valley?

Military Installation Development Authority. "Home." Accessed June 20, 2025. https://midaut.org/.

O'Malley, Michael. "Chairlift conversation with D. Uchtdorf." *Author's personal files*, March 2018.

Transportation

Parley's Canyon and I-80

Eyewitness. "America on the Move." Accessed June 20, 2025. https://www.archives.gov/exhibits/eyewitness/html.php?section=24.

Klein, Christopher. "The Epic Road Trip That Inspired the Interstate Highway System." *History*, June 29, 2016. https://www.history.com/articles/the-epic-road-trip-that-inspired-the-interstate-highway-system.

Strack, Don. "Summit County Railroad of 1871." *Utah* Rails, December 13, 2024. https://utahrails.net/utahrails/summit-county-rr-1871-1881.php.

Strack, Don. "The Golden Pass: A History of Transportation in Parleys Canyon, Utah." *Utah Rails*, April 17, 2025 https://utahrails.net/articles/parleys.php.

Weaver, Sydney. "Utah State study shows Summit County wildlife crossing success." *KPCW*, September 17, 2025. https://www.kpcw.org/summit-county/2025-09-17/utah-state-study-shows-summit-county-wildlife-crossing-success

Driving in Snow

Discount Tire. "How Do Winter Tires Work." Accessed April 11, 2026. https://www.discounttire.com/blog/how-do-snow-tires-work

Highway Patrol. "Driving Tips." Accessed June 20, 2025. https://highwaypatrol.utah.gov/winter-driving/driving-tips/.

Utah Motorsports Campus. "Home | Burt Brothers Motorpark." Accessed June 20, 2025. https://www.utahmotorsportscampus.com/.

Just What Are Those Trucks Hauling?

Associated Press. "Deadly semi-truck fire closes westbound I-80 at Parley's Canyon." *KUTV*, February 23, 2017. https://kutv.com/news/local/deadly-semi-truck-fire-closes-westbound-i-80-at-parleys-canyon.

Holst, Thomas. "Insight: Uinta Waxy Crude Oil Flows Out Of State, Spurring Possible Economic Growth In State" *KEM C. Gardner Policy Institute*, May 8, 2023. https://gardner.utah.edu/blog/blog-uinta-waxy-crude-oil-flows-out-of-state-spurring-possible-economic-growth-in-state/.

Maffly, Brian. "Disputed rail project seeking to ship eastern Utah oil to more lucrative markets clears hurdle with $21 million funding boost." *The Salt Lake Tribune*, June 13, 2019. https://www.sltrib.com/news/environment/2019/06/13/disputed-rail-project/.

TownLift. "Semi rollover on I-80 closes lanes and sends driver to hospital." *TownLift Park City News*, May 19, 2024. https://townlift.com/2024/05/semi-rollover-on-i-80-closes-lanes-and-sends-driver-to-hospital/.

Utah SGID. "Utah environmental incidents." Last Modified July 1, 2025. https://opendata.gis.utah.gov/datasets/892f7efacb8b4643b8e111a33d34a7f0_0/about.

Dodge Camper and Tesla Slalom

Ellis, Rich and Neighbors of Park City. "Park City struggles with labor shortages as housing costs soar." *TownLift, Park City News*, April 3, 2024. https://townlift.com/2024/04/park-city-grapples-with-labor-shortages-as-housing-costs-soar/.

A Prime Place to Get a Traffic Ticket
American Association of Motor Vehicle Administrators and Utah Driver License
    Division. "Utah Driver Handbook." 2023. https://dld.dev.utah.gov/wp-
    content/uploads/Driver-Handbook-V2-2023.pdf.
High Valley Transit. "The Bob: Bobsled Express." Accessed April 11, 2026. https://
    www.hvtutah.gov/sr224-brt
Summit County Utah. "Fine Schedule | Summit County Justice Court, Utah."
    Accessed June 20, 2025. https://www.summitcountyutah.gov/541/Fine-
    Schedule.

Stop Signs and Wheaton Way
GPS 40.624549, -111.493330

The Salt Lake City International Airport and Walkathon
"2026 Report: U.S. Airports With the Longest and Shortest Walking Distances."
    KURU Footwear, April 14, 2026. https://www.kurufootwear.com/blogs/
    articles/airport-walking-distances.
Fox News. "Salt Lake City International ranked in Top 10 worldwide for punctuality
    in 2025." Accessed April 11, 2026. https://www.fox13now.com/news/local-
    news/northern-utah/salt-lake-city-international-ranked-in-top-10-worldwide-
    for-punctuality-in-2025.
Larson, Andy and Paighten Harkins. "Why is it so expensive to fly out of SLC? More
    importantly, what can be done about it?" *Salt Lake Tribune*, April 7, 2026.
    https://www.sltrib.com/news/2026/04/07/salt-lake-city-airport-airfares/.
High Valley Transit. "Bus Routes." Accessed June 20, 2025. https://www.hvtutah.gov/
    bus-routes.
Utah Transit Authority. "Schedules and Maps." Accessed June 20, 2025. https://www.
    rideuta.com/rider-tools/schedules-and-maps.

Civics and Politics

Schools
Herinkova, Eva. "Trailside Elementary ranks 10th in state." *Park Record*, December 10,
    2024. https://www.parkrecord.com/2024/12/09/trailside-elementary-ranks-
    10th-in-state/.
Park City Education Foundation. "Home." Accessed June 20, 2025. https://pcef4kids.
    org/.
Spiewak, Jim. "Lawmakers tighten rules after year one in education voucher program."
    KUTV, June 4, 2025. https://kutv.com/news/local/lawmakers-tighten-rules-
    after-year-one-in-education-voucher-program.

Weller, Kristine. "New 'report card' shows Park City students perform better than state averages." *KPCW,* October 9, 2024. https://www.kpcw.org/park-city-school-district/2024-10-08/new-report-card-shows-park-city-students-perform-better-than-state-averages.

Weller, Kristine. "Why Park City third graders have the best literacy rates in the state." *KPCW*, January 8, 2026. https://www.kpcw.org/park-city-school-district/2026-01-08/why-park-city-third-graders-have-the-best-literacy-rates-in-the-state.

Williams, Jenna and Taylor Throne. "Tracking Utah's K-12 education funding." *Voices for Utah Children*, October 1, 2024. https://utahchildren.org/newsroom/speaking-of-kids-blog/tracking-utahs-k-12-education-funding.

U.S. News and World Report. "U.S. News Best High Schools Rankings." Accessed April 28, 2026. https://www.usnews.com/education/best-high-schools/rankings-overview.

Crime

CrimeGrade.org. "The Safest and Most Dangerous Places in Summit County, UT: Crime Maps and Statistics." Accessed April 11, 2065. https://crimegrade.org/safest-places-in-summit-county-ut/.

"NHTSA: Utah's .05% law shows promise to save lives, improve road safety." *NHTSA*, February 11, 2022. https://www.nhtsa.gov/press-releases/utah-lower-impaired-driving-law-study.

Weller, Kristine. "Summit County underage drinking rates more than double Utah average." *KPCW*, January 27, 2024. https://www.kpcw.org/summit-county/2024-01-27/summit-county-underage-drinking-rates-more-than-double-utah-average.

Werner, Dave. "Utah's 05 BAC law reduces crashes." *Adirondack Daily Enterprise*, December 10, 2023. https://www.adirondackdailyenterprise.com/opinion/columns/safety-on-the-roads-by-dave-werner/2023/12/utahs-05-bac-law-reduces-crashes/.

Park City Mayors

Gendron, Jane. "Meet Nann Worel, the first woman to lead Park City." *Park City Magazine,* February 22, 2024. https://www.parkcitymag.com/news-and-profiles/2022/06/madame-mayor.

Gill, Tony. "Former Park City Mayor Andy Beerman Looks Back." *Salt Lake Magazine*, September 15, 2022. https://www.saltlakemagazine.com/park-city-mayor-andy-beerman/.

Hamburger, Jay. "Dana Williams, a 'real town' mayor, retires after 12 years." *Park Record,* December 31, 2013. https://www.parkrecord.com/2013/12/31/dana-williams-a-real-town-mayor-retires-after-12-years/.

Hamburger, Jay. "Former mayor recalls 'crazy exciting' award of Winter Olympics of 2002." *Park Record*, July 23, 2024. https://www.parkrecord.com/2024/07/23/former-mayor-recalls-crazy-exciting-award-of-winter-olympics-of-2002/.

Hamburger, Jay. "Park City's outgoing mayor acknowledges he accumulated 'enemies' while in office." *Park Record*, May 13, 2024. https://www.parkrecord.com/2021/12/31/park-citys-outgoing-mayor-acknowledges-he-accumulated-enemies-while-in-office/.

Hamburger, Jay. "Williams versus Olch, nuff said." *Park Record,* October 31, 2009. https://www.parkrecord.com/2009/10/30/williams-versus-olch-nuff-said/.

Jackson, Laura. "Park City picks – former Mayor Dana Williams' insider guide." *Mountain*, May 13, 2024. https://mountainparkcity.com/park-city-picks-former-mayor-dana-williams-insider-guide/.

Weller, Kristine. "Park City's new mayor Ryan Dickey to prioritize Bonanza Park, SR-248 projects." *KPCW*, November 29, 2026. https://www.kpcw.org/park-city/2025-11-28/park-citys-new-mayor-ryan-dickey-to-prioritize-bonanza-park-sr-248-projects.

Taxation and Budgets

Bergeson, Heather. "Summit County council approves nine-figure budget for 2026." *Townlift*, December 16, 2025. https://townlift.com/2025/12/summit-county-council-approves-nine-figure-budget-for-2026/.

Doefler, Grace. "Heber accepts tentative $87 million budget; tax hike not expected." KPCW, May, 7, 2025. https://www.kpcw.org/heber-city/2025-05-07/heber-accepts-tentative-87-million-budget-tax-hike-not-expected.

Hatcher, Clara. "Wasatch County finalizes, adopts 2026 budget." *Park Record,* December 19, 2025. https://www.parkrecord.com/2025/12/19/wasatch-county-finalizes-adopts-2026-budget/.

Maletesta, Parker. "Park City Council approves $98 million budget." *KPCW,* June 13, 2025. https://www.kpcw.org/park-city/2025-06-13/park-city-council-approves-98-million-budget.

United States Census Bureau QuickFacts. "Wasatch County, Utah. Census Bureau QuickFacts." https://www.census.gov/quickfacts/fact/table/wasatchcountyutah/PST045224.

"Utah Code Title 59, Chapter 12 - Sales & Use Tax Act: Combined Sales And Use Tax Rates" *State of Utah*, 2025. https://files.tax.utah.gov/tax/salestax/rate/26q2combined.pdf.

Utah State Tax Commission. "Utah State Tax Commission: Annual Report 2021-2022." *Utah State Tax Commission*, 2022. https://tax.utah.gov/commission/reports/fy22report.pdf.

Walczak, Jared, Andrey Yushkov, and Katherine Loughead. "2025 State Business Tax Climate Index." *Tax Foundation*, October 31, 2024. https://taxfoundation. org/research/all/state/2025-state-tax-competitiveness-index/.

Gerrymandering – A Liberal's Lament

McKellar, Katie. "Another Utah Senate district topples as signature removals continue in failed Prop 4 repeal." *Utah News Dispatch*, April 8, 2026. https:// utahnewsdispatch.com/2026/04/08/senate-district-falls-signature-removals-continue-in-failed-prop-4-repeal/.

Seariac, Hanna. "The Utah Supreme Court rules on Amendment D, votes will not be counted." *Deseret News*, September 26, 2024. https://www.deseret.com/ politics/2024/09/25/amendment-d-ruling.

Stern, Emily A. "Utah trolled with 4,000 hoax reports of trans bathroom ban violations within days of reporting form launch." *The Salt Lake Tribune*, May 6, 2024. https://www.sltrib.com/news/politics/2024/05/03/utah-trolled-with-4000-hoax/.

The News Fix

Deseret News. Accessed June 20, 2025. https://www.deseret.com/.

KPCW. "Local News." Accessed June 20, 2025. https://www.kpcw.org/local-news.

Malatesta, Parker. "Park City Television shutting down after 35 years." *KPCW*, November 29, 2022. https://www.kpcw.org/park-city/2022-11-28/park-city-television-shutting-down-after-35-years.

Park Record. Accessed June 20, 2025. https://www.parkrecord.com/.

The Salt Lake Tribune. Accessed June 20, 2025. https://www.sltrib.com/.

TownLift. "TownLift Park City News." Accessed June 20, 2025. https://townlift.com/.

Wealth and Real Estate in Park City

Air Quality and Where to Live

Carleson Ringholz, Raye. *Diggings and Doings in Park City*. University of Utah Press, 1972.

The Skiing/Real Estate Interface

Deer Crest Master Association. "Home Page." Accessed June 20, 2025. https://www. deercrest.com/.

Extell Development. "Deer Valley East Village." Accessed June 20, 2025. https://extell. com/portfolio/deer-valley-east-village.

The Colony Homeowners Association. "Home." Accessed June 20, 2025. https:// thecolonyhoa.org/.

The Four Seasons

Evan Bennet. "Four Seasons ~ Vivaldi." 2011. Video, 41 mins., 59 secs. https://www. youtube.com/watch?v=GRxofEmo3HA.

Subsidence Versus Sinkhole

Park City Board of Realtors. Accessed June 20, 2025. https://parkcityrealtors.com/.

Park City Museum. "Daly West Mine." Accessed June 20, 2025. https:// parkcityhistory.org/mining/daly-west-mine/

The Time to Wealth Disclosure with a Side Helping of Diversity

O'Malley, Michael. "Conversation on chairlift." *Author's personal files*, March 2025.

NIMBY and BANANA and CAVE

Rogers, Don. "Park City to burn slash piles on Treasure Hill." *Park Record,* November 14, 2023. https://www.parkrecord.com/2023/11/13/park-city-to-burn-slash-piles-on-treasure-hill/.

Water and Weather

Where Does Our Water Come From?

Bloch, Emily. "Why Is Everyone Suddenly Obsessed With Dirty Sodas?" *Bon Appétit,* September 27, 2024. https://www.bonappetit.com/story/what-is-dirty-soda?s rsltid=AfmBOoo9tTaieSM07OQ2erXFYD557SW6FMWuCxYHwg2jGdiM cbLOnwkW.

Coleman, Christine. "Park City Community Foundation Launches Food Waste Collection Program as Part of Its Zero Food Waste Initiative for Summit County." *Park City Community Foundation*, June 3, 2024. https://parkcitycf. org/zero-food-waste-launch/.

Engage Park City. "The future of Empire Creek." Accessed June 20, 2025. https:// engageparkcity.org/empire-creek.

Noble Predictive Insights. "Utah Pulse Check: Voters take legislative temperature." *Noble Predictive*, March 21, 2025. https://www.noblepredictiveinsights.com/ post/utah-pulse-check-voters-take-legislative-temperature.

Park City. "Water Division." Accessed June 20, 2025. https://www.parkcity.org/ departments/public-utilities/water-division

Snyderville Basin Water Reclamation District. "Annual Comprehensive Financial Report." Accessed June 20, 2025. https://www.sbwrd.org/financial/reports/.

Snyderville Basin Water Reclamation District. "Service Area." Accessed June 20, 2025. https://www.sbwrd.org/wp-content/uploads/2017/03/ServiceArea.pdf.

Summit Water Distribution Company. "About." Accessed June 20, 2025. https://www. summitwater.us/about/.

Utah State Legislature. "H.B. 81 Fluoride Amendments." 2025. https://le.utah.
gov/~2025/bills/static/HB0081.html.

The Mighty Weber
"DWR makes changes at Weber River tubing spot." *Utah Division of Wildlife Resources*,
May 20, 2024. https://wildlife.utah.gov/news/utah-wildlife-news/1904-dwr-
makes-changes-at-weber-river-tubing-spot.html.

Jordanelle Reservoir
Utah State Parks. "Jordanelle State Park." Accessed June 20, 2025. https://stateparks.
utah.gov/parks/jordanelle/.

Lake Effect, Pineapple Express, and the Powder Buoy
Jim Steenburgh. "Home Page." Accessed June 20, 2025. https://www.inscc.utah.
edu/~steenburgh/home/.
Milligan, Mark. "Glad you asked: Utah's Hydrologic Cycle." *Utah Geological Survey*,
August 10, 2023. https://geology.utah.gov/map-pub/survey-notes/glad-you-
asked/utahs-hydrologic-cycle/.
Powder Buoy. "About." Accessed June 20, 2025. https://powderbuoy.com/about/.

Aspens in the Fall
Grant, Michael and Jeffry Mitton "Case study: The Glorious, Golden, and Gigantic
Quaking Aspen." *Nature Education Knowledge* 3, no. 10 (2010). https://www.
nature.com/scitable/knowledge/library/case-study-the-glorious-golden-and-
gigantic-13261308/.
Jones, John R., and Norbert V. DeByle. "Other physical factors." *US Forest
Service Research and Development*, 1985. https://research.fs.usda.gov/
treesearch/27784.
Utah State University. "Quaking Aspen." Accessed June 20, 2025. https://extension.
usu.edu/rangeplants/shrubs-and-trees/aspen-quaking.
Wikipedia. "Pando (tree)." Last modified June 13, 2025. https://en.wikipedia.org/
wiki/Pando_(tree).

Wait, What? They Can Make Snow Above Freezing?
Backyard Snowstorm. " Snowmaking Weather Chart." Accessed June 20, 2025.
https://backyardsnowstorm.com/snowmaking-weather-chart/.
Weather.gov. "Temperature - Dry Bulb/Web Bulb/Dew Point." Accessed June 20,
2025. https://www.weather.gov/source/zhu/ZHU_Training_Page/definitions/
dry_wet_bulb_definition/dry_wet_bulb.html.

The Risk of Wildfire

Bergeson, Heather. "Utah adjusts wildfire preparedness program, delays homeowner fee to 2027." *Townlift.* March 16, 2026. https://townlift.com/2026/03/utah-adjusts-wildfire-preparedness-program-delays-homeowner-fee-to-2027/.

Mountainland Association of Governments. "PRE-DISASTER MITIGATION PLAN for Summit, Utah, and Wasatch counties." 2022. https://hazards.utah.gov/wp-content/uploads/2022-Pre-Disaster-Mitigation-Plan-for-Summit-Utah-and-Wasatch-Counties.pdf.

Qiu, Minghao, Jessica Li, Carlos F. Gould, et al. "Mortality Burden From Wildfire Smoke Under Climate Change." *National Bureau Of Economic Research*, April 2024. https://doi.org/10.3386/w32307.

Thomas, Connor. "Final report: Logging accident sparked Wasatch Back's Yellow Lake Fire." *KPCW*, January 9, 2025. https://www.kpcw.org/state-regional/2025-01-09/final-report-logging-accident-sparked-wasatch-backs-yellow-lake-fire.

Wildfire Risk to Communities. "Wildfire risk in Utah." Accessed June 20, 2025. https://wildfirerisk.org/explore/overview/49.

Recreation, Your Health and Wellbeing at High Altitude

Ten Seconds of Kindness: Trail Etiquette

Mountain Trails Foundation. "About Us." Accessed June 20, 2025. https://mountaintrails.org/mission/.

U.S. National Park Service. "Hiking etiquette." Accessed June 20, 2025. https://www.nps.gov/articles/hikingetiquette.htm.

Volmrich, Jeff. "10 Seconds of Kindness - with Charlie Sturgis - ATBS #34." *All Things Big and Small*. Audio, 46 mins., 9 secs. 2020. https://redcircle.com/shows/ac556e39-2f3e-4711-b354-ffb69de5e9e9/ep/19d9b034-694b-440b-8ff4-e22cdac0539f

Paddleboarding and Mussels

"Boating this summer? Take the mandatory course, pay fee to prevent spread of aquatic invasive species." *Utah Division of Wildlife Resources*, April 5, 2024. https://wildlife.utah.gov/news/utah-wildlife-news/1864-boating-this-summer-take-the-mandatory-course-and-pay-fee-to-prevent-spread-of-aquatic-invasive-species.html.

Utah Division of Outdoor Recreation. "Boating Education." *Utah Outdoor Recreation*, February 1, 2025. https://recreation.utah.gov/boating/boating-education.

Mountain Biking and Other Mayhem

Advanced Solutions International, Inc. "Industry Stats." Accessed June 20, 2025. https://www.nsaa.org/NSAA/Media/Industry_Stats.aspx.

Boltz, Adrian J., Aliza K. Nedimyer, Avinash Chandran, Hannah J. Robison, Christy L. Collins, Sarah N. Morris. "Epidemiology of Injuries in National Collegiate Athletic Association Men's Ice Hockey: 2014–2015 Through 2018–2019." *NIH National Library of Medicine*, July 2021. https://pmc.ncbi.nlm.nih.gov/articles/PMC8293892/.

Carmont, Michael R. "Mountain bike Injuries?: An Overview. In Springer." *Sports Injuries,* 2014. https://doi.org/10.1007/978-3-642-36801-1_217-1.

Evans, Margaret. "Head First - Horse Riding Accidents And Concussions." *Horse Journals*, September 14, 2023. Horse Journals. https://www.horsejournals.com/life-horses/head-first-horse-riding-accidents-and-concussions.

Forrester, Mathias B. "Pickleball-Related Injuries Treated In Emergency Departments." *Journal of Emergency Medicine* 58, no. 2 (2019). https://doi.org/10.1016/j.jemermed.2019.09.016.

Fowler, Helsel, Vogt. "Skiing vs. Snowboarding: Which Sport Causes More Injuries?" Fowler | Helsel | Vogt. October 26, 2023. https://www.fhvlaw.com/blog/2023/october/skiing-vs-snowboarding-a-comparative-study-of-wi/.

Health Research Funding. "19 Important Bungee Jumping Death Statistics." Accessed June 20, 2025. https://healthresearchfunding.org/19-important-bungee-jumping-death-statistics/.

Kekelekis, Afxentios, Zoe Kounali, Nikolaos Kofotolis, Filipe Manuel Clemente, and Eleftherios Kellis. "Epidemiology of Injuries in Amateur Male Soccer Players: A Prospective One-Year Study." *Healthcare* 11, no. 3 (2023). https://doi.org/10.3390/healthcare11030352.

NSC. "Skateboarding Safety." 2024. https://www.nsc.org/community-safety/safety-topics/child-safety/skateboarding-safety?srsltid=AfmBOopySPB9d3vk55Sr4QtmeTePmPOMmqVkKVpmzVpzvKvhJ4HkdXvU.

NSC Injury Facts. "Sports and Recreational Injuries." 2024. https://injuryfacts.nsc.org/home-and-community/safety-topics/sports-and-recreational-injuries/.

Skydive California. "How Safe is Skydiving?" Accessed June 20, 2025. https://skydivecalifornia.com/blog/skydiving-statistics/#:~:text=Skydiving%20is%20an%20inherently%20risky,1%20fatality%20in%20200%2C000%20jumps.

Weisenthal, Benjamin M., Christopher A. Beck, Michael D. Maloney, Kenneth E. DeHaven, and Brian D. Giordano,. "Injury rate and patterns among CrossFit athletes." *Orthopaedic Journal of Sports Medicine* 2, no. 4 (2014). https://doi.org/10.1177/2325967114531177.

Wikipedia. "Fire-fighting sport." Last modified March 23, 2025. https://en.wikipedia.org/wiki/Fire-fighting_sport.

E-Biking on Streets and Singletrack Trails

American Association of Motor Vehicle Administrators. "UTAH DRIVER HANDBOOK." 2023. https://dld.dev.utah.gov/wp-content/uploads/Driver-Handbook-V2-2023.pdf.

Bergeson, Heather. "E-motorcycle crackdown coming to Summit County as new Utah law takes effect May 6." *Townlift*, April 6, 2026. https://townlift. com/2026/04/sheriffs-office-warns-of-increased-enforcement-after-new-e-motorcycle-law-passes-in-utah/.

Herink, Petr. "Summit Bike Share provided more than 23,000 rides in 2025." *Park Record*, January 16, 2026. https://www.parkrecord.com/2026/01/16/summit-bike-share-provided-more-than-23000-rides-in-2025/.

Malatesta, Parker. "Park City sticking with existing e-bike singletrack ordinance." *KPCW*, May 24, 2024. https://www.kpcw.org/park-city/2024-05-24/park-city-sticking-with-existing-e-bike-singletrack-ordinance.

Manson, Pamela. "Speed limit set for bikes on trails as a safety measure." *Park Record*, August 6, 2024. https://www.parkrecord.com/news/speed-limit-set-for-bikes-on-trails-as-a-safety-measure/.

Thomas, Connor. "Slow your roll: 15 mph limit on Snyderville Basin bike paths, too." *KPCW*, July 12, 2024. https://www.kpcw.org/summit-county/2024-07-11/slow-your-roll-15-mph-limit-on-snyderville-basin-bike-paths-too.

Utah State Legislature. "Utah Code Section 41-6A-1115.5." Accessed June 20, 2025. https://le.utah.gov/xcode/Title41/Chapter6A/41-6a-S1115.5.html#:~:text=(4),(7).

Weller, Kristine. "Park City students can learn about e-bike safety, earn certificate before law changes." April, 20, 2026. https://www.kpcw.org/summit-county/2026-04-20/park-city-students-can-learn-about-e-bike-safety-at-an-afterschool-course-april-27.

Zukowski, Dan. "Electric scooter and e-bike injuries have soared since 2017, study says." Smart Cities Dive, July 29, 2024. https://www.smartcitiesdive.com/news/ebike-electric-scooter-micromobility-injuries-soared-since-2017-ucsf-study/722610/.

The Rail Trail

"From Echo To Park City: The story of Union Pacific Park City Branch." *UtahRails. net*, April 23, 2025. https://utahrails.net/articles/up-park-city.php.

Bonanza Flat

Gorlinski, Robert. "Mining Claim Map - Gorlinski_s_general_map_of_Park_City_mines.pdf." *Park City Museum,* 1900.

Malatesta, Parker. "Paid parking coming to Bonanza Flat trailheads this summer." *KPCW*, February 10, 2025. https://www.kpcw.org/park-city/2025-02-07/paid-parking-coming-to-bonanza-flat-trailheads-this-summer.

Utah Open Lands. "Bonanza Flat Conservation Area." Accessed June 20, 2025. https://www.utahopenlands.org/landscapelandingpage-bonanzaflat.

Wikipedia. "Henry H. Blood." Last modified July 30, 2024. https://en.wikipedia.org/wiki/Henry_H._Blood.

The Atmosphere, Altitude Sickness, and Team Melanoma

Alberty, Erin. "Utah's melanoma rate tops the nation." *Axios Salt Lake City*, July 25, 2023. https://www.axios.com/local/salt-lake-city/2023/07/05/utah-skin-cancer-rate-ranks-highest-cdc.

American Cancer Society. "Cancer Facts & Figures 2023." 2024. https://www.cancer.org/research/cancer-facts-statistics/all-cancer-facts-figures/2023-cancer-facts-figures.html.

Hypoxico. "Altitude to Oxygen chart." Accessed June 20, 2025. https://hypoxico.com/pages/altitude-to-oxygen-chart.

Stein Eriksen Lodge. "U.S. Best Ski Hotel." Accessed June 20, 2025. https://www.steinlodge.com/blog/wsa-2021.

"U.S. Standard Atmosphere: Temperature, Pressure, and Air Properties vs. Altitude." *The Engineering Toolbox*, March 27, 2025. https://www.engineeringtoolbox.com/standard-atmosphere-d_604.html.

Hospitals, Clinics, and Senior Care

Coalville & Kamas Health Centers. "About Us." Accessed June 20, 2025. https://ckdocs.com/index.php/about-us/mission-statement.

Intermountain Health. Park City Hospital. Accessed June 20, 2025. https://web-ih-sc-prd-hdl-wus2.azurewebsites.net/locations/park-city-hospital.

Intermountain Health. "Park City InstaCare." Accessed June 20, 2025. https://web-ih-sc-prd-hdl-wus2.azurewebsites.net/locations/park-city-instacare.

Park City Senior Citizens. "About." Accessed June 20, 2025. https://parkcityseniors.org/about/.

Peoples Health Clinic. "About Us." Accessed June 20, 2025. https://peopleshealthclinic.org/about-us/#mission.

Redstone Health Center. "Redstone Health Center (Park City)." Accessed June 20, 2025. https://healthcare.utah.edu/locations/redstone-park-city.

STAT+MD Urgent Care. "STAT+MD Urgent Care Park City Utah." Accessed June 20, 2025. https://statmdurgentcare.com/location/park-city/.

Thomas, Connor. "Summit County life expectancy, overall health exceeds state average." *KPCW*, August 2, 2024. https://www.kpcw.org/summit-county/2024-08-02/summit-county-life-expectancy-overall-health-exceeds-state-average.

Gyms, Spas, and Sports Programs

Basin Recreation. "Open Play." Accessed June 20, 2025. https://basinrecreation.org/the-fieldhouse/open-play/.

Basin Recreation. "The Fieldhouse." Accessed June 20, 2025. https://www.basinrecreation.org/the-fieldhouse/.

F45 Training. "F45 Park City." Accessed June 20, 2025. https://f45training.com/studio/parkcity/.

Hotel Park City. "Spas in Park City." Accessed June 20, 2025. https://www.
    hotelparkcity.com/spa.html.
Marriot. "The St. Regis Deer Valley." Accessed June 20, 2025. https://www.marriott.
    com/en-us/hotels/slcxr-the-st-regis-deer-valley/spa/.
Montage Dear Valley. "Spa Montage Dear Valley." Accessed June 20, 2025. https://
    www.montage.com/deervalley/spa/.
Orangetheory Fitness. "Park City, UT." Accessed June 20, 2025. https://www.
    orangetheory.com/en-us/locations/utah/park-city/1678-west-redstone-center-
    drive
Park City Boxing Club. "Home." Accessed June 20, 2025. https://parkcityboxing.
    com/.
Park City. "Park City MARC & Recreation." Accessed June 20, 2025. https://www.
    parkcity.org/departments/park-city-marc-recreation-home.
Pure Barre. "Pure Barre Park City." Accessed June 20, 2025. https://www.purebarre.
    com/location/park-city-ut.
Silver Mountain Sports Club & Spa. "Home." Accessed June 20, 2025. https://www.
    silvermountainspa.com/#new-page.
Stein Eriksen Lodge. "The Spa at Stein Eriksen Lodge." Accessed June 20, 2025.
    https://www.steinlodge.com/spa/.
Yuldoshboev, Shakhzod. "Healthy hotspots: 25 most physically active counties in
    the U.S. Northwell Health Newsroom." October 23, 2023. https://www.
    northwell.edu/news/the-latest/25-most-physically-active-counties-in-us.

Avoiding Organ Recitals
O'Malley, Michael. "Conversations with Harry B. Richardson." *Author's personal files*,
    March 2024.

Churches and Liquor
Churches, Synagogues, and Other Places of Worship
Chabad Lubavitch of Park City. "About." Accessed June 20, 2025. https://www.
    jewishparkcity.com/templates/articlecco_cdo/aid/1971250/jewish/About.
    htm.
St. Mary's Catholic Church Park City. "Home." Accessed June 20, 2025. https://www.
    stmarysparkcity.com/.
Temple Har Shalom. "Welcome." Accessed June 20, 2025. https://www.
    harshalomparkcity.org/.
Tischner, D.J. "The LEAST MORMON counties in Utah are. . ." *Cat Country 107.3
    and 94.9*, April 6, 2024. https://catcountryutah.com/the-least-mormon-
    counties-in-utah-are/.
The Church of Jesus Christ of Latter-day Saints. "Ward." Modified May 3, 2011.
    https://newsroom.churchofjesuschrist.org/article/ward#.

Utah Islamic Center. "Home." Accessed June 20, 2025. https://utislamiccenter.org/.

Utah Liquor Laws and the Pricing Gambit

"Dept. of Alcoholic Beverage Services 2025 Annual Report." *DABS*, June 30, 2025. https://abs.utah.gov/wp-content/uploads/90th_Annual_Report_2025.pdf.

Sullivan, Jack. "Brigham Young and 'Valley Tan' Whiskey." https://pre-prowhiskeymen.blogspot.com/2016/08/brigham-young-and-valley-tan-whiskey_18.html.

Pints for the People

Cider Guide. "Utah Cider Map & Directory." Accessed June 20, 2025. https://ciderguide.com/cider-maps/united-states/utah-cider-map-directory/.

Hamburger, Jay. "Park City-area man indicted in fraud case centered on brewery investments." *Park Record,* May 12, 2024. https://www.parkrecord.com/2020/09/04/park-city-area-man-indicted-in-fraud-case-centered-on-brewery-investments/.

Knight, Marina. "Fire up the shots: Park City challenged as Breck takes back shot ski World Record." *TownLift, Park City News*, December 20, 2024. https://townlift.com/2024/12/fire-up-the-shots-park-city-challenged-as-breck-takes-back-shot-ski-world-record.

Leonard, Collin. "Park City man who defrauded investors of $1.7M in brewery scheme is sent to prison." *KSL.com*, July 12, 2024. https://www.ksl.com/article/51066693/park-city-man-who-defrauded-investors-of-17m-in-brewery-scheme-is-sent-to-prison.

U.S. Securities and Exchange Commission. "Mine Shaft Brewing, LLC et al." Accessed June 20, 2025. https://www.sec.gov/enforcement-litigation/litigation-releases/lr-25149.

Weaver, Sydney. "Canadian ski area breaks shot ski record." *KPCW*, April 11, 2025. https://www.kpcw.org/state-regional/2025-04-11/canadian-ski-area-breaks-shot-ski-record.

Weller, Kristine. "Park City locals and visitors reclaim shot ski world record — for now." *KPCW*, October 12, 2025. https://www.kpcw.org/park-city/2025-10-11/park-city-locals-and-visitors-reclaim-shot-ski-world-record-for-now.

Critters

Bark City

Morgan, Ryan. "Only in Boulder: A home for pet 'guardians.'" *Colorado Daily*, July 31, 2009. https://www.coloradodaily.com/2009/07/31/only-in-boulder-a-home-for-pet-guardians/.

O'Malley, Michael. "Summit County Animal Control GRAMA request." *Author's personal files.* 2024.

Summit Park Homeowners Association. "Pets." Accessed June 20, 2025. https://summitparkutah.net/wp-content/uploads/2022/12/Pets.pdf.

World Population Review. "Dog Ownership by Country." Accessed June 20, 2025. https://worldpopulationreview.com/country-rankings/dog-ownership-by-country.

Wyman, Rich. "Dog Park Debate – Letter to the Editor." *Park Record*, April 18, 2007. https://newspapers.lib.utah.edu/ark:/87278/s6n9106k/22586636.

Moose, Elk, and the Occasional Bear

Iyah SGID. "Utah Moose Habitat." Accessed June 20, 2025. https://opendata.gis.utah.gov/datasets/e66c061ebd4346e3b16ed8786f5d5d78_0/explore?location=39.016863%2C-111.927692%2C-1.00.

U.S. National Park Service. "Staying Safe Around Bears." Accessed June 20, 2025. https://www.nps.gov/subjects/bears/safety.htm.

"Utah Wildlife Board approves 2024 big game hunting permits, changes to shed antler gathering." *Utah Division of Wildlife Resources*, May 3, 2024. https://wildlife.utah.gov/news/utah-wildlife-news/1882-wildlife-board-approves-2024-big-game-hunting-permits-and-changes-to-shed-antler-gathering.html.

Wild Aware Utah. "Elk." Accessed June 20, 2025. https://www.wildawareutah.org/wildlife/elk/.

Rattlesnakes and Ticks in Park City?

Davis, Ryan S. and Ricardo A. Ramirez. "Ticks and Tickborne Diseases of Utah: What you should know." *Utah State University Extension and Utah Plant Pest Diagnostic Laboratory*, 2017. https://epi.utah.gov/wp-content/uploads/Ticks-and-Tickborne-Diseases-of-Utah.pdf.

Gustman, Meredith. "Sharing your yard: snakes." *TownLift, Park City News*, April 30, 2021. https://townlift.com/2021/04/sharing-your-yard-snakes/.

Mayo Clinic. "Poison Ivy Rash." Accessed June 20, 2025. https://www.mayoclinic.org/diseases-conditions/poison-ivy/diagnosis-treatment/drc-20376490.

Sonoma Ecology Center. "The Real Numbers On Rattlesnake Bites." May 10, 2019. https://sonomaecologycenter.org/the-real-numbers-on-rattlesnake-bites/.

Thomas, Connor. "Ticks reemerge as warm weather arrives in Summit County." *KPCW*, May 30, 2024. https://www.kpcw.org/summit-county/2024-05-30/ticks-reemerge-as-warm-weather-arrives-in-summit-county.

University of Utah Health. "Poison Ivy. Poison Control." August 30, 2021. https://poisoncontrol.utah.edu/plant-guide/poison-ivy.

Utah Department of Health and Human Services, Utah Public Health Lab, Division of Wildlife Resources, et al. "Tick surveillance annual report 2022." Utah Department of Health and Human Services, 2022. https://epi.health.utah.

gov/wp-content/uploads/DHHS_TickSurveillanceReport_FINAL.pdf.

Sandhill Cranes, Magpies, and Mountain Bluebirds
All About Birds. "Mountain Bluebird." Cornell Lab of Ornithology. Accessed June 20, 2025. https://www.allaboutbirds.org/guide/Mountain_Bluebird/.
All About Birds. "Sandhill Crane." Cornell Lab of Ornithology. Accessed June 20, 2025. https://www.allaboutbirds.org/guide/Sandhill_Crane/overview.
Journals of the Lewis and Clark Expedition. "September 17, 1804." Accessed June 20, 2025. https://lewisandclarkjournals.unl.edu/item/lc.jrn.1804-09-17.
Lyric Wild Bird Food. "The Thieving Black-billed Magpie." Accessed June 20, 2025. https://www.lyricbirdfood.com/birding-hub/behavior/the-thieving-black-billed-magpie/.
O'Malley, Michael. "Recollections of one of Deer Valley's first female ski instructors." *Park City Museum*, February 28, 2024. https://parkcityhistory.org/recollections-of-one-of-deer-valleys-first-female-ski-instructors/.
Thomas Jefferson's Monticello. "From the Trail to Monticello." Accessed June 20, 2025. https://www.monticello.org/thomas-jefferson/louisiana-lewis-clark/framing-the-west-at-monticello/from-the-trail-to-monticello/.
Utah State University | Swaner Preserve & EcoCenter. "Live Pressure Webcam." Accessed June 20, 2025. https://extension.usu.edu/swaner/webcam.

Beaver Believers
Park Record Staff. "Dead beavers raise concern for tularemia awareness." *Park Record*, April 15, 2024. https://www.parkrecord.com/2024/04/15/dead-beavers-raise-concern-for-tularemia-awareness/.
Wikipedia. "Beaver." Last modified May 22, 2025. https://en.wikipedia.org/wiki/Beaver.

Marmots, Potguts, and Ermine
Animal Diversity Web. "Mustela erminea (ermine)." Accessed June 20, 2025. https://animaldiversity.org/accounts/Mustela_erminea/.
UPR Wild About Utah. "The Shape of Wildlife in Winter." January 26, 2012. https://wildaboututah.org/tag/ermine/.
Utah Conservation Data Center. "Utah Natural Heritage Program." Accessed June 20, 2025. https://fieldguide.wildlife.utah.gov/?species=mustela%20erminea.
Wikipedia. "Marmot." Last modified June 2, 2025. https://en.wikipedia.org/wiki/Marmot.
Wikipedia. "Uinta ground squirrel." Last modified June 5, 2025. https://en.wikipedia.org/wiki/Uinta_ground_squirrel.

Wildlife Bridges and Underpasses

Bissonette, John A., Christine A. Kassar, and Lawrence J. Cook. University of Nebraska - Lincoln. "Assessment of costs associated with deer–vehicle collisions: human death and injury, vehicle damage, and deer loss." *Human–Wildlife Interactions* 61 (2008). https://digitalcommons.unl.edu/cgi/viewcontent.cgi?article=1060&context=hwi.

Siu, Wai. Y., "Wildlife Crossing Ahead: Costs And Benefits Of Avoided Collisions." The Center for Growth and Opportunity at Utah State University, 2023. https://www.thecgo.org/research/wildlife-crossing-ahead-costs-and-benefits-of-avoided-collisions/.

UDOT. "Traffic Statistics." Accessed June 20, 2025. https://www.udot.utah.gov/connect/business/traffic-data/traffic-statistics/.

Utah Wildlife Migration Initiative. "Crossing Structures." April 10, 2024. https://wildlifemigration.utah.gov/land-animals/crossing.

Art, Music, Film, Museums, and Things You Have to See to Believe
Public Art and Art by the Public

Hughes, Locke. "Take a Self-Guided Tour of Park City's Public Art Works." Visit Park City. September 26, 2023. https://www.visitparkcity.com/blog/stories/post/take-a-self-guided-tour-of-park-citys-public-art-works/

Summit County Utah. "Public Art in Summit County, UT | Celebrating Local Artists & Installations." Accessed June 20, 2025. https://www.summitcounty.org/249/Public-Art.

TownLift. "Summit County announces major public art project for Jeremy Ranch roundabouts." *TownLift, Park City News*, December 19, 2023. https://townlift.com/2023/12/summit-county-announces-major-public-art-project-for-jeremy-ranch-roundabouts/.

Galleries

Arts Council Park City Summit County. "CREATE PC Local Artist Collective." Accessed June 20, 2025. https://www.pcscarts.org/create-pc

Kimball Art Center. "About Us." Accessed June 20, 2025. https://kimballartcenter.org/about-us/.

Mangelsen Images of Nature Gallery. "Biography." Accessed June 20, 2025. https://www.mangelsen.com/biography.

Mountain Trails Gallery. "About Us." Accessed June 20, 2025. https://mountaintrailsgalleries.com/about-us/.

The Music Scene, or Rage Against the CPAP Machine

Forum Fest. "Schedule of Events." Accessed June 20, 2025. https://forumfest.com/schedule-of-events/.

Mountain Town Music. "About." Accessed June 20, 2025. https://
mountaintownmusic.org/about/.

Park City Performing Arts. "Our Mission." Accessed June 20, 2025. https://www.
parkcityinstitute.org/our-mission.

Stay Park City. "Music." Accessed June 20, 2025. https://stayparkcity.com/how-to-pc/
music/.

Celebrities, Sundance, and Other Festivals

Arts Council Park City Summit County. "Events Calendar." Accessed June 20, 2025.
https://www.pcscarts.org/event-calendar.

Clyde, Tom. "More Dogs on Main: Hasta la vista, Sundance." *Park Record*, April 5,
2025. https://www.parkrecord.com/2025/04/05/more-dogs-on-main-hasta-
la-vista-sundance/.

Must-See Museums

Alf Engen Museum Foundation. "Ski History Museum Exhibits." Accessed June 20,
2025. https://engenmuseum.org/ski-history-museum-collection/.

Natural History Museum of Utah. "Visit NHMU." Accessed June 20, 2025. https://
nhmu.utah.edu/visit.

Park City Museum. "About the Park City Museum." Accessed June 20, 2025. https://
parkcityhistory.org/about/.

Summit County Utah. "Echo Canyon Church | Historic Church in Summit County,
Utah." Accessed June 20, 2025. https://www.summitcounty.org/141/Echo-
Canyon-Church.

Summit County Utah. "Summit County Historical Museum – Explore Utah's Rich
History & Cultural Heritage." Accessed June 20, 2025. https://www.
summitcounty.org/191/Summit-County-Historical-Museum.

Utah State University | Swaner EcoCenter. "Mission & History." Accessed June 20,
2025. https://extension.usu.edu/swaner/mission-and-history.

The Film Series

Charnes, Joanna. "Thanks from the Arts Council – Letter to the Editor." *Park
Record*, January 12, 1995. https://newspapers.lib.utah.edu/ark:/87278/
s6q854vj/22827094.

Park City Film. "Mission and History." Accessed June 20, 2025. https://parkcityfilm.
org/about/mission-history/.

Thomas, Connor. "What does a post-Sundance Park City arts scene, economy look
like?" *KPCW*, January 25, 2026. https://www.kpcw.org/sundance-film-
festival/2026-01-23/what-does-a-post-sundance-park-city-arts-scene-
economy-look-like.

Visit Park City. "Park City Film." Accessed June 20, 2025. https://www.visitparkcity.
com/listing/park-city-film/15174/.

Things You Have to See to Believe

Deer Valley. "Intermountain Health Freestyle International Ski World Cup." Accessed June 20, 2025. https://www.deervalley.com/things-to-do/activities/world-cup.

Kamas City. "Kamas Valley Fiesta Days." Accessed June 20, 2025. https://www.kamascityut.gov/o/kamas/page/fiesta-days.

Oakley Rodeo. "FAQs." Accessed June 20, 2025. https://oakleyrodeo.com/faqs/.

Summit County Fair. Accessed June 20, 2025. https://summitcountyfair.org/index.php.

Utah Ski Joring. "Ski Joring Utah." Accessed June 20, 2025. https://www.skijoringutah.com/collections/2024-skijoring-utah-teams.

The Future is Here

The Once and Future Olympics

International Olympic Committee. "Salt Lake City Utah 2034 - Olympic Winter Games." Accessed June 20, 2025. https://www.olympics.com/ioc/olympic-games/salt-lake-city-utah-2034.

O'Malley, M. "Notes from tour of Park City water treatment plant." *Author's personal files*, June 12, 2025.

US Ski and Snowboard. "USANA Center of Excellence powered by iFIT." Accessed June 20, 2025. https://www.usskiandsnowboard.org/about/usana-center-excellence-powered-ifit.

Weintraub, Daniel. "Olympics bus system ought to receive a gold medal." *Deseret News*, February 16, 2002. https://www.deseret.com/2002/2/17/20630218/olympics-bus-system-ought-to-receive-a-gold-medal/.

Salt Flat City

Great Salt Lake. "Great Salt Lake Strategic Plan." Accessed June 20, 2025. https://greatsaltlake.utah.gov/great-salt-lake-strategic-plan-2.

Instagram. Utah Business. https://www.instagram.com/utahbusiness/p/DF_XYcHSbsJ/.

KEM C. Gardner Policy Institute. "Great Salt Lake Strike Team." February 3, 2025. https://gardner.utah.edu/great-salt-lake-strike-team/.

Salt Lake Chamber. *Public Policy Guide*. January 10, 2025. https://issuu.com/saltlakechamber/docs/publicpolicyguide_2025_digital.

Staff. "Utah business leaders put up $30M in race to save the Great Salt Lake before the Olympics." *KPCW*, April 14, 2026. https://www.kpcw.org/state-regional/2026-04-14/utah-business-leaders-put-up-30m-in-race-to-save-the-great-salt-lake-before-the-olympics

Utah State University. "Strike team: Utah making progress on Great Salt Lake." Effective January 14, 2025. https://www.usu.edu/today/story/strike-team-utah-making-progress-on-great-salt-lake.

Utah State University. "The Great Salt Lake." Accessed June 20, 2025. https://www.usu.edu/ilwa/projects/great-salt-lake/.

Things to Change

Jet-One. "Goodfellas Night Club Scene - Copacabana - Henry Hill" YouTube, 2012. https://www.youtube.com/watch?v=4aQ4Vj1OtjQ.

Kemo Sabe. "Kemo Sabe Locations." Accessed June 20, 2025. https://www.kemosabe.com/page/locations.

Lorelli, Matt. "The Countless Ways To Bump a Chairlift." *Unofficial Networks*, October 15, 2021. https://unofficialnetworks.com/2021/10/15/how-to-bump-a-chairlift/.

"Maine Moose and Winter Ticks." Maine Department of Inland Fisheries & Wildlife. https://www.maine.gov/ifw/fish-wildlife/wildlife/species-information/mammals/moose-winter-ticks.html.

Things We Love (and Some We Fear)

O'Malley, Michael. "Random musings." *Author's personal files*. 2025.

Challenges

Droste, Keith A. "Mayflower Mine - Hot, Wet and Payable Gold." Powerpoint. *Author's personal files*. 2019.

Kem C. Gardner Policy Institute. "The Evolving Landscape of Utah's Short-Term Rental Market." October 23, 2024. https://gardner.utah.edu/utahs-short-term-rental-market/.

Leaver, Jennifer. "Insight: The Good, the Bad, and the Ugly: Addressing Utah's Short Term Rental Market Growth." KEM C. Gardner Policy Institute, April 19, 2022. https://gardner.utah.edu/blog/blog-the-good-the-bad-and-the-ugly-addressing-utahs-short-term-rental-market-growth/.

Thomas, Connor. "Summit County's new short-term rental hotline sees 18 calls in first 2 months." *KPCW*, April 2, 2026. https://www.kpcw.org/summit-county/2026-04-02/summit-countys-short-term-rental-hotline-received-18-complaints-this-year.

Wood, James. "*Housing Needs Assessment: Unincorporated Wasatch County, Heber, and Midway.*" 2017. https://www.summitcountyutah.gov/DocumentCenter/View/6628/Final-Housing-Needs-Assessment-Wasatch-County--2017-PDF.

Wood, James. *Park City's Housing Needs Assessment 2021*. Park City Affordable Housing Program. 2022. https://www.parkcity.org/home/showpublisheddocument/72312/637907261125170000.

The source for miscellaneous dollar value conversions throughout the manuscript is https://www.in2013dollars.com/us/.

www.ingramcontent.com/pod-product-compliance
Lightning Source LLC
Chambersburg PA
CBHW070547130626
46556CB00001B/47